brother Sam

brother Sam

THE SHORT, SPECTACULAR LIFE OF SAM KINISON

bill kinison with steve delsohn

William Morrow and Company, Inc.
New York

It is the policy of William Morrow and Company, Inc., and its imprints and affiliates, recognizing the importance of preserving what has been written, to print the books we publish on acid-free paper, and we exert our best efforts to that end.

Library of Congress Cataloging-in-Publication Data

Kinison, Bill.
     Brother Sam : the short spectacular life of Sam Kinison / Bill Kinison with Steve Delsohn. — 1st ed.
       p. cm.
     Includes index.
     ISBN 0–688–12634–0 (alk. paper) : $22.00
     1. Kinison, Sam. 2. Comedians—United States—Biography.
I. Delsohn, Steve. II. Title.
PN2287.K669K56 1994
792.7′028′092—dc20   93–42974
[B]   CIP

Printed in the United States of America

First Edition

1 2 3 4 5 6 7 8 9 10

I dedicate this book to my three brothers—Sam, Richard, and Kevin. Who can say they've been where we've been, seen what we've seen, and done what we've done? This book is also dedicated to my mother, Marie, the original screamer, to Sherry, the love of my youth, and to Ginger, the love of my life.

B.K.

For Emma and Mary Kay, who bless me with their love.

S.D.

Acknowledgments

Thanks to Paul Bresnick and Ben Ratliff, our smart and gracious editors. Thanks to our agent, Frank Weimann, for his work ethic and loyalty. Thanks to Cheryl Booth for her all-world transcription.

Contents

brother Sam

Prologue

SATURDAY NIGHT IN MANHATTAN. STUDIO 8H AT NBC'S HEAD-quarters in 30 Rockefeller Plaza. The set of *Saturday Night Live.* October 18, 1986. And my brother Sam was pushing the limits again.

He was *always* pushing the limits, always going too far and speaking too freely. But that was Sam's appeal. People never knew what he might say next. Sometimes even Sam didn't know. He opened his mouth and outrageousness just came out.

Within network television, *SNL* producer Lorne Michaels was one of Sam's earliest boosters. Lorne's show had gotten tame since losing John Belushi and Dan Aykroyd. In trying to restore its rock-and-roll spirit, Lorne had booked Sam four times in less than a year. Everything had gone smoothly on Sam's first three appearances. The trouble started that Saturday night, shortly before the live broadcast, at the program's dress rehearsal.

Sam rehearsed two bits that he'd done before in clubs, but never on television. One poked fun at President Reagan's war on drugs. The other targeted greedy televangelists, ending up with a riff about Jesus' last words on the cross. Drugs and religion—two subjects Sam knew intimately. A preacher's son and a former preacher himself, Sam never even smoked pot until he was twenty-five. Now he was thirty-two, famous and riding high and partying hard.

The moment he finished rehearsing, the NBC censors called Sam into a glass-walled conference room. As his older brother, his confidant, and his soon-to-be personal manager, I watched from outside the room a few feet away. The meeting was brief. Nobody seemed irate. For one time in his life, Sam didn't say much. Lorne Michaels was quiet too. The NBC censors seemed to be calling the shots.

It was almost 11:30 P.M. With the live show beginning in just a few minutes, Sam filled me in as we hurried back to his dressing room. On the live broadcast, he said, the censors just told him not to do either bit. Not the one on drugs, not the one on religion.

I asked Sam, "What did you say?"

"Nothing," he said. "I didn't say anything either way."

"So what are you gonna do?"

"I'm gonna do 'em."

"That's up to you, Sam. But just know that it may cost you. They told you not to do it. They're gonna be pissed."

"I'm doing them, man. They're funny."

"Yeah, well, I hope you know what you're doing."

Sam smiled his cocky, I'm-in-control smile, which frequently meant he was not in control at all. Still, I felt proud of him. Sam had been in the big time less than a year. It would have been easy to play it safe, just go along, kiss the censors' asses and cover his own. I thought it took courage for Sam to hold his ground. Courage, and maybe some craziness.

In a leather coat down to his ankles, black high-top gym shoes, and his trademark beret, Sam walked onstage a few minutes past midnight. Then he defied the NBC censors.

"It's tough, man," he told SNL's viewers. "The drug war is on. They've got the pot, there's no more pot—the pot is *gone*! And

now they want to make us stop smoking crack: 'Please stop
smoking crack, please stop smoking crack.' All right, we'll make
you a deal. We'll stop smoking crack . . . IF YOU GIVE US THE
POT BACK! WE'LL TRADE YOU THE CRACK FOR THE POT!''

Sam wasn't completely fooling around. Back in Los Angeles,
he'd been having trouble buying good weed.

After loud, surprised laughs from the studio audience—Nancy
Reagan was telling people to "just say no"—Sam segued to his
bit on religious greed and hypocrisy.

"Things aren't conservative enough, now Pat Robertson wants
to be in the White House. A preacher in the White House. I
don't have enough nightmares already? This guy wants to be in
the White House . . . because *Jesus* told him. Jesus woke him up
and went: 'Pssst. Pat, Pat. Yeah, it's Jesus, man. Hey, I want you
to run for president.' '' Sam winked at the camera, as if to say
bullshit.

"These guys kill me, you know? I watch these guys on television, because they're on cable, and they're on like *half* the channels, so you end up watching them. But these guys look you
right in the eye, like you're not gonna doubt 'em. They're like:
'JESUS TOLD ME TO!' NOW WHAT? And they're so eloquent
with it, you know? I like their style, they're really smooth.'' Sam
slipped into the voice of a rural televangelist: '' 'You know, I
remember when the Lord spoke to me . . . and said to go into
radio. And it was about this time Jesus said, "Expand your ministry into the television area." And that was about the time Jesus
spoke to me and said to put out a satellite, so the government
couldn't control our transmissions. And it was about that time
that Jesus came to me and began to explain to me the nonprofit
corporation principle. Then Jesus told me to build an amusement
park. . . . ''

Letting his anger show, Sam resumed speaking in his own
voice. "I'm sitting here listening, going: 'Hey! What did *Santa*
Claus have to say about it, huh? What was the *Easter* Bunny's

input?' I mean, I read the Bible, I follow the calendar. I think it's been about two thousand years since Jesus said *anything* to anybody." Banging the head of his microphone on the stage, making the startling sound of crucifixion, Sam said, "Yeah, I think his last words may have been 'NOT THE OTHER ONE! NOT THE OTHER ONE!' "

Sam screamed, "Thanks a lot!" and ran off the stage. As usual, he killed. And yet I could picture the NBC censors, watching him on their monitors, mouths gaping open, saying, "Who the fuck does this guy think he is?"

In every market except the West Coast, Sam's performance was broadcast fully intact. But out West, where the show aired at 11:30 P.M. Pacific Coast Time, NBC radically censored him. First, as Sam did his bit on the drug war, NBC cut off his sound. For twenty-six seconds, his mouth moved but nothing came out. Later, when he talked about Jesus' last words on the cross, the censors let him start building toward his punch line. But before Sam could actually say it—"NOT THE OTHER ONE! NOT THE OTHER ONE!"—NBC suddenly cut to him thanking his audience.

Nobody hollered at Sam when he came offstage. Nobody even commented. So we left New York in the morning without even knowing what had happened. While Sam flew to Washington, D.C., for a concert date, I flew home to Rockford, Illinois. The day after that, as planned, I moved to Los Angeles with my wife, Sherry, and my daughter, Ginger. Sam never trusted many people in Hollywood. For the past five years he'd been asking me to manage him. Finally, recently, I'd accepted his offer.

With Sam out on the road, and my own family just getting settled here in L.A., I was planning to join him on tour in a couple weeks. Then I heard two big pieces of news:

Sam had been censored out West for his jokes about Jesus and drugs.

Sam was now banned for life from appearing on NBC. Brandon Tartikoff had released that statement himself.

Not only was *SNL* on NBC, so was *Late Night with David Letterman* and *The Tonight Show*. Sam couldn't afford to be banished from all these shows. No rising comedian could.

I didn't know how serious NBC was, and I didn't want Sam to go blasting off to the press. I told my wife he was in trouble, I needed to meet him much sooner. Sherry had known Sam since he was a kid. She knew he had a big mouth and could easily make things worse. She told me she understood. But Sherry also seemed disappointed in me.

Later that week, I flew to meet Sam in Norfolk, Virginia. Sherry and Ginger stayed at Sam's rented house in the Hollywood Hills. Because I got too wrapped up in my brother's life, it wasn't the last time I put his needs in front of my family's. This was also probably the first major blow to my marriage.

From *CNN* to *Good Morning America* to *People* magazine, the entertainment media clamored for Sam's response: How did he feel about his banning from NBC? This was all new to Sam. He'd never been in a controversy before, and it wasn't as if he'd planned out this first one. Though Sam liked to *pretend* he was always in charge, he rarely planned anything. On the contrary, Sam was pure emotion. When people met him face to face, they were usually struck by how *uncalculating* he was.

But now that the uproar had started, Sam was enjoying it. I knew he was dying to talk to the press, so I told him before his concert in Norfolk, "You've already got plenty of publicity out of this. You just pissed off two big guys, Brandon Tartikoff and Lorne Michaels."

Sam said, "You think they're really that pissed? I didn't cuss or anything."

"I don't know," I said. "Maybe Brandon and Lorne kind of

liked it. It might be only the censors who're upset. Either way, maybe they'll change their minds if we don't provoke them. So let's not do any interviews."

To my surprise, Sam acquiesced, and we managed to stonewall the media. But Sam couldn't stop himself when he got onstage. That night, he told a packed house in Norfolk, "Yeah, maybe I did get censored, but I did it for you! Fuck them! Fuck NBC! *You* are my people, and I *command* you. I COMMAND YOU!"

As Sam kept thumbing his nose at a powerful network, his audience ate it up. They *wanted* Sam to be bad. Sometimes they felt like shouting at big shots too.

Later that week, as our tour bus headed south toward the Carolinas, Lorne Michaels surprised us with a phone call. He spoke to Elliot Abbott, Sam's manager, who I was supposed to replace when this crisis died down. Elliot told me what Lorne had told him: Just as NBC expected, there'd been a flood of angry letters since Sam's spot on *SNL*. Lorne said there was a twist, however. Almost every letter supported Sam, while condemning NBC for the censorship of an artist.

"Lorne said some people are not even writing letters," Elliot said. "They're just sending shit into NBC."

I said, "What do you mean? Like, garbage?"

Elliot said, "No! They're sending shit! Human shit, in envelopes!"

Sam and I figured these weren't even his fans, but a handful of First Amendment lunatic fringe. Regardless, the attendant publicity wave was fantastic for Sam's career, as freedom of speech proponents now rallied around his "cause."

Sam thought it was funny. He never spent much time discussing the First Amendment. He just liked to say what he thought.

Lorne called us again a few days later. He wanted Sam back on his show. He'd already cleared it with Brandon Tartikoff. Only this time, Lorne invited Sam to be the guest host.

Sam didn't hesitate or gloat. He just said, "Let's do it."

On November 15, four weeks after NBC banned him for life, Sam flew back into New York and hosted *Saturday Night*. At 11:30 P.M., the camera opened on Dana Carvey. He was sitting behind a desk, demurely dressed in drag as the wildly popular Church Lady.

Carvey said, "Hello, I'm the Church Lady and I'm here to inform you that I will not be appearing on *Saturday Night Live* this evening. I'm sorry, I am protesting the selection of the guest host. As you may already know, a few weeks ago Mr. Samuel Kinison was fortunate enough to be chosen to perform his funny little comedy routines on *Saturday Night Live.* Instead, he said some naughty things about crack and Christ. Some things that might come out of the mouth of, oh, oh I don't know . . . I don't know who it would be . . . maybe . . . *Satan?*"

After prattling on about Sam and Satan and sin, the Church Lady changed her mind. It wasn't enough to protest the show. She had to stop this "dirty little sex show."

Leaving her desk and storming backstage, she found Sam standing next to a statuesque blonde. It was Seka, the famous porn star, wearing high heels and a nightie, and feeding Sam grapes. Knowing that he had NBC by the balls, Sam had insisted she join him on the show. They'd recently met in Chicago, and Sam was aching to sleep with her. He figured something like this—getting Seka a cameo on *Saturday Night Live*—might help do the trick.

The Church Lady chided Seka for hanging around with Sam. Then she turned, frowning, toward him.

Sam cut in before she could lecture him. He said, "You know what you need?"

"What's that?" the Church Lady asked.

Sam grinned at Seka. "Well, what you need is what I was just about to give to *her.*"

The Church Lady said, "*Well,* I have no idea what you're talking about."

Sam said, "I call it a real touch from God."

Turning his back to the camera, so no one could see his lips, Sam grabbed the Church Lady, bent her over his knee, and gave her a massive fake kiss.

The Church Lady popped back up looking totally flustered. Also a little sexed up.

Sam screamed: "LIVE FROM NEW YORK! IT'S SATURDAY NIGHT!"

After the credits rolled, Sam ran back out for his opening monologue. Not to worry, he told the audience. NBC's censors were on vacation. They'd invited him back with the promise he could say anything. No interference, no pressure. While Sam was still discussing all this freedom, two New York cops rode their horses onstage. Surrounded on either side, Sam looked at the mounted policemen. He looked at the audience. He looked at the horses.

"Well," Sam said, "I guess NBC kept their word."

After an hour of skits, Sam came back out by himself to do his stand-up act. A two-time failure at marriage, a guy who once got called by Marvin Mitchelson on Christmas Eve, he was already known for his darkly comic views of romance and sex.

Sam said, "Yeah, I been taking a lot of heat lately for some of my religious jokes, some of my jokes about women. But I love women, women know that, I love religion—CAN'T GET ENOUGH! I used to be a preacher, I used to be a minister, and people think I changed overnight, and I didn't. It wasn't like I just woke up one day and said, 'HEY, FORGET THE BIBLE! WHERE'S THE PARTY?' It was a little more gradual than that, it took a little more time, it took a lot of *women* to disillusion me. *But . . .* I don't want to leave the impression that all women are bad, that all women are bitches from hell. Don't want to do that. I love women . . . I just choose the wrong ones. I choose *psycho-*

bitches. I look for women I *know* are gonna bust me up good. Come on, man, who can resist that? Who can resist that emotional pain? Yeah, they all have the same line, they're so sweet: 'I'm not gonna hurt you like all the others. Really, I'm not. I'm gonna introduce you to a whole new level of *pain*! They were *amateurs*! They were *lightweights*! YOU'RE IN THE BIG LEAGUES NOW! Yeah . . . I'm gonna make love to all your friends. I'm gonna leave you about eight, ten grand in debt, run up all your credit cards, get your phone disconnected, and then talk you into giving me your *car*! *Ha-ha-ha-ha-ha!*' "

Shortly before 1:00 A.M, the cast joined Sam onstage to say good night. Sam had one arm around Seka and the other around his buddy Dennis Miller. As the credits rolled, everyone else was shaking hands, waving good night, quietly talking. Not Sam. He was still shouting into the camera: "I'd just like to tell all the women that have been in my life . . . you did the right thing. Yeah, you did the right thing. YOU LEFT! LIVE WITH YOUR-SELF!"

And that was pretty much Sam his entire life. One more laugh from the crowd. One more grab for attention.

Preacher's Kids

ORN IN YAKIMA, WASHINGTON ON DECEMBER 8, 1953, SAM
arrived in the midst of a family crisis. He was three weeks
old when the ministry blackballed our father.

Up until then, Samuel Earl Kinison was a Pentecostal preacher
affiliated with the Church of God. With his freethinking sermons,
he quickly drew record crowds to his church just outside Yakima, but as he became a star to his congregation, he started to
threaten the power structure above him.

In several respects they considered him an outlaw. Contrary
to most Church of God ministers, he believed in the gifts of the
Holy Spirit: faith-healing, prophecy, the interpretation of unknown tongues. Before joining the ministry at age thirty-five, my
father had hoboed on freight trains, sold automobiles, owned a
dance hall and some dump trucks. Most shocking of all to his
peers, he was nineteen years older than his pretty wife, Marie.

One morning in late December of 1953, with a Church of God
overseer sitting ominously behind him, my father preached as I
sat in the pews with my older brother, Richard, our mother, Marie, and our new baby, Sam. After my father's sermon, the overseer stood up and declared, "This pulpit is vacant." The

congregation went silent, then started to shout, then rushed the stage to attack the overseer. My father picked up a chair over his head, protecting the man who had just kicked him out of the ministry.

The next morning I watched from our front window as a black sedan pulled up to our home and four somber men in heavy black overcoats ushered my father inside it. They were men from the church, but to me they looked like the gangsters I saw in movies. I burst into tears, certain they'd harm my father or take him away forever.

When our father came back to our house, he said we were moving. Within a few weeks, the Church of God mailed letters to other pastors, saying they could be banished, too, for allowing my father to preach inside their churches. As our father lost his pulpit and part of his pride, our mom had a nervous breakdown. Sam was still in his first few months of life. I had just turned five.

From living in a comfortable house, next door to our neighborhood bank president, we moved into a government-subsidized housing project in Peoria, Illinois, where our grandparents lived. The housing project was crime-infested, we were abruptly poor and money was chronically tight. Some days, Sam and I wore pajama tops with our jeans.

In Peoria, my grandparents' friends pulled their car out of their garage, my father set up a few metal chairs, and he started preaching again to much smaller crowds. Later he bought an old building and opened his own Pentecostal church. This time he stayed independent.

Soon there were four Kinison boys—Richard, myself, Sam, and Kevin. We craved acceptance, like all kids, but instead we grew up feeling like social outcasts, rejected by children at school who didn't think we were cool. How could we be cool? We were known all over town as "the preacher's kids."

Worse, at least to us, our father's church was Pentecostal. Sam and I used to joke that everyone in our church was either sick, poor, or old: sick people hoping to get well, poor people hoping for wealth, old people fearing their death and hoping to make things right first. It was a potent combination—poor, pious, and Pentecostal—and Sam and I both grew up with low self-esteem. I never said it out loud, but I thought of myself as white trash. I suspect Sam did too.

As Sam got older and started looking for trouble, some people we knew said he just had a "natural-born wild streak." In truth, Sam was a mild little boy until he was three years old. Then, one morning while I was at school, he chased his rubber ball into a street, where a semi-truck struck him flush on the side of his head. A few days later, the doctor gave our family the awful news. Sam had been diagnosed with 30 percent brain damage.

Sam was confusing to me when he came home from the hospital. He looked exactly the same—the damage was all internal—but he acted very different. A quiet kid until then, almost passive, Sam was now ornery and aggressive. Much less in control of his emotions, he was suddenly prone to temper tantrums. Sam had physical changes as well after the accident. He started drooling again, even heavier than he had when he was an infant. He'd also feel shaky and dizzy, and would often go to our mother so she would hold him. Sam also resumed wetting his bed, and continued wetting his bed until age thirteen. Sam and I never discussed this, just as we never discussed his brain damage, but I know that his bedwetting shamed him and made him feel peculiar. Sam never slept at his friends' houses, or had them sleep at our church, for fear he would be discovered.

As Sam turned into another little boy, increasingly defiant and unhappy, my father would frequently say about our future: "Sam will get in trouble and Bill will bail him out." Though we both had mixed emotions about being preacher's sons, Sam and I idolized our father. We fulfilled the roles he prophesied for us, and performed them the rest of our lives.

*   *   *

We lived in the housing projects until Sam entered first grade, then my father bought an old Methodist church and the six of us moved in there. The building was enormous, with about twenty rooms, spread over three different levels. My family lived upstairs in what used to be Sunday-school rooms. On the main floor my father preached. In the basement, our father would feed the bums who had crawled inside during the night. Having bums inside her home unnerved our mom, so our dad found an old picnic table and started bringing their sandwiches to them outside. Sam *loved* our father for this.

He wasn't too pleased about living inside a church. Sam used to lie, tell other children he lived next door with our neighbor Mr. Kelly, but no one stayed fooled for long, and Sam would hear it just about every day: "You live in a *church*?" Sam would then ask our mom, "Why can't you and dad do something else? How come dad is a preacher?"

Out of all four Kinison boys, Sam chafed the most at being a preacher's son, because Sam always had the hardest time fitting in. Sam never cared about school. Although he was already husky, he never liked sports. This may have been because I was already the family jock. I started at guard on all our school basketball teams, and I later became a state champ in wrestling. Sports gave me an outlet for my anger. It gave me some popularity. Sam never had that in his childhood. The one time he tried out for football he quit after two weeks. In wrestling, Sam lasted two practices.

He was a great petty thief, though. One time Sam removed a locked door from its hinges, stole the money inside, then put the door back in place before our parents came home. He'd also steal from old ladies who sat in a park near our church. Sam would crawl up behind them on his belly, reach quietly under their bench, and snatch their purses. As Sam graduated to shoplifting—mostly toys that our parents couldn't afford—the same neighborhood cop kept pulling up to our church steps in his squad car. Pretty soon, we were calling Officer Upholls by his first name: "Hey, Dad, Red's here for Sam again."

What Sam enjoyed most as a child was television and movies. By eleven, he was already dreaming vaguely of someday becoming an actor. Sam's childhood hero was Richard Kimble in *The Fugitive*. Sam didn't just relate to him, he thought *he* was Richard Kimble. It could have had something to do with our living inside a church. When the public keeps streaming in and out your front door, it's hard for a kid to feel rooted—especially one as troubled as Sam. Almost every day, he dressed in all black, and his only childhood hobby was making monsters. Even then, my brother felt drawn to darkness.

After school one afternoon in 1966, when Sam was twelve and I was seventeen, my father pulled me aside in the church. He told me to break the string he held in his hand. After I did, he held four strings tautly together and said I should try breaking that. When the four strings held tight, my father said, "That's how strong you boys will be if you stay together. No one can break you four boys if you stick together."

A few months later, our family was ripped apart. Although our father didn't want to, our mother finally convinced him they should divorce.

Their marriage had started in controversy. My mother was just sixteen when they snuck off and got married. When her father found out, he carried a gun for almost a year, vowing to shoot my dad the first time he saw him.

Nobody got shot, and for twenty-two years the marriage survived, but toward the end our parents were constantly fighting. My mother made it clear she was tired of being broke, tired of not living inside a real house, tired of our father's jealous comments, as she stayed youthful and pretty while he kept feeling older and more insecure. One night, as she kept railing, he hit her. First Sam and I heard them argue, then we heard our mother call him the magic words—"you son of a bitch." Sam got scared and told me I'd better go in there, since normally I made the peace. Before I could, our dad knocked our mother cold with a single punch. Then he caught her in his arms before she could hit the floor.

By the morning we all went to court, Sam and I had decided we wanted to live with our father. He was the family star, the beloved preacher whose sermons people hung on. He was also much more lenient than our mom, who Sam and I always felt was the toughest one in our family.

The judge asked Richard, the oldest boy, who he wanted to live with.

"I'm going with Bill," Richard said.

"Well, who is Bill?" the judge asked.

"I'm Bill," I said. "I wanna go with my father."

To Sam's shock and dismay, the judge never asked him where *he* wanted to live. So each parent would have two kids, the judge ordered Sam and Kevin to stay with our mother.

It was a messy and bitter divorce. Our mother, trying to justify her divorce to the church, wrote letters to dozens of preachers saying that our father had cheated on her—that's why the judge had granted her a divorce. She told the same thing to our church board. It wasn't true—they'd gotten divorced on other grounds—but inside the church the gossip spread quickly. For the second time in his life, our father was banned from the ministry. He took a job driving a city bus in Peoria. He was fifty-five years old.

Sam was crazy about our dad and crushed by our new arrangement, as our father, Richard, and I moved six miles away, while Sam, Kevin, and Mom stayed in the church. Richard moved back to the church in about a month, but I stayed with our father, so Sam vented most of his anger on me. Before this, Sam had always looked up to me: I got good grades, I could play ball, I once punched out a young Marine for picking on Sam. But now that I'd left our home, Sam felt betrayed and abandoned by me. I don't think he ever completely forgave me.

Since Sam *couldn't* get mad at our dad, he turned the rest of his anger on our mother. Why, Sam wanted to know, did she have to send those letters and ruin his name in the ministry? Why hadn't she settled for just a divorce?

Suddenly being raised in a fatherless home, Sam started stealing more frequently from our mom. One afternoon, after she caught him taking her missionary money, my mother gave Sam his whipping and then called me. "Sam needs some discipline," she said. "Can you come over here, Bill?"

To me, a hotheaded athlete, discipline back then meant physical threats. "I'll beat the shit out of you, Sam!" I screamed at him in the church. "You don't steal from your mother!"

"Mind your own business!" Sam shouted back. "You're the one who left, man."

When we'd both yelled ourselves out and Sam ran upstairs, I found my mother and started right in on her. She knew, better than anyone, how much Sam resented anyone in authority.

"I'm his brother," I complained. "Why do *I* have to discipline him?"

Sam told our mother that night when they were alone, "I'm sorry I stole again, Mom, but I'll take care of you now. I'm the man of the house now." He was twelve years old.

By the time Sam entered eighth grade, he was cutting as many classes as he attended. Our mom started dropping him off at school, but that didn't work either, because Sam would stroll in the front door and flee out the back. Sometimes he'd skip school altogether, hitch a ride downtown, and watch movies in near-empty theaters. Some days Sam would wait for my father along his city bus route. After they'd ridden around together all day on his bus, our dad would issue Sam halfhearted reprisals: "Now listen, boy, today was fun. But tomorrow you go back to school."

Sam turned thirteen on December 8, 1966, just a few months after my father and I moved out. Shortly thereafter, my mom caught Sam having sex with a girl up in the choir loft. The rebellion was on.

In 1967, when Sam was almost fourteen, my mother started dating a guy named Roger. Richard and Kevin and I all instantly disliked him. Sam *despised* him, of course, because Sam never did anything halfway. Roger played a mediocre guitar, but he thought he was Chet Atkins. After playing a simple riff, he would look straight at Sam and say, "How'd you like that, boy?"

Roger began riding Sam harder and harder, until one day I heard he had gone too far—he had slapped around both Kevin and Sam. When Kevin told me what happened, I drove straight to our church in a rage with a baseball bat pulled from my closet. I stalked past my mother and right up to Roger, told him to follow me into the Sunday-school room. Walking in front of Roger I felt myself trembling, getting excited, feeling the heat.

"I heard what you did," I told him inside the classroom. "You touch my brothers again, ever, I'll break both your legs with this bat. The only reason you still got balls is 'cause I kept my father away." It was true. When he learned Roger had put his hands on his boys, my father started talking about castration.

Sam took his own revenge that Christmas. For exactly $5, he bought Roger a smoking jacket at the Salvation Army, disguised it inside a nice box, and added a festive bow. As Roger opened his gift on Christmas Eve, as his eyes filled with tears that Sam could be so forgiving, Sam screamed, "I got it at Salvation Army! It cost me five bucks!"

Just kicked old Roger's ass.

When I graduated from high school in 1967, I thought I'd be drafted that summer and sent off to Vietnam. But I hadn't been called by that fall, so I enrolled at a junior college in Peoria. In 1968 I finished my freshman year, intending to transfer to the University of Illinois. That fall, I entered the ministry instead.

I never quite saw it coming, yet the psychic pull to preach had always been strong. As preacher's kids we had all heard it for years: You have to carry the mantle. That's why God *made* you a preacher's son. He wants you to spread his Word.

Although our father himself never pushed us, at certain emotional moments his true feelings surfaced. When Sam was seven and I was twelve, I once thought our father might die from a diabetic coma. To my intense relief, and to my surprise, I woke up one morning and found him upstairs cooking breakfast. I asked him what happened, why he had slept for so long. "The Death Angel came to my bed," my father told me. "He said it was my time to leave, but I told the Death Angel no. I said God has promised me things I haven't seen happen. He promised me I would see my four boys preach. Until I've seen that, I'm not dying."

One fall afternoon in 1968, I was struck by a powerful feeling while standing alone in my rented apartment. I wanted to follow my father into the ministry. He was getting older and might not be around long; I did not want to disappoint him. A caretaker by nature—Sam would say "controlling"—I also felt the urge to help other people. But mostly my motives were selfish. Through preaching, I hoped I could heal myself. I wanted some happiness in my life.

If I joined up with any religious organization, I felt one day they'd fuck me over and throw me out, just as they had my dad. Meanwhile, my older brother, Rich, had been preaching the past two years. I asked him how he felt about teaming up. Rather than pastor one church as our father had done, we could enter the evangelical field. This meant we would drive from city to city, holding revivals, and whatever money we raised would be split with the church where we preached. Richard jumped at the chance to preach with his brother. At age nineteen, I became a traveling evangelist.

Since our parents never had money, our economic expectations were low, and so we were both amazed when we saw we could make decent livings. A natural showman, Richard could burn down the house without even preparing. All I had at the start was an athlete's stubborn will, and a fierce commitment to learning my craft. I worked sixteen-hour days, analyzing scriptures, preaching to motel-room mirrors, writing out my sermons in meticulous detail.

Our messages and our beliefs were mostly derived from our father's. Once he'd left the Church of God and become independent, he had undergone a radical transformation. In stark contrast to most Pentecostal preachers, he stopped using fire and brimstone to keep people coming to church. In fact, he started to tell people there *was* no hell. "God loves you," he told his congregations, "so how *can* there be a hell? Why would he punish the people he loves? There is no hell. We're all going to heaven."

Richard and I also preached of a more compassionate God, and right out of the gate the Pentecostals responded. After preaching our first revival without owning decent clothes, within five months we were rocking and rolling. Billing ourselves as the Kinison Brothers, we were soon wearing nice suits, preaching revivals with two thousand people, driving from state to state in my new Pontiac LeMans. In our busiest months, we were earning more than our father had made in a year.

Peoria. Summer of 1968. The summer before Sam's sophomore year in high school.

When I stopped home from the road, Mom seemed especially anxious about Sam's future. Fearing he'd flunk out of high school when he returned that fall, she also disliked the crowd he was running with that summer. Before Sam could get into serious trouble, I suggested she get him away from East Peoria. For his sophomore year, I recommended she send him to Pinecrest Bible Training Center, a Pentecostal boarding school in Utica, New York, which I'd briefly attended myself after one year of preaching. At age fifteen, what Sam lacked most was discipline and direction, and Pinecrest was more than strict. It was a place out of Dickens. There was no dating between the sexes. No holding hands. For first-year students like Sam, no sitting at tables with girls in the school cafeteria. It was a new institution with shaky financial support, and its food was donated by local stores. The best thing about meals was that they were served in small portions.

And yet Sam enrolled and loved it. Everywhere he looked he saw preachers' kids, so he no longer felt like such a freak. He made two or three long-haired buddies—Sam called them "the cool guys there"—and they taught him to play guitar while sitting around in the dorms. At age sixteen, Sam even had his first affair with an older woman, a twenty-one-year-old college student named Sonia. They snuck off the school grounds and made love in the woods under blankets.

For a kid with no plans and no real prospects, Sam seemed unusually happy when he returned home that summer. He showed up with an old guitar, a gift from a Pinecrest pal. All summer long he attacked it, getting better and better each day, and it struck me then for the first time: My younger brother might have a kind of raw genius. If he could just focus himself . . .

For the first time, too, Sam started dreaming out loud of becoming a rock-and-roller. One night at the church, our whole family sitting around except for our father, Sam said to our mother's boyfriend, Roger, the self-styled hot-shit guitar man, "My guitar is upstairs. Mind if I try yours?"

Grinning, Roger handed it over. Sam strummed the exact same

riff that Roger always did. Roger said, "Yeah, that ain't half bad, boy." Then, as Roger leaned forward for his guitar, Sam took one long step back and started to *jam*.

Buried Roger a second time.

One hot, sticky night in August, Sam ran away from home. He split late one night with just his guitar, some clothes, and a Bible. He and Mom had been fighting, but there hadn't been any huge blowouts. No one ever really knew why Sam cut out. But there it was, Sam playing Richard Kimble at age sixteen.

Sam never returned to school once he ran away, and this lack of education intensified his self-doubts. Even though he received an equivalency diploma from his one year at Pinecrest, Sam never believed he'd earned it. "Man," he would say, "I don't even think my diploma's legit. I don't think I even graduated from high school."

For the next two years, nobody in our family except our father knew Sam's whereabouts. An anguished part of me feared that Sam was in jail, or dead, but something in my father's composed behavior, how he kept saying "I'm sure Sam is okay," made another part of me think they were actually keeping in touch. We later found out it was true. Sam was calling him all along, and our dad was mailing Sam money every so often. Sam knew that if our father told the rest of us where Sam was, our mother would call the police. So Sam made our father swear not to tell us, or else Sam would break contact off with him too. My father kept his promise. For two years it remained their unbroken trust.

Then, in the summer of 1971, in a church one Sunday night in Oklahoma City, Richard and I were preaching our weekly live radio broadcast. Sam was hitching a ride with a trucker in another part of the state, the trucker was changing channels, and Sam heard our voices over the radio! After finding out from the church where we were staying, he called us the next morning in our hotel room.

"I'm here," he said, some nervousness in his voice, like we might kick his ass for running away.

"Where is here?" I asked, feeling only a rush of relief.

"Oklahoma City. I just got dropped off. Can you guys pick me up at the capitol building?"

We spotted Sam before he saw us. He stood crouched on the capitol steps, glancing around, looking thinner and longer-haired than I recalled. We all rushed into a circle, overcome with emotion, hugging and crying and saying how great we all looked.

Inside my car Sam couldn't sit still. First thing he wanted to know: "Is Mom gonna kill me?" We said she probably was, and Sam refused to drive with us back to Tulsa, where our mother had moved since he left. I wanted to surprise her, burst in the door with Sam, but Sam insisted I pull over and call her. After she promised not to kill him, Sam's entire body seemed to relax, but his mouth kept moving all the way back to Tulsa.

The night he left Peoria, Sam said he'd hitched to Virginia Beach, Virginia, where his two closest Pinecrest friends lived. Dressed like a beatnik, he sang religious folk songs and played guitar in Christian coffeehouses. Leaving behind his friends, Sam traveled on impulse, hitching all the way north to New York and then south again back to Virginia. When he ran out of the money our father sent him, he zoomed out of diners without paying for meals. He frequently slept outside, in stairwells or on beaches, but some nights he stayed in benevolent preachers' churches. One evening in New York, in a snowstorm becoming a blizzard, he thought he was freezing to death. Dropped off on the side of the New York State Thruway, Sam could not thumb another ride. Two hours later—not knowing the thruway had just been shut down—Sam lost hope and sat down in the snow. A state cop making one last run probably saved his life.

Although he and our mother made peace, Sam quickly felt

restless again. In less than a month he went straight back on the road, traveling with me and Rich as we crisscrossed the country preaching. I'm sure the notion of preaching had crossed his mind, but Sam settled for playing piano at our revivals. Amazingly, he taught himself. Learning to play on out-of-tune church pianos, in *three weeks* he had churchgoers up on their feet clapping and singing. Sam always knew he was not the main act, though, and he looked many times as if he yearned to be preaching. But he never did.

I figured he was still scared to. Sam grew up in church, watching the father he worshiped enrapture his crowds. As for Richard and me, we were rising stars in the evangelical field. We'd already been courted by Jimmy Swaggart, and we'd turned Swaggart down, since we figured we didn't need him. Then, feeling cocky, we'd both walked around for weeks saying, "Swaggart *this.*"

How could Sam compete in a family of preachers like ours? How could a kid who felt like a loser hope to succeed?

Spreading **the Word**

ON MARCH 4, 1972, WHILE DRIVING THROUGH CENTRAL ILLI-
nois on my way to Chicago, I arrived in the city of Decatur
around 10:00 P.M. My father lived there now and I wanted
to surprise him.

At age sixty-two, he had rejoined the ministry and remarried.
His wife left us alone after showing me to his bedroom. It was
blazing hot, unnaturally hot for a March night in Illinois, and my
father perspired as he slept. He'd shaken off his covers. On his
sheet I noticed a circle of blood. While I stood there, just looking,
my father stirred and woke up and covered himself. I realized
I'd embarrassed him.

We stayed up and talked for an hour or so, avoiding the subjects of sickness and aging, his hemorrhaging ulcers, the round
red spot on his bedsheet. I told him I planned on marrying
Sherry, the woman I'd known for years and had recently fallen
in love with. In the morning, I said, I'd be driving to Chicago
in my new Buick Electra. Once I got there, I'd ask Sherry to
marry me.

"I'm not buying any more rings, boy," my father said, playing
comedian. A few years before, when I was still broke, he'd

bought me a ring for a girl I later broke up with.

We slept late the next morning and ate a leisurely breakfast, then I showed my father my new Electra.

"I've preached for thirty-two years and I never owned a car that nice," he said. "Mind if I take it for a spin?"

I felt my heart twitch. "Sure, Dad, of course."

He drove slowly, complimenting my car, then he pulled back in front of his home. I couldn't wait to see Sherry, pop the big question, but my father seemed to have something he needed to say. We sat in the car a few moments, a silence building between us.

"I'm dying," he said.

"What?"

"I am, son. The Lord woke me up a few weeks ago. He told me it won't be long before he takes me. I want you to preach my funeral."

"Dad. What are you talking about? You'll end up burying all of us."

But my father persisted. He made me promise to preach his funeral, and to tell the other three boys how much he loved them, and that he would look out for them from the other side. He didn't think he'd have time to see them again himself.

I gently agreed, still disbelieving him. He kissed my cheek, got out of my car and climbed the steps of his house. Before he walked in he turned around to wave. There were tears streaming down his face.

Then I understood: He *was* going to die. This was the last time I'd see him.

I went to my father and held him and kissed him goodbye.

He died seven weeks later in Zanesville, Ohio. After first passing blood at a Midwestern preachers' convention, he was driving back to Illinois with a few other preachers. He asked them to stop at a Howard Johnson's, went inside the men's room and collapsed. He died that afternoon of bleeding ulcers. My father was sixty-two.

I learned the news from his wife, but at first she softened the story, trying to spare me. She said he'd died of a heart attack. She said he went suddenly, without any suffering.

Sam was finishing up a Christian retreat in Virginia. He expected our dad to pick him up the next day. Together, they would drive back to Illinois.

I called Sam in Virginia, not knowing how to say it.

"What are you doing, Sam?"

"I'm all packed up. Dad's coming tomorrow."

"Well, ah, he's not gonna make it."

"What do you mean?"

"He had a heart attack this morning."

"What? Is he gonna be all right?"

"No, Sam. He died this morning."

On the other end of the line, I heard Sam screaming and sobbing, throwing a fit of despair. He was eighteen.

I prepaid an airline ticket so Sam could fly home for the funeral. The night before the funeral, we picked up Sam at the airport in Champaign, Illinois. I drove my new car and Sam sat shotgun. Kevin, Richard, and my father's stepson, Johnny, filled the backseat. On the ninety-minute drive back to Decatur, we went through the tears, the laughter, the memories, the knotted throats and the silence.

"I'm entering the ministry," Sam blurted out. "I was his namesake, and now he passes the mantle down to me."

The following morning, I told my fiancée, Sherry, I couldn't go through with it: I could not preach my father's funeral. Although Sherry told me I could, I didn't believe her. My father's church was too small to accommodate the crowd, so the service was moved to a larger church nearby. He was a well-loved man, and the mourners spilled out the doors anyway. I gathered myself, and I kept my last promise to him, but I preached that day in a blur. Our father had gone too soon.

At age eighteen, Sam came along preaching with Richard and me, joining the colorful world of traveling evangelists, which is not unlike the world of stand-up comedians: You develop your message, take it out on the road, and hope that you make a connection with your audience. Rather than comedy clubs, there are churches. There are pastors instead of promoters. Whatever money a traveling evangelist raises, he splits with the church where he is guest-preaching. If he doesn't bring in much money, he probably won't get asked back.

Having Sam traveling with us made it all a lot more fun. Bizarre things seemed to occur when Sam was around.

One night in Hamilton, Ohio, a distressed man burst into the church while Sam was preaching.

"I'm demon-possessed!" the man screamed. "I want you to cast out the demons!"

After praying for him, Sam told the man, "Okay, brother, all right. Now you are delivered."

"No!" the man screamed at Sam. "Nothing came out!"

Sam prayed again, but the man insisted the demons still churned inside him.

Sam had this strange anointing oil he used. Most Pentecostal preachers use olive oil, by itself, but Sam never liked the smell, so he mixed it with Brut cologne.

Sam turned back to the troubled soul, still yelling that he was possessed.

"Tell you what I want you to do," Sam said. "I want you to drink this. Then I'll pray for you again."

The man drank Sam's brew and threw up on the stage. But once he caught his breath, he was delighted. "The demons are out! The demons are out!"

One night at a church in Chicago, while waiting for Sam and

me to arrive, the pastor there asked his people to come up and give testimonials. When Sam and I showed up, the pastor's wife looked frantic. "You'd better get in there," she said.

We stepped inside, and a man was standing stark naked up on the platform, shouting about the fire he felt inside him. He had just stripped off his clothes to escape the terrible heat.

"Fire!" he bellowed. "It feels like fire inside my bones!"

Sam and I hurried toward him, not certain how to proceed, but hoping to calm him down. The moment he saw us coming, he bolted off the stage and into the long center aisle. As Sam and I chased a nude man all over the church, his balls were swinging, his arms were flailing, and we started hearing shouts from the ladies out in the crowd: "Don't touch him, don't touch him! He's a true prophet! He's a true prophet!"

"I'll tell you, folks, God is wonderful. He's kind. He has to be, folks. He *has* to be merciful, really, any way you look at it. Hallelujah. Praise God . . . because, honey, we're no longer in the likeness of Adam. Now we're beginning to look just like HIM! We're not clothed with coats of skins, but we're beginning to be clothed in *His* glory—we're beginning to be clothed in the likeness of HIM! Because I'm finding out, once you put on Christ, you CAN'T take it off! Once you begin to walk in this light, this light will never leave you or forsake you, 'cause I'm going to walk out this door, but the SPIRIT is always there! Anytime you want to *call* on Him, anytime you want a blessing from *God,* honey, you don't need to say SEND me the blessing, you can say, Lord, I AM your blessing!"

—Sam Kinison preaching at age nineteen

Sam could always rouse an audience, and sometimes he even had flashes of brilliance. More frequently, though, he'd have a terrific meeting going, and then find some way to self-destruct.

It was almost as if he heard some internal whisper: You're a loser, kid. Why fight it?

Sometimes Sam would get too excited and go too fast, and a cardinal rule of preaching is Always to preach clearly, since you may be talking to people who've never been inside a church. Sam also knew he could coast with Rich and me drawing large crowds, so he never developed good work habits. All in all, Sam struggled in the ministry because deep in his heart he never wanted to preach. Sam felt he had to, to please his dead father.

His single greatest weakness was raising funds, for both himself and the churches where he was preaching. When most traveling evangelists see that their crowd is transfixed, they will ask for donations. When Sam had his audience enthralled, he usually told a joke or a funny story. I saw Sam have people clutching their sides, literally stepping into the aisles to regain their composure.

"That was pretty funny, huh, Bill?" Sam would say after his service.

"Yeah, Sam, it was. So funny you laughed your money right out of church."

While this never endeared him to pastors, the people seemed to enjoy him. Like the rest of our family, Sam preached an idealistic gospel. He told people not to spend their lives waiting for the physical return of Jesus Christ, because "Jesus is inside you. You can make friends with him. You can talk to him every day." He told factory workers making $100 a week that they could lift themselves up and be wealthy someday, not because God could work a miracle for them, but because they could work miracles for themselves. He said there was no hell, only a heaven. It was all very liberal, very radical, and another reason why I excelled as a preacher and Sam essentially flopped: I could diplomatically phrase these strange-sounding notions. Sam always gave people a much straighter dose.

*   *   *

While we were traveling together, Sam got hold of a comedy tape by an obscure black comedian named Rudy Ray Moore. "Man, you gotta hear this guy," Sam told me. Rudy Ray Moore spoke in X-rated rhyme, so Sam and I would sneak off and listen to him in private. Being preachers and all.

Sam also got turned on to Richard Pryor, a fellow Peorian. We'd sit around howling at Sam's all-time favorite comedy album, *Bicentennial Nigger.* Sam went nuts at Pryor's famous old-time preacher routine: "Now, I'd like to make some apologies to you, because last Sunday a spiritual thing happened. A nice family came, the Walker family, brought in their son, they asked me, 'Can you heal our son?' Well, I apologize because he's a big waterhead boy, and I wasn't gonna touch the motherfucker. Get the nigger a big hat or something—leave me alone! And some of the deacons come down on me for that."

In Pentecostal circles, Sam was becoming known as a major cutup himself. Once, Sam detected a scam artist in his crowd, a young guy who was "donating" bogus checks during church, then asking old ladies for "loans" after church ended, since he'd just given away his last red cent. Sam called the guy out of the crowd and told him he wanted to pray for him.

"But first," Sam said, "I want you to take off your coat and lie on the stage. Lie on your back for me, brother."

After the guy lay down, Sam grabbed a pitcher of ice water and drenched him. Hundreds of people gasped, but that was typical Sam, even in the ministry. He loved to shock and break rules.

He'd also do just about anything for a laugh. One Halloween night in St. Louis, after Sam and I had attended a prominent preacher's birthday party, we went out to eat with a dozen well-known ministers. At the restaurant most of the patrons wore Halloween costumes, hoping to win that night's contest. Although dressed in regular clothes, Sam secretly added his name to the list. When they called out "Sam Kinison," he went up on the little stage, turned his back to the room, dropped his pants, shot a moon, and screamed, "I'm just an ASS!"

Everyone cracked up, including the big-time preachers—and Sam lost his chance to ever be booked at their churches. Preachers like funny guys too. But they don't necessarily want them praying over the sick.

In 1975, Sam got married at age twenty-one. He met Gail, nineteen, in Ohio, when they both sang in the same church quartet. Sam idealized Gail, a demurely dressed Baptist, as the innocent childhood sweetheart he'd never had. They'd been dating only three weeks when he told me he wanted to marry her.

But Sam, married, did not stop being Sam. After their wedding reception, we all checked into the same Ohio hotel. With Sam and Gail leaving in the morning on their honeymoon, I and a few other guys went to say goodbye.

"I'll be there in a minute," Sam said when we knocked on the door.

Sam came to the door in his dress shirt, tuxedo jacket and tie, no pants, and a steaming hard-on.

"What's going on, guys?" he said.

On his honeymoon in Tampa, Sam made a few extra bucks preaching a revival. When I saw him two weeks later he seemed severely distressed. I asked him what happened on his honeymoon.

"Not much, man," Sam said. "Not much at all. I found out she slept with her old boyfriend the night before we got married."

"What? Gail? How did you find out that?"

Sam told me he'd conned her.

That Gail slept with her old boyfriend, the night before her wedding, I found astounding. That Sam conned her into confessing did not surprise me at all. As a preacher, Sam was straight as an arrow. In his personal life, Sam was the greatest con man I ever knew.

Sam said Gail acted fidgety all during their honeymoon. He sensed she'd cheated on him, and the night which made the most sense, the only recent night they hadn't spent together, was the night before they were wed. But Sam wanted proof, so he told Gail, "I can't keep this inside anymore. This one girl that was in our wedding . . . I slept with her the night before we got married."

Gail said she understood. That same night, just to make sure she really loved Sam, she had slept with her old boyfriend.

"I was LYING, you bitch!"

In Peoria, Sam asked me what he should do. I told him he had two choices. "Get rid of her now, or if you can handle it, it may never happen again. Everyone makes mistakes."

Although the marriage survived, it was already precarious. And in fairness to Gail, Sam didn't exactly foster a wholesome relationship. One outrageous night in Fairborn, Ohio, where they lived in a small apartment, Sam and Gail swapped partners with another preacher and his wife. Afterward I asked Sam how things had worked out.

"At first it seemed like a great idea," Sam said. "We were all in one bedroom and I made love to his wife. But we finished up before Gail and the other guy did. So I stood there and looked, and this guy had a foot-long dick. And my wife is taking it all, and she's *liking* it."

I almost told Sam to stop. He was really in pain over this.

"Now you want to pull the guy off," Sam said. "But you can't, because you just did *his* wife. Man, I won't ever do that again."

To go with his sexual worries, Sam had financial anxieties too. Just after marrying Gail, he'd stopped preaching with Rich and me. Sam seemed to feel it was time to be his own man, but he still lacked even a shred of responsibility, and once he went on his own he barely scraped by. Instead of working harder, instead of any honest self-appraisal, Sam mostly blamed me for his troubles. Mixed in with Sam's love for me there was still a lot of resentment. Though at some level he knew it was never that simple, I think Sam saw himself as the bad seed and me as the good.

Sam said I should have opened more doors for him in the ministry. After Richard and I preached a church, Sam thought I could pick up the phone and book him a crusade there too. But church pastors could count on me and Rich, while Sam might show up two hours late, or not at all, or show up on time but deliver a sloppy sermon. Despite his reputation, I *did* talk Sam's way into dozens of churches. But Sam seemed to forget this.

It was partly my own fault, for coddling him. With our father dead, I was treating Sam more like a son than a brother. Sam knew this about me, and used it. Each time he ran out of cash, he called me up for a loan. Soon I was sending him $200 every few weeks. It was only a stopgap, Sam always said. There was always something big on the horizon.

"Just get me through next week," Sam would tell me. "It's a done deal, I'm preaching St. Louis next week. I'll pay it *all* back then. I'm right on the verge, man."

In 1977, Gail and Sam took a brief vacation to Los Angeles. One evening, in West Hollywood, they went to the famous Comedy Store on Sunset Boulevard. Richard Pryor was there, working out material for a concert film. Sam and Gail sat riveted in the front row. As Sam later said, that was the night that stand-up took hold of his heart.

He got a steady job offer later that year from the same Chicago church where we'd once chased the naked man with the flapping balls. The pastor had recently died, and his widow asked Sam to replace him. Wanting a steady income, however small, Sam accepted and moved to Chicago. When their budget and her nursing job permitted, Gail flew or drove in from Ohio.

Sam pastored at 918 Belmont Avenue, in a part of Chicago so rough that he carried a .38 pistol in his briefcase. Occasionally he found other uses for it. Sam once invited a traveling evangelist to one of his revivals. By his final night in Chicago, the evangelist still needed bus fare to get him to his next town.

"All the man needs is fifty dollars," Sam told his small crowd of twenty or so.

But when Sam passed around the plate, it only filled up with coins. Sam pulled out his .38, fired two rounds into the ceiling, and yelled at the crowd, "The man says he needs some money to get out of town!" The congregation coughed up.

In this hard-edged Chicago neighborhood, it didn't take long for the people to warm up to Sam. He was a character, and yet he was real. And rather than traveling around from city to city, Sam was seeing the same friendly faces night after night. I'd never seen him so happy before in the ministry.

It all unraveled one weekend when Gail flew in. Though she'd planned on flying home too, Sam got a few unexpected days off, so they drove back to their apartment in Fairborn, Ohio. When Sam and Gail walked up to their front door, they found a teddy bear propped against it. Pinned to the bear's chest was a note from a man expressing his love for Gail. With Sam working in Chicago, Gail was having an affair with the guy who cleaned her carpets.

Sam said Gail admitted this freely, but I didn't believe him. In his heartbreak and rage, I figured Sam slapped her around.

Either way, Gail also revealed to Sam that he'd seen the guy one time. When Sam was in town, the carpet cleaner had brazenly knocked on their door. He wanted a glimpse of Gail's husband.

"Excuse me," the guy had said when Sam came to the door himself. "Do you have a red truck for sale?"

"You got the wrong place," Sam had told him.

Now, in a state of violent despair, Sam drove to the carpet cleaner's apartment.

"Do you have a red truck for sale?" Sam asked as the guy

opened his door. Then Sam pulled out his .38 and pressed it beneath the guy's chin. "I want everything she gave you," Sam demanded.

The carpet cleaner went rummaging through his apartment, pulling out pie pans, shirts, religious paperback books—and love letters written by Gail.

Later that week, Sam was supposed to be preaching a meeting with me, but he never showed up or called. One week after that he appeared in Peoria. Sam brought the love letters with him; I read some myself at his prodding. I could see why Sam felt destroyed. Gail had written a few while sitting in church in Chicago, listening to Sam preach.

Sam read those particular letters over and over, flagellating himself. I'd never seen him so openly wounded.

Getting hit by a truck at age three was the greatest physical trauma of Sam's childhood. Emotionally, our parents' divorce was Sam's most wrenching blow. Still scarred by that experience, Sam's own divorce was devastating to him. Though their marriage was unconventional, Sam really loved Gail. He always called her "the first love of my life." And Gail was a Baptist, a choir singer, and Sam tended to see the world in black and white. If he couldn't trust Gail, then who could he trust?

That winter, the chip on Sam's shoulder bigger than ever, we both knew his days in the ministry were numbered. We just delayed telling each other.

Sam returned to the church in Chicago, but soon had a falling-out with the pastor's widow. He hit the revival circuit again, preaching churches which I set him up in, but Sam was a ticking time bomb. While preaching in Dallas, he slept with the pastor's wife. In Phoenix, Sam and another minister were spotted in a diner with two young women they'd preached to that evening. Nothing sexual happened that time, but in both cities the result was the same. Brother Sam was all through around there.

A few months later, in February 1978, Sam stopped in Rockford. He seemed lost and confused and worn down. In seven years as a preacher, Sam had never earned more than $5,000 in any one year. His marriage had just ended in disillusion, and as Sam put it, "divorce does not look good on a spiritual résumé." Sam still needed our dead father's approval. But he also needed a whole new life.

"It's no use anymore," he told me in Rockford. "I can't make it, man. I can't even pay my bills. What am I gonna do?"

"What have you always wanted to do?"

"I don't know."

"No. I mean what have *you* always wanted to do? Forget that your dad was a preacher, your brothers are preachers, forget all that psychology you were raised with. What have *you* always wanted to do?"

"I've always wanted to be a comedian."

Sam had never said this to me before. Still, I wasn't very surprised. From the beginning, Sam had been funny. He'd always been starved for attention. And at this point in his life, Sam had little left to lose.

"I'll tell you what, Sam," I said. "I think you should give it a shot. If it doesn't work out, you can always come back to the ministry, tell 'em the devil made you do it."

"You think I can do it? Wow, when should I start?"

"You're twenty-five. If you're gonna do it, do it soon. Pick a date, and after that date, no matter what happens, even if you have to pump gas, promise yourself you won't fall back on preaching. You have to commit to this, Sam."

"That's what I'll do, man," Sam said, his voice excited.

Sam set his no-preaching deadline for July 1. By then our mother had married A. D. Marney, another preacher, a man just as kind and decent as our father, and considerably more prosperous. That spring, Sam was preaching the church they pastored together in Tulsa when he got a phone call from Terry Marrs, an attractive woman he'd met while preaching in Houston. Terry read him a newspaper ad for a comedy school down there. Sam was poor, he was divorced—he didn't need any prodding.

Within a few days, Sam drove the five hundred miles from Tulsa to Houston, where he was the most improbable student at the week-long comedy school. A *preacher* who wanted to make it in stand-up comedy? A round guy with thinning hair and a lifetime of failure behind him?

And none of that meant a thing. Because Sam was flat-out funny. *Naturally* funny. Funnier than anyone else in his class. Even funnier than his instructors.

Of course, he was also still broke. But our mother loaned him some cash, and that summer Sam moved to Houston and found his true calling.

Comedy King of Texas

"Sam Kinison has obviously never heard the term soft-spoken. Easily the most manic and audacious of the aspiring funnymen, he will apparently do or say anything to get a laugh, collapsing onto the stage in an impression of Peter Sellers having a heart attack while playing Inspector Clouseau, and tearing up the joint in a dead-on-target parody of a tent revivalist. His act has no unity but it has frenzy to burn, and you can't help laughing at the all-out, bludgeoning outrageousness of it."

—*Houston Post,* July 13, 1979

By my first trip down to Houston that October, Sam was the comedy god at a club called the Comedy Annex. He was juggling three women. After almost twenty-five years of feeling small-time, Sam was finally taking his first walk in the sun.

Still, he barely had an act yet, only five or six lightweight minutes. Initially, Sam relied on sight gags, props, and redneck characters based on people who had attended our father's church. Sam did one early bit called "the fucking cops," where he ran into a crook's apartment, yelling, "Up against the wall!

We're the fucking cops!'' Then Sam the ''fucking cop'' started pumping the crook from behind. On one April Fools' Day, he beat the head off a baby doll, then whipped the torso out into the crowd. ''April Fool!'' he shouted. ''It was *already dead!''*

It wasn't exactly Richard Pryor. But Sam understood that. As an artist, he knew he was merely a baby. Slowly, Sam's repertoire grew, and his fundamental thoughts about comedy changed. ''I first went up with props and characters that make me wince to think about them now,'' Sam told a reporter in one of his earliest interviews. ''If there is one thing I learned in the ministry, it's that you've got to get people's attention, but you also have to have the concepts and information to back up that kind of an attitude once you have their interest. Anyone can go out onstage and start beating people over the head with rubber chickens. That'll get people's attention; real comedy doesn't just make people laugh and think, but makes them laugh and *change.''*

That was a very tall order, but Sam had some confidence now, some momentum. His first big comedic breakthrough came when he performed a bit on a topic that most comedians wouldn't touch: the family dynamics of Mother Mary, her husband, Joseph, and their little Baby Jesus.

''It all goes back to Jesus . . . he's got to be up in heaven freaking out at all the interpretations of things they *say* he said. He didn't even *know* he was the son of God. As soon as he was born, as soon as he could speak the language, his mother said, 'You're the son of God. When you were born the angels came, and the stars stood in one place, the wise men brought gifts, and the whole world's been waiting for you to come and do great things.' '' Sam replied in the sweet voice of a baby: '' 'Really? Me? Are you sure?'

''Everyone but Joseph. Joseph's walking around going, 'Yeah, you better be the son of God, I'll tell you that. You had *better* be him, little mister. And you better be the *only* son of God!' ''

Sam spoke here as Joseph, a jealous husband, talking to Mary. " 'You understand what I'm saying, honey? I got enough problems without running a fucking family full of God's kids. Okay? You sure it was God, right? Did he have any ID? He just said he was an angel and you guys went in the garden? Last time I take a fucking job out of town, I'll tell you that.' Talk about a test of the guy's faith, man. He's going to work, and these fucking dicks are working next to him: 'Hey, Joseph, how's the son of God, pal? Hee-hee-hee.' And Joseph comes back home to Mary: 'Now I'm not saying you're lying, honey, but you don't know the kind of shit I go through at work. So let me make sure I got this straight. An angel came . . . and visited you in the garden . . . and *did* you? Am I getting this right?' "

The first night I saw Sam perform this bit, for just eighty people or so, I went back to Tulsa and told my mother and brothers, "This isn't another tangent. I don't know how long it will take, but Sam is gonna be big."

Sam's first year in Houston, the *Dallas Morning News* named him the Funniest Man in Texas. It was Sam's first serious accolade as a comic, and he finally had some cash in his pocket too. Performing mostly in Houston, with a few college-town gigs around the state, he earned close to $20,000 that year, four times what he'd earned during any one year in the ministry.

As I became more familiar with his act, sometimes I'd watch the crowd instead of Sam. I could see the people trying to figure him out. Is he kind of cute or offensive? Good-hearted or twisted? One night he'd grab a beer off someone's table and fling it at a wall without saying a word, until someone would laugh just to break the tension. Some nights Sam passed around a hat, just like in church, badgering the crowd into donating enough money so that all the indigent comics could eat Chinese food. Several times, I saw Sam pretend to sodomize guys in his audience. This was in Houston, no less: pointed boots, pickup trucks, gun racks. These cowboys strode into the Annex with their dates, had a cold one or two, sat through a few other comics. Next thing they knew, they were rolling around on a dirty nightclub floor, getting dry-humped by Sam. It cracked up the crowd every time, but I always braced for a fight. Not one guy ever swung at Sam, though. Up on a stage, he seemed bigger than he really was. He also seemed tightly wound. When Sam mounted the cowboys, they mostly just laughed and blushed and tried to get away.

Sam rarely cursed before moving to Houston. Not even in private conversation. Now, in front of an audience, he was referring to Baby Jesus as "fuckin' Baby Jesus." I found myself wincing, and I told Sam several times after his show: "Hey, man, you're funny without saying 'shit' and 'fuck' all the time."

Sam always replied the same way. "We're not in church anymore, Bill."

In Houston, there were no limits on Sam at all. "It was like a breakout," he told an interviewer. "The ministry's a hard thing to live up to. And then, suddenly, not to have to live up to any of it—no one knows a thing about you, about your past. Nobody comes up and goes, 'Reverend Kinison' or 'Brother Kinison'—it was fucking great. To get up in front of people and go, 'Hey, fuck you'—it was amazing. It was probably why I got into the vulgarity so much, because it was just such a trip to be able to live it out."

Now that Sam was locally famous, he could also sleep with more women than ever before in his life. My first visit there, he had three affairs going at once: with Terry Marrs, an actress named Kate Connelly, and a comedy fan he picked up at the Annex. Although Terry Marrs was the prettiest by far, she was too dominating for Sam. A divorced businesswoman with one young daughter, Terry tried talking Sam out of stand-up and into something more stable. Sam didn't want to lose her completely, but once he saw that other women liked him, he started ducking

Terry whenever he could. Terry represented stability to Sam, and a stroke for his ego because she looked fine on his arm. But Kate Connelly meant good times.

Kate was not as attractive as Terry Marrs, and so Sam could always relax more around her. Outgoing and intelligent, Kate worked next door to Sam in an improv troupe. Unhappily married to a Houston policeman, she moved out of their house soon after meeting Sam. Sam kept his own apartment, Kate took a small loft near the club, but they frequently spent their evenings and mornings together. Sam was in heaven. For most of his life he'd been waking up alone.

In fellow Annex comedian Carl LaBove, Sam also met a best friend who would stick by him through anything. When they first started getting tight, Carl would hang out all night at Sam's apartment, then secretly crash in his car because he was broke. Sam finally said, "Hey, how come you never invite me to your place?" Carl told him, slightly embarrassed, "Man, I sleep in my car." Carl instantly moved in with Sam and they became razor-close. It wasn't until later that Sam told Carl *why* he'd first befriended him. Among other stand-ups in Houston, Sam considered Carl his sole competition.

Our youngest brother, Kevin, lived with Sam and Carl too. The rest of our family felt Kevin should go to college, but Sam had a strange control over Kevin ever since childhood, when they'd both stayed with our mom while Rich and I went with our dad. It irritated me when Sam persuaded Kevin to join him in Houston. Sam didn't know he would be an instant success. He wanted Kevin there so Kevin could get a real job and cover their bills. Once Kevin did find work, at a clothing store, he sometimes stole clothes for Sam to wear in his act. In Houston, Sam also began telling Kevin that one day he'd help him break into stand-up, or else into the movies. I was in Houston on Kevin's twenty-first birthday, the night he got up and tried stand-up. A talented drummer and basketball player, the best-looking

Kinison boy and the only one six feet tall, Kevin was no comedian. Few people are. But Sam kept making him hollow promises anyway.

One night, after Sam saw Rodney Dangerfield in concert, Rodney dropped in at the Annex. Rodney saw Sam go up, then he pulled Sam aside and told him he thought he was funny. Even before this, the other young comedians looked up to Sam. Even more of a big shot now with Rodney's validation, Sam found himself clashing with Steve Moore, the Annex creative director. A stand-up himself, Moore still performed at the Annex, but he was pure whitebread. And then there was Sam, talking nasty up there, attacking every convention—and killing the crowd every night. As the young Annex comedians split into camps, Moore tried pressuring Sam into sanitizing his act. One night he banned Sam for two weeks for smashing a barstool onstage.

Sam had the fever. He couldn't wait two weeks to perform. The night after getting banned, Sam held a mock crucifixion directly across the street from the Annex. He took off his clothes, put on a towel, and doused his body with ketchup. Then, with help from a few other comics, he tied himself to a convenience-store sign. The Annex crowd, watching Sam through a large picture window, rushed outside to see what the madman was up to. By the time the Houston media and police came, Sam had been hanging there for an hour, shouting, *"Help! They're crucifying me! They're crucifying my talent across the street!"*

Two weeks later, his banishment over, Sam returned in a limo and packed out the house.

Sam found more than notoriety, women, and his best friend Carl in Houston. At age twenty-five, he discovered liquor and drugs.

Until then, Sam had never so much as smoked a joint. At first, he was so innocent. Marijuana would make him so paranoid, sometimes he would call Kate at her apartment, warning her that he'd just gotten high at the Annex. "I'm walking to your house now," he'd tell Kate. "If I don't show up soon I want you to come and look for me." Sam thought he might pass out or forget the way, even though Kate only lived about seven blocks from the club. And it wasn't even good pot!

Once Sam understood that smoking pot couldn't kill him, he got high first thing every morning, graduating from joints to two-foot-high bongs filled with wine. Sam also tried acid in Houston, dropping it his first time with our brother Rich. Walking the streets in the early-morning darkness, they spotted a garbageman and thought he was a werewolf. Sam and Rich ran for their lives and forgot where they'd parked their car. They had to go back for it later.

Sam also took his first Quaalude and snorted his first cocaine, but his drug of choice was liquor. Before this, I'd never seen Sam drink even a beer. Now that he'd started, I felt his drinking might soon grow into a problem. Sam was hopelessly undisciplined. Hopelessly imperfect. That's what made Sam so human. But sometimes that was his curse.

In early 1980, for the second straight year, Sam was named the Funniest Man in Texas by the *Dallas Morning News*. Although pleased, Sam was already plotting to get out of Houston. He made several driving trips out to Los Angeles, to see the top stand-ups perform at the fabled Comedy Store, and to try to schmooze its owner, Mitzi Shore. One night Sam, Kevin, and I all saw Robin Williams play there. "The guy's a fucking genius," Sam kept saying repeatedly after the show. I took it as a good sign: Sam seemed inspired by Robin and not freaked out.

Shortly thereafter, Sam returned to Houston, where it ended for him at the Annex when he and Steve Moore had a fistfight. After Moore loudly threatened Sam with another suspension, they took their hard feelings outside to the parking lot. Although

Moore had a better build, Sam got in the first blow. He charged Moore and pinned him into a parked car, then kept driving his knee into Moore's stomach and thigh, until Moore started convulsing. Moore wound up with busted ribs, a bruised spleen, and a leg broken in two places.

His Annex relationship severed, Sam asked Kate Connelly to move with him to L.A. Kate replied by asking Sam to go with her to New York, where she wanted to act in the theater. Sam let Kate win the argument. They moved to a small flat in the city, but after one month Sam felt miserable.

"I can't do this," he told her, not knowing the city and not having any connections. "If you love me," Sam challenged her, "you'll come with me to L.A."

When Kate chose the theater and New York, Sam seemed destroyed. I was surprised. I hadn't known his feelings for Kate ran that deep.

"My heart never broke like that before," Sam told me later. "I loved her more than Gail, man. My heart hurts just to think of her."

A Screamer Is Born

IN THE SUMMER OF 1980, SAM ARRIVED IN L.A. WITH MAJOR IN-
tentions: Go straight to the Comedy Store, the legendary club
on Sunset Strip. Ingratiate himself with its owner, Mitzi Shore.
Knock her out with his talent. Impress the Hollywood heavy-
weights. Vault straight to the front lines of stand-up comedy.

After dominating in Houston, Sam thought it would happen
fast. Six months, Sam told me. Maybe a year. Instead, he described his move to L.A. as a "swan dive into fucking hell."

Mitzi Shore didn't think he was funny. She also found him too
dirty. Mitzi wanted Sam to try playing clean, but he wasn't capable yet. Sam was a star in Houston. When he struggled in L.A.,
his fragile self-confidence broke. Feeling all the old rage and
bitterness growing inside him, Sam couldn't help himself when
he got onstage. The obscenities just came out.

For his first several months at the Comedy Store, a meat market
of stand-ups, Sam performed only on Monday nights. These were
called Animal Nights, because anyone with a pulse could stand
up and do five minutes. Since Sam didn't impress her the first
time, it took Mitzi Shore several more weeks just to come back
and see him again. Mitzi didn't like him the second time, either.

Sam kept hanging around the Store anyway, pestering Mitzi, charming her, kissing her right on the mouth, trying to con her. Although Sam was still stuck in Animal Night, Mitzi broke down and gave him a job as a doorman.

Sam wasn't sure how to feel about that. The Funniest Man in Texas, he was now showing Angelenos their seats. Sam was also making minimum wage. On the other hand, what a place for a young comic to work. While working the door on weekends in the Main Room, Sam saw dozens of superstar comedians. They'd be working out material for *The Tonight Show,* or for a concert film, or a special on HBO. Sam watched Eddie Murphy, Steve Martin, Billy Crystal, Robin Williams, Jay Leno. Those nights, Sam said he could forget he was a doorman. He could ride all night on his dreams.

Some nights after closing, if Sam had cocaine, he found he could even party with major celebrities. The first time he met Robin Williams, back when Robin still used, Sam told me Robin's opening words were "Hey, got any blow?" Robin blew Sam off as soon as Sam's coke was all gone. Sam didn't even mind. He was a nobody, snorting blow with a star! To Sam, everything was still new and romantic—Hollywood, show business, drugs. He wasn't famous yet. The pressure was low. Sam's appetites were growing, but not yet enormous. Life hadn't gotten insane.

Along with Kevin and Carl, Sam rented a one-bedroom apartment at Oakwood Gardens in Burbank, mostly because he heard Johnny Carson had lived there when he first moved to L.A. They all shared an old Buick Regal, but they seldom had money for gas, so they frequently walked the five miles to the Comedy Store. This was no level walk, either. Between Burbank and West Hollywood there were mountains. Famished by the time they got to the Comedy Store, they'd scrounge orange wedges and olives from the bar. Sometimes they stole tickets from the office, then scalped them outside to people strolling down Sunset. They ate a lot of cheap hot dogs and greasy burgers.

But Sam wouldn't quit. He seemed to know he was running out of options: Make it as a comic, or make it at nothing.

As he told the *Los Angeles Reader,* one of the first local publications to admire him, "There must be some 250 comedians out in L.A. No matter where you were before you came here, you start at the bottom. You take a number. The important thing is that you find a stage and you go up and perform on it. That has to be the priority of your life. If you're broke, you go up. If you haven't eaten that day, you go up. And once you're up, you make it worth all the hell you had to go through to be there."

"I got a real depressing letter from my folks about two weeks ago, because I haven't been taking real good care of my money. They said, 'Sam, we can't send you any more money. You're out of control, you don't know what the fuck you're doing with your cash. And . . . you're old enough to be on your own.' I said, 'Oh, okay' . . . and I called them. I said, 'Mom, get Dad on the phone too, wake him up, I know it's late, but I want you both to hear this. You know, before I was your little son, before I was your baby, before I was your *loan,* I was a free spirit in the next stage of life. I walked in the cosmos, not imprisoned by a body of flesh, but free, in a pure body of light. There were no questions, only answers, no weaknesses, only strengths, I was light, I was truth, I was a spiritual being, I was a God . . . But you had to FUCK and bring my ass down HERE. I didn't *ask* to be born! I didn't call and say: 'Hey, please *have* me so I could work in a fuckin' Winchell's someday!' Now you want me to pay my own way? ". . . FUCK YOU! PICK UP THE FUCKIN' CHECK, MOM! PICK IT UP!"

By the time he performed "Letter from Home," in 1981, Sam had graduated from Animal Nights to being an unpaid regular. Although still performing for free, he could now count on two or three five-minute spots during the week. Some people were shocked by "Letter from Home," since most children don't say "fuck you" to their parents in front of a live audience. Around the Store, people started calling Sam a "shock comedian." Sam liked the image. He cultivated it. But unlike so many other shock comedians, being shocking for Sam wasn't an act. Sam had always been shocking. He was a shocking preacher.

Sam drew "Letter from Home" from his chronic financial frustrations. Much of his rage at the time was directed at me. In Houston, our relationship had never been more relaxed. Sam didn't begrudge my success as a preacher—he had some success of his own. But once show business and L.A. began chewing him up, Sam and I reverted to all our old patterns. I started sending him money, caretaking him, assuming the role of his parent. Sam resumed feeling both gratitude and resentment.

One day we had a blowup at Sam's apartment in Burbank. Even though Richard, Sherry, and I were all staying with him, at his insistence, he'd been gone for two straight days when his landlord banged on his door. He angrily demanded two months' rent. Otherwise, he said, he would lock up Sam's apartment.

I thought: That's pretty strange. I've been sending Sam rent money every month.

Then it struck me: Sam's been spending the money on drugs.

After Rich and I paid the landlord, Sam still didn't appear until the next day.

I said, "Sam, you're not even paying your rent! You're partying on it, man! Every month, like a thousand dollars free money!"

He denied it. Sam always denied it. And I could always see through him.

"That's it," I said. "I'm not paying your drug bills. It's over. I'm not paying anyone's rent who's not using it for rent!"

Later that afternoon, still in Sam's apartment, I felt my anger rising again. Lounging around were four perfectly healthy guys: Sam, Carl, Kevin, and another stand-up from Houston named Bill Barber.

"I can't fuckin' believe this," I said. "You got four able guys here, and not one of you can get a fuckin' job? You're at the Comedy Store at night—fine. What's wrong with getting a job during the daytime?"

Kevin mumbled something about getting a job as a waiter. Sam, Carl, and Barber just looked at me—like I was a raving idiot. Man, they were *comedians.* They lived for the rush they got on the stage—the emotional orgasm. Everything before that, and everything after, was just killing time. Get a day job? They'd rather starve. They'd rather blow my money on drugs.

Though I stopped paying their rent, I kept sending them about $500 a month. It made me sick to think of those guys not eating. When Sam was clean and sober he seemed appreciative, and he loved showing me off: "This is my brother, Bill. Had I taken care of myself, had I gone to school, this would be me." But when alcohol or cocaine brought out his rage, sometimes Sam laid into me: "Mr. fuckin' Goody-Goody, back in Illinois. With your house and your cars. You don't give a shit if I eat! I'm in *hell* out here, and you don't give a fuck, man!"

At times, I felt so bitter toward him I could barely form words. No one could push my buttons the way that Sam could.

"I was married for TWO FUCKIN' YEARS! Twenty-four hours a day, three hundred and sixty-five days each fucking year, I was married. I been married twice, that's how smart I am. Yeah, my second wife—oh my fuckin' . . . oh shit . . . oh man. I married her just to piss another woman off. Very dumb, stupid, high, drunk thing to fuckin' do."

Sam meant he married Terry Marrs to spite Kate Connelly. In truth, Sam married Terry to get his bills paid.

Even then, Terry had to talk him into it. While still living in Houston, she called Sam in L.A. and told him he'd gotten her pregnant. Terry wanted them to get married and have the baby. Sam consented to marriage, but only if Terry would put off having a child. Terry aborted the baby early in her pregnancy, she and Sam were married in Houston, and Terry and her daughter moved into his Burbank apartment. Carl moved out, but still spent many nights crashed out on their living-room floor. Kevin stayed where he was, on the couch.

An account executive in Houston at Arrowhead Water, Terry had landed a transfer out to L.A. In return for working full-time to support Sam and her child, Terry wanted a diligent husband. Instead she got a roller coaster named Sam, who would leave in the afternoon for the Comedy Store, then not return home for three days. When Sam did drop back into her life, he turned their apartment into a crash pad for comics. Terry was almost as stubborn as Sam, though. She thought she could change him. When she couldn't, they hardened toward each other quickly. Sam slept with other women. Terry demeaned him constantly, even in front of our mother. In a Texas accent that Sam had once found sexy, she started to call him a loser. "You're the biggest loser I know. You bring all your loser friends home, they take up the entire floor. You're not gonna be a comedian, you ain't never gonna be nothing. You're nothing but a doorman."

Terry was small but fiesty. A few times, when they fought, she and Sam both threw punches. One night, while Sherry and I were at their apartment, Terry called him a loser and Sam suddenly popped her in the mouth. I jumped on Sam's back and pinned his arms. Sherry hustled Terry outside the apartment. "Take your daughter," Sherry told Terry, "and move back to Texas. Start living a normal life. Sam doesn't want you out here. It's not gonna get any better."

But Terry and Sam stayed trapped right where they were. One day they fought all morning and afternoon. They fought as Sam stalked out the door. When Sam stepped onstage that night at the Comedy Store, he was still seething.

Spotting a man and woman in the front row, Sam asked, "You guys in love? You gonna get married?"

"Yeah, I think we will," the man said.

Sam slowly moved several steps closer. "Gonna get married, huh?"

"I guess so, yeah."

"Tell you what," Sam said calmly. "Before you get married, I want you to make me a promise. I want you to remember this face." Sam leaned over, until he was inches from the man's face. Then Sam opened his mouth and screamed at the top of his lungs: "Oh! OH! AAAAUGH!"

The crowd at the Comedy Store erupted.

Sam did it again the next night he performed, and the next, and each time the crowd roared. From the rage he'd been feeling inside from fighting with Terry, Sam discovered his comic trademark: a blood-curdling, gut-level primal scream.

It wasn't just the scream that made this an important period for Sam. As he talked onstage about his terrible love life, as he started baring his soul, Sam made his performance *personal*. He let his audience *feel* his anger and grief. Some people call that honesty. And that's what began to set Sam apart.

"Yeah, I was pissed off for a while, I was bitter, then I met this little tiny lesbian, only this tall. It was out in California, where you can meet women like that. She was like the first really gentle pretty one I'd ever met. Most lesbians are like: 'Hi there, my name's Alice? I own my own security business?' But this girl was beautiful, she was so cute and pretty: 'I just love women. I think men are indulgent and selfish and they just think of theirselves, and I love women.' I said, 'I agree with you. I love women too. If I was a woman, I'd probably love a woman too, rather than have a fuckin' guy in my life.' So we started going out, started living together. It was funny, though, man. She came up to me one night, she goes: 'Would you mind if I brought another woman into our bed?' Now what fucking *guy* is gonna mind, huh?"

"Lesbians Are Our Friends" was inspired by Cory Yugler, Sam's first bisexual lover. Before meeting Cory, Sam was mostly still in his boy-does-girl phase. Afterward, as he once told *Esquire* magazine, Sam became "addicted to deeply intimate three-way sex. Four is bad choreography, five a sports event."

An acting student, voracious reader, and budding script supervisor, Cory physically resembled Nastassja Kinski. After meeting one night at the Comedy Store, they started spending most evenings at Cory's Westwood apartment, even though Sam was still married to Terry Marrs. Soon, Sam and Terry were splitting up. They tried it again, then separated for good around 1983. With the bogus promise he'd join them soon in Houston, Sam persuaded Terry to move back there with her daughter. Once Terry left, Sam moved out of his Burbank apartment and never called her. There was no talk of divorce for the time being.

One night, after three-way sex with another woman, Cory Yugler confided in Sam: "You're really not very good at eating pussy. It's like you're painting a fence with your tongue—up and down, up and down. Try licking the alphabet in capital letters."

Sam's lack of technique was comedy's gain. In a matter of weeks, he was doing his "Alphabet" riff at the Comedy Store.

"There's no sex education for men. I never got any. No one ever set me hip to anything. The government doesn't send you a pamphlet or anything, you know, on how to lick pussy. Mom and Dad are no fucking road map, all right? Nobody helps you, you're on your own, you gotta learn your own technique. That's why a lot of guys are pretty bad at it. They don't know anything about licking pussy—why would they know? Most guys got like one stroke, you know. They think they're painting a fence or something. The girl's going, 'JESUS CHRIST, AM I BEING LICKED OR WEATHERPROOFED HERE? *Hey!* What the fuck is THIS?' But . . . I like to help. If you don't mind, I'd like to submit a plan to you. What you do, guys, is, you lick the alphabet. *Lick* that fuckin' alphabet. Lick the alphabet, man. It makes you *ap-*

pear creative . . . it's an easy diagram to remember . . . she thinks you're from fuckin' Europe or something. IT WORKS! And do plenty of capital T. On the big letter chart, this is the favorite letter. 'More T, more T! More capital T!' Just trying to help folks, okay? Oh yeah, Dr. Ruth can do it, but I'm a fuckin' asshole. Is that the game here?''

Nobody calls it the "casting couch" anymore, but it's still an open secret in the entertainment industry: Some people use sex to advance their careers. In the wild old days at the Comedy Store, there were female stand-ups sleeping with male stand-ups, in exchange for better spots in the nightly lineup. There were also young male comics sleeping with Mitzi Shore. Sam and I knew several guys ourselves. Sam might have slept with Mitzi, too, and just never told me. Sam was as nakedly ambitious as anyone there.

By 1983, Mitzi had a relationship with Argus Hamilton, a comedian at her club who also played *The Tonight Show.* He would later sober up, and talk about his transformation in *Rolling Stone,* but back then Argus was still an alcoholic. One night, outside the Comedy Store, while several other comedians stood around watching, a drunken Argus started shoving Mitzi. Sam, alone, rushed to Mitzi's defense, bullrushing Argus and knocking him down.

That very instant, Sam's stock began to rise at the Comedy Store. Mitzi introduced him to more Hollywood big shots. She asked Sam's opinion of other comics, at one point so often that several comics resented it. Finally, after three years of rebuffs, Mitzi made Sam a paid regular. This meant he could perform every night, and performing for Sam was narcotic. He could play weekends. And he could play the historic Main Room.

Almost every night Sam performed last, after the crowd had seen twenty or so other comics. Some people said Sam went up last because he was so outrageous and so profane—if he went up earlier, there'd be no one left in the club by the time he came off. Some people said he was too dynamic—none of the other stand-ups wanted to follow him. That part might have been true, but the main reason Sam went last was economic. "Sam Kinison will be up later on in the evening," the Comedy Store announcer would keep repeating all night. It kept people in their seats and buying more cocktails.

Often beginning his act at one or two in the morning, Sam drew an extremely colorful crowd. Porn stars. Strippers. Prostitutes. Drug dealers. Bikers. Junkies. Night people. Packing out the Comedy Store after midnight, underground Hollywood turned Sam into a cult star.

Sam started coming onstage with a new opening bit, which his then-buddy Andrew Dice Clay helped him create. When Sam first moved to L.A., he'd actually performed in a sports coat and tie. Dice suggested a more ominous look—leather jacket, dark sunglasses, on some nights a dark hat or beret. Later, Dice also helped Sam develop his signature introduction. "Ladies and gentlemen," the emcee would announce, "Sam Kinison!" Puffing a cigarette, Sam would walk out slowly in leather coat and dark glasses. He'd just stare at the crowd, without speaking. He'd smoke and stare a long time, until people felt edgy. Finally, Sam would say gently, "You have a good time tonight, folks? You've seen a lot of other comedians? They were funny? They made you laugh? Some you may want to see *again*. Well, I'm a little different." Sam would remove his dark glasses, let the crowd see his face. "My name is Sam. Sam Kinison. YOU'RE GONNA WISH TO GOD YOU'D NEVER SEEN ME! Oh! OH! AAAAUGHH!"

"Did you see Manson's interview? Did you see that? Was that too funny? This guy is fucking gone. He's been in the hole for like fourteen fucking years. He was already sick going in. He's on a comeback—yeah. They pulled him out and said, 'Charlie, why'd you do it?' " Sam, in a small, sniveling voice: " 'I heard the album. I heard that goddam *White Album.* Why don't we do it in the road? Whadda you think he was sayin', man? No one will be watching us.' And you're sitting there going: IT'S A FUCKIN' ALBUM! YOU WERE ON ACID, MANSON! IT'S A FUCKIN' ALBUM! YOU'D have gotten the same message out of the *Monkees,* you fuckin' dickhead." Sam, again as a shaky-voiced Manson: " 'Don't you hear what he's sayin', man? Hey hey, we're the Monkees. Hey hey, we're the Monkees, people say we monkey around. How *clear* does he have to say it, man? Last train to Clarksville, whitey.' IT'S THE MONKEES! THEY WEREN'T EVEN A REAL GROUP! YOU FUCK!"

"There was like a pack of us, four or five, we'd scrape all our money together to buy enough pot and Oki-dogs. They were this two-foot-long hot dog wrapped in a burrito with pastrami, chili, cheese, for a dollar twelve. I was living with whoever had an apartment. It was an amazing struggle."
—Sam on his early days in L.A.

One night in 1983, Sam called me in Rockford. He sounded depressed, almost despondent. He said he'd stopped paying his bills at a storage facility. It had confiscated what few possessions he had, including some cherished letters our father had written to him. Then Sam mentioned, almost in passing, that the LAPD had impounded his car.
I said, "Why'd they do that?"
"Too many parking tickets, man."
"Why didn't you call me? Why lose a *car* on parking tickets? Why lose your letters from Dad, your personal stuff?"
"I didn't think you'd send me the money."
"Since when?"
"It doesn't fuckin' matter. I'm not getting attached anymore to anything material."

Later that year, a few weeks before Christmas, Sam called me from New York City. He was staying with Carl and Carl's girlfriend, Christy, at her parents' small flat. Could I come to New York, Sam wanted to know, to check out two guys he'd met there? They both owned East Coast comedy clubs, Sam said. They were promising him they could break him into the big time. In exchange, Sam had to let them manage his career.

I flew into New York, and Sam looked like crap. He'd been snorting and drinking all week with the two guys who wanted to manage him. The moment Sam said it was their cocaine, I knew there could be trouble. Because even though Sam sounded serious when he called me, the truth was coming out now. He had no real intention of letting these guys manage him. He was stringing them along in return for doing their blow.

On our way to meet them, Sam dropped another bombshell. He said these guys had friends in organized crime. I didn't believe him. Sam said, Yeah, they were both aware of our uncle, a high-ranking Mafia member in the Midwest. When I met them myself, I figured Sam was probably right. Their whole manner said Mob.

I told Sam after the meeting: "You're fucking with serious guys here. Get your ass on a plane and get back to L.A. If they find out you're jerking them off, you're gonna have a real problem."

Two weeks later, Sam never showed up in Madison, Wisconsin, where he, Sherry, and I were supposed to be spending the weekend. Sam was still in New York City, partying hard at bars and comedy clubs, bullshitting guys with possible links to organized crime. One night, all of them doing cocaine at one guy's apartment, one guy said something like "Hey, time to put up or shut up. Are we going in business, or not?" Sam told them no. They made a threat. Sam said fuck you. One guy pinned Sam down while the other guy beat him unconscious. Sam was alone when he came to. He stumbled outside and went and got Carl

LaBove. They returned to the apartment carrying knives. Luckily for everybody involved, the apartment was empty. When Sam sobered up, he got scared. For a long time he stayed away from New York.

By the spring of 1984, Sam and Robin Williams had gotten much tighter. Sam decided he wanted to live in a house, but no one would rent him one after running his credit, so Sam asked Robin to sign a lease for him. Robin agreed. Sam moved into an A-frame house off Mulholland Drive, in the Hollywood Hills. It was also around this time that Sam and Robin began performing together. As Sam told a reporter, "Robin watched me from the back of the room for about a month, and then we began to work out together onstage, trying to top each other with improv bits. And let me tell you, that is not easy to do. Robin is quick. Very quick. A Jedi."

The first time I saw them sharing a stage, Sam looked like an awestruck pupil and Robin destroyed him. Intensely embarrassed, Sam took me around to the back of the Comedy Store. He asked me what I thought he'd done wrong. This was completely unlike him—Sam never let anyone tell him about his act—but since he'd asked I said, "Well, he's a lot more aggressive than you up there. He's getting you to react to him. This is Robin Williams, you aren't gonna beat him like that. Jerk *him* into *your* thing. You can't lay back with this guy."

The next time I saw them onstage, a uniformed Green Beret sat in the audience. Returning prisoners of war had been filling the nightly news shows. Moving upstage toward the Green Beret, Sam said, "You know something, Robin? These POW guys are pussies. Oooh, I spent four hundred and eighteen days. Oooh, oooh, I was a prisoner." Sam edged even closer, speaking directly now to the Green Beret. "Lemme tell you something, man. You wanna know what torture is? Don't give me this four hundred days shit. I was married for TWO FUCKIN' YEARS!"

When the laughter died, the soldier's voice cut through the darkness. He said, "I'll bet you guys didn't even go. Did you?"

When they're not performing, most comics have massive inferiority complexes. They've used humor all their lives as a method of self-defense. Robin Williams is the *only* self-confident stand-up I've ever met. But at that moment I looked at Robin and he seemed frightened: This guy is a Green Beret. If I drill him, like any other heckler, will he snap? Is he gonna climb up here and kick my ass?

Sam seized the moment. He ad-libbed, "No, no, I didn't go over there to Vietnam. I was TWELVE at the time, you ass!"

The Green Beret laughed. Sam went blasting off on another riff. It was a critical moment for Sam, the first time he got the best of Robin Williams. Sam still felt completely inept in his personal life. But after that night, he knew he could rock with anyone up on a stage.

As the word spread through Hollywood—somebody fresh and strange is working the Comedy Store—major stars starting calling in to see what time Sam would go up. Among Sam's early admirers were Lauren Hutton, Alan Thicke, Stephen Stills, Phil Collins, Eric Clapton, Dan Aykroyd, Richard Lewis, Bob Saget, Eddie Murphy, Richard Belzer, Rodney Dangerfield, Steve Martin, and Randy Newman. One unforgettable night, Sam performed with Richard Pryor in the front row. Pryor later came backstage and complimented Sam's spot. They talked about preachers and Peoria. They developed warm feelings for one another. Sometimes they shared cocaine.

I first met Pryor myself at Mitzi Shore's pink mansion, just a few hundred yards uphill from her Comedy Store. A crash pad for struggling stand-ups, it was also a wild after-hours spot for anyone in the business who partied hard. One morning there, about 3:00 A.M., Richard Pryor pulled out a huge round rock of cocaine, tightly wrapped in a $100 bill. He chipped off some lines with a pocket knife, then he and Sam snorted blow until after sunrise.

Even after the Hollywood stars embraced him, the top managers and agents kept Sam on a steady diet of cruel rejection. The more time I spent around Hollywood, the less surprising I found this. Contrary to the myth, there *are* no starmakers in Hollywood. In Hollywood, where everyone covets what they don't have, everybody is working for their next job, which means they can't be bothered to break in anyone new, no matter how promising that performer might be. I saw this again and again, when agents and managers came to watch Sam at the Comedy Store. He made their stomachs hurt. He made them laugh until they cried. They knew he was truly original. But for years nobody signed him. For years.

Something else about Sam made mainstream Hollywood nervous. Both as a person and a performer, he inspired strong feelings in people. One night in the Main Room, after Sam offended someone, a liquor glass whizzed toward the stage. Sam threw up his right hand and the glass cut open his palm. Sam stared at his blood, then jumped off the stage and barged into the crowd, demanding to know what imbecile had thrown it. Everyone pointed to Gallagher's sister, whose brother had played there that night in a smaller room. Sam dragged her from her seat and out toward the door, then he went back for her friends. The whole time she kept shouting, "I'm Gallagher's sister! I'm Gallagher's sister!"

Sam growled, "Bring him over here too! I'll beat *his* fuckin' ass!"

The story made the rounds. It fueled Sam's renegade image. It didn't move him closer toward hitting the big time.

It was a weird, frustrating, up-and-down time. Friendly with all the stars, a star in his own right on Sunset Strip, Sam was still unknown to the general public. He was also perpetually broke, and the comedy business had boomed in the early eighties. Performing in concert, recording albums, starring in sitcoms or movies, a leading comic could earn well over $1 million a year. Even I told Sam sometimes when his frustrations mounted: "Important industry people will be here tonight. Maybe you oughta lay back just a little bit. Just for tonight."

"Okay, man," Sam would agree. He would start out playing it clean, playing it safe, and he'd get a few giggles from tourists. Then he'd spot some celebrities in the crowd, or a woman he wanted to sleep with. Experiment over. He'd start riffing on serial killers and Satan, crucifixion and cunnilingus. The crowd would be gasping for air. The stars would be grinning at him. The managers and agents would tell me after the show: "Your brother is very funny. But where will I put his act?"

In late 1984, Sam was evicted from the house which Robin Williams had signed the lease on. Sam had stopped paying his rent.

As I helped Sam move out his belongings, he told me, "This is the last time I'm doing this, man. I'm not getting connected to my stuff anymore. My physical stuff. I don't care anymore." When Sam turned thirty-one that December 8, he did not even have his own place, so Mitzi Shore gave him a room at her pink mansion.

A few weeks later, Rodney Dangerfield tracked down Sam on the phone. Calling Sam from the Comedy Store. Rodney said he and HBO were arranging another *Young Comedians' Special,* at Rodney's own club, Dangerfield's, in Manhattan. Rodney wanted Sam, but Sam told Rodney he didn't do contests. Rodney told him it wasn't a contest. Sam said it sounded like one.

Rodney hung up with Sam and called me in Rockford.

"You gotta talk to your brother," he said.

"About what?"

"I want him on this HBO special. It's already full, but I want Sam. I'm at the Comedy Store. I'll go upstairs and bump somebody right now."

"Sam won't do contests."

"It's not a contest! What is it with you two guys? It isn't a contest—it's a showcase! He ain't gonna win anything. It's a showcase, I tell ya. He can get up and be seen all over the country."

I called Sam and told him it wasn't a contest. He still sounded hesitant. Since getting his ass kicked there, Sam had avoided New York for almost a year. Sam had a pretty wild imagination. He thought there might be a contract out on his life.

I told Sam I felt strongly that it was all over, and that he would be safe. I reminded him that we had friends too. I promised I'd go there with him.

"Let's do it," Sam said.

I called back Rodney. He went upstairs at the Store and aced out another comic. Sam and I never found out who Rodney bumped.

Sam had been doing stand-up for seven years, and he still hadn't gotten his break. He tried staying fatalistic about the HBO gig, but he couldn't control his excitement. Unlike network television—with all its conservative watchdogs and powerful sponsors—no one at HBO would try censoring him. On HBO, an outlaw comic like Sam could really cut loose.

Sam said he didn't need me in New York; he wasn't afraid anymore. Sounding happy and straight, he called me from his hotel after taping his spot at Dangerfield's. Sam said the audience gave him a standing ovation, he thought he did great, but he wasn't even sure when the show would be aired. Back in L.A. a few days later, Sam called Rodney to thank him again. In the same conversation, Rodney asked him why he didn't play at Dangerfield's more often. Sam hemmed and hawed and then told Rodney the truth. He'd been frightened to come to New York since getting knocked out there.

Sam and I never knew what phone calls Rodney made. But the following week, the two guys who'd punched out Sam showed up in Los Angeles. They apologized to Sam behind the Comedy Store.

Pain and Success

WE TOOK A FAMILY SKI TRIP THAT CHRISTMAS TO RED MOUNTAIN, Nevada. My brother Kevin kept saying he wanted to lose more weight, so he could start modelling again at the Barbizon Agency in Los Angeles. I told Kevin he already looked too thin, but other than that he seemed his usual self—outgoing, charming, and spoiled. His whole life our family had pampered Kevin; we still thought of him as our baby. Kevin exploited this. In his own words, he was always a "taker, not a giver."

A few months later, in February of 1985, Kevin, Sam, and Carl were house-sitting for a friend. One night, while partying, Sam and Carl told Kevin they'd come right back with some food. Three nights later they still hadn't returned.

Kevin called Jim Carrey at the Comedy Store, asking Carrey to come pick him up. Sam's most devoted fan, Kevin hung out at the club and knew all the comedians. He and Sam and I were especially close with Carrey.

Carrey brought Kevin back to the club, made several phone calls, and finally tracked down Sam.

"You better get in here fast," Carrey told him. "Your brother is acting weird, Sam. I was scared riding with him."

When Sam arrived at the Store, Kevin alternated between being utterly lucid and incomprehensible. Kevin had suffered a psychiatric disorder.

Even before that week, Kevin was starving himself so he could model again. The house they were all staying at had no food, so he may not have eaten at all for three straight days. Once Sam and Carl went out and Kevin was by himself, I also feared that he'd taken some powerful drug. Angel dust perhaps, or PCP.

Sam was guilt-stricken for leaving Kevin alone. Then, the day after picking up Kevin at the club, Sam arranged for him to fly back to Tulsa. This made Sam feel even worse, as if he had bailed out on his younger brother. But Sam could barely take care of himself. He thought Kevin should be near our mom and her husband, A.D.

Before Kevin's flight out of Burbank Airport, he and Sam and Jim Carrey killed time at the Glendale Galleria. As Sam and Kevin were crying in each other's arms, some punks ridiculed them. Sam, Kevin, and Carrey got into a brawl. Although Kevin could always fight, Sam called me and told me that night: "I had one guy on the ground and I looked over at Kevin, and he was just getting hit. He never swung back. He never turned loose on the guy. It was like watching another person."

In Tulsa, Kevin refused to see any doctors. He insisted he was fine, and that everyone else had changed. I thought maybe I'd have a chance. When Kevin was a boy I taught him how to play basketball. I protected him from bullies the way I protected Sam. But none of this mattered. I could not persuade Kevin to see even one doctor. All these years we had treated him as our child, and this made watching his suffering even more painful.

On March 22 we all gathered in Tulsa, where Carl married his longtime sweetheart, Christy. Sam was best man. Our stepfather, A.D., presided over the ceremony. It was a joyous occasion when our family needed one.

Three days later, back in Los Angeles, Mitzi Shore threw Carl and Christy out of her mansion. They'd been secretly sleeping in Sam's room when he wasn't there. At Mitzi's mansion, comedians could behave like animals. They could trash the place, drink and snort and smoke pot around the clock. But wives and girlfriends were forbidden to live there.

When Sam learned what had happened, he left the mansion too. Then he started asking around to see how Mitzi found out about Carl and Christy. Several comics told Sam, "It was Dice Clay." Mitzi herself may have confirmed this to Sam. Sam had really liked Dice until then, but this happened at an emotional time for Sam, and Sam was intensely loyal to Carl and Christy. Although few people knew it, this was the real beginning of Sam's feud with Dice Clay. It also strained his already ambivalent feelings toward Mitzi Shore.

Sam called me that spring from a hotel room in Toronto, where he'd hustled a modest gig at the Yuk Yuks comedy club. Even over the phone, I always knew when Sam was coked up or drunk. Stone sober, and weeping, Sam said he'd just read the last page of *Wired,* Bob Woodward's biography of John Belushi.

A big fan of Belushi's talent, Sam had met him a few times at the Comedy Store, in the summer of 1981, when Belushi dropped in during the filming of *Neighbors.* In 1982, Belushi had died of a drug overdose at the Chateau Marmont on Sunset.

"I just finished the book," Sam said, crying. "It sounds too close to me, Bill. I'm not ending up like that, man."

We talked for another ten minutes and then said good night.

One month later, at a mutual friend's apartment, I found Sam snorting cocaine off the back cover of *Wired.*

"This is for John," Sam said, as he looked up from his next blast. "I owe it to John, man."

"Let's see," I told Sam. "A month ago you were crying about it, now you're doing lines off it. I guess you've adjusted."

* * *

One night that summer, Sam's ostensibly steady girlfriend, Cory Yugler, discovered a phone number in his pocket. Cory knew Sam was an outrageous flirt, but this time she got angry. First, Sam tried to lie his way out of it. Then the confession came gushing out: He'd just had a one-night stand with a woman he'd met at the club. After they went through the tears and the reaffirmations, Sam thought Cory had forgiven him.

A few weeks later they made a trip to New York. Then Sam had to get back home for a gig at the Comedy Store. Cory would hang out with friends and fly home a few days later.

Sam arrived at Newark International with the usual terror he felt before stepping on any airplane. Sam was certain that one day he'd die in a plane crash. Over the years he'd tried Quaaludes, liquor, and pot to quell his fear, but nothing had worked.

On this particular night, a metal detector went off as Sam passed through with his carry-on bag. He was so mellowed out on pot and 'ludes, Sam thought someone else was in trouble.

Airport security shoved him against a wall, pulling their weapons and shouting, "He's got a gun!" The Newark police charged Sam with attempting to carry a loaded .38 onto an airplane. As terrified of jails as he was of airplanes, Sam told the police he'd been set up by his girlfriend. According to Sam, it was Cory who'd packed his luggage for him that night.

Sam's attorney called me in Buffalo, where I pastored a church that year. I called the Newark district attorney, explained that I was a preacher, and talked her into putting Sam on probation. Every week for one year, Sam would have to keep her apprised of his whereabouts and activities.

Sam told *Premiere* magazine: "The gun in the fucking bag may be the coolest thing that's ever been pulled on me. It was an act of passion. I really hurt her, so she was going to get me back." Privately, he was furious at Cory. For all his walks on the wild side, this was Sam's first serious brush with law enforcement. It shook him up.

When he and Cory broke up over the incident, Sam reacted the same way he did whenever he lost a woman he honestly cared for. He plunged into depression and went on a nasty binge.

In show business, in life, one day can make such a difference. Sam's life changed forever on August 3, 1985, the night HBO broadcast *Rodney Dangerfield's 9th Annual Young Comedians' Special.* Other young comics made strong showings that night, especially Louie Anderson and Rita Rudner, who Sam probably liked most out of all the female stand-ups.

But even Louie and Rita couldn't touch Sam.

He was more than the nastiest, naughtiest, darkest. Sam was the one who didn't remind you of any other comic you'd ever seen. He was the one people quoted the next day to friends.

Rodney made the introduction himself. "Here's a guy who is rather unusual, and I love people who are different, you know? When I say rather unusual, you'll know what I mean when you meet him, okay? We all love him here. Let's have a nice warm reception for Sam Kinison."

Sam walked out in an overcoat down to his knees. It was a gift from Yanna Widmark, an old girlfriend of Sam's and Richard Widmark's daughter. Richard Widmark had worn the coat on *Madigan,* one of Sam's favorite TV shows when he was a kid. Sam thought it might bring him luck.

"Well, I'm sorry I'm late," Sam started off. "I was supposed to be here a little earlier, but I just spent the last two hours at a 7-Eleven, going, 'MARLBORO! MARLBORO! CIGARETTES! SMOKEY-SMOKEY! How the fuck did you get this job? I shoulda shot your ass in Da Nang when I had the chance!' "

Just that quickly, Sam had the audience under his spell. Who is he? What will he say next?

In his six-minute HBO spot, Sam also targeted marriage:

"I'm going around the country, I'm trying to get as many people as I can *not* to get married. I've been married, and I'm just trying to help. Anyone here who's never been married? You never been married? What's your name? Michael? Well, Michael, if you ever think about getting married, if you ever think you've met the right woman, you want to settle down and change your life, will you do me a favor, Mike? Remember this face. AAAAUGH! AUGGGHH! AAAAUGHH! Because if you get married, Mike? That's gonna be your fuckin' face every morning."

Hen-pecked husbands talking to friends on the telephone:

"Hello, guys? Yeah, listen, I gotta cancel out, I can't make it. Nah, I'm not gonna be able to go. SHE'S GOT MY DICK! Nah, she won't give it to me, I been talking to her all day. Yeah, she got the spare too. Well, she's upset. I tried to sneak out of the house with it this morning, I was halfway out of the driveway, she came running out of the house, and I had to give it to her right there on the street. Huh? Okay, I'll ask her, hold on. Honey? It's the guys. No, they just called to say they're all taking theirs. No, I just wanna take mine 'cause I don't want to stand out. Okay, dear. Guys? She said no fuckin' way. She said no way, the dick stays here. Do me a favor, if you guys see me working on the yard and stuff, around the house next week, will you do me a favor, do you love me? KILL ME. STRANGLE ME, SHOOT ME, RUN ME OVER—WHATEVER IT TAKES! I'M IN HELL! OH! AAAUGH!"

And the pitch-black routine that people talked about most:

"I'm like anyone else on the planet, I'm very moved by world hunger. I see the same commercials, with those little kids, starving, and very depressed. I watch these things and I go, Fuck, I know the *film* crew could give this kid a sandwich! There's a director five feet away going, 'DON'T FEED HIM YET! GET THAT SANDWICH OUTTA HERE! IT DOESN'T WORK UNLESS

HE LOOKS HUNGRY!' But I'm not trying to make fun of world hunger. Matter of fact, I think I have the answer. You want to stop world hunger? Stop sending these people food. Don't send these people another bite, folks. You want to send them something, you want to help? Send them U-Hauls. Send them U-Hauls, some luggage, send them a guy out there who says, 'Hey, we been driving out here every day with your food, for, like, the last thirty or forty years, and we were driving out here today across the desert, and it occurred to us that there wouldn't *be* world hunger, if you people would LIVE WHERE THE FOOD IS! YOU LIVE IN A DESERT! YOU LIVE IN A FUCKIN' DESERT! NOTHING GROWS OUT HERE! NOTHING'S GONNA GROW OUT HERE! YOU SEE THIS? HUH? THIS IS SAND. KNOW WHAT IT'S GONNA BE A HUNDRED YEARS FROM NOW? IT'S GONNA BE SAND! YOU LIVE IN A FUCKIN' DESERT! GET YOUR STUFF, GET YOUR SHIT, WE'LL MAKE ONE TRIP, WE'LL TAKE YOU TO WHERE THE FOOD IS! WE HAVE DESERTS IN AMERICA—WE JUST DON'T LIVE IN 'EM, ASSHOLE!''

Within one stunning week, the HBO spot propelled Sam from local noteriety into national stardom. Reviewing the show in the *Washington Post,* Tom Shales singled out Sam as "the one discovery on the program," and "the one comic on the show with a little ferocity to him." As for the flood of phone calls, the first important one came in from Marty Klein, president of the Agency for the Performing Arts. Best-known for helping Steve Martin cross over from stand-up into movies, Klein had also represented Steven Wright, Andy Kaufman, Rick Moranis, Pee-wee Herman, John Candy, Rodney Dangerfield, and Martin Mull. From his Hollywood office on Sunset, Klein called Sam at a comedy club in Colorado Springs.

"We want to sign you," he told Sam.

"I've been waiting for this phone call for ten years," Sam replied.

The rest of that August the offers came in a rush. HBO wanted Sam for his own one-hour special, with an option to finance three more. David Letterman, an old friend of Sam's from the Comedy Store, offered Sam a six-show commitment. Warner Bros. Records pitched a deal for four comedy albums. Lorne Michaels called from Manhattan, wanting Sam to become the first nonhosting comic in history to perform stand-up on *Saturday Night Live.* Then Rodney Dangerfield came through for Sam again. He wanted Sam in his next feature film, a comedy in the works called *Back to School.* Rodney said he and the writers would insert a few cameo scenes for Sam.

Sam got so hot, so fast, from one six-minute performance, that it all seemed slightly bizarre. And even with all the sudden acclaim, Sam's emotions were characteristically divided. Mostly, he was elated. But at times Sam was bitter and brooding. He'd created no new material for this gig. At the Comedy Store, he'd been killing crowds for years with the same exact stuff, and mainstream Hollywood knew it. *Sam* hadn't changed at all—everyone else had. Now that he had a national television credit, everyone in Hollywood wanted to be his pal. Everyone told him, We always knew you could do it.

"Why did it *take* so long?" Sam said. "Were they fuckin' blind until now?"

I agreed with Sam about Hollywood. As a whole, the industry struck me as a bunch of wimps. Still, I also told Sam one night that summer, "A lot of it was your own fault. You wasted a lot of time, man. You'd make an important contact, get a meeting, then get fucked up and blow it off. Or you'd show up two hours late. You'd have made it a lot sooner if you were straight."

Sam took offense. "No, man," he said angrily. "It took *everything* I went through to get me here today."

"Including the partying?"

"That's right."

"So it doesn't matter what you do, how you act, as long as the end comes out right."

"Yeah. The ends justify the means."

To Sam, it was all part of one necessary whole. Live hard, perform hard. I felt that was a cop-out, that the main reason Sam partied so hard was to try and dodge real life and avoid certain feelings. Sam, at least on the surface, never conceded this. And once the public found out he used liquor and drugs, Sam used his image as an excuse to continue. That's right—Sam was never "trapped" by his image. That's a show-business cliché. Sam's image was very convenient for him.

"That's what my fans expect out of me," Sam would tell me, typically when he was hammered. "I'm an outlaw, man! You don't break any rules, Bill! Gotta start breaking some rules, bro!"

Sometimes I'd walk in on Sam getting blitzed with his less successful comedian friends. I'd try getting him to ease up, because those guys could sleep away the entire next day, but Sam had an engagement.

"Hey, man," Sam would slur, "we're partying out for a reason. If we get *one* idea tonight, it's been worth it."

In the weeks after the HBO spot, as it became clear his career was about to explode, I wondered if Sam was emotionally equipped. Even when nobody knew who he was, Sam never learned how to pull back. How would he now?

The Beast

SAM ALWAYS LIKED CALLING HIMSELF "THE ROBERT REDFORD OF comedy." He meant that he was the Natural. Unlike most comics, Sam never sat down and wrote out his routines. Never. Instead, Sam did his stand-up the same way he'd preached—extemporaneously. He always had some idea of where he would start and end, but no clue at all where his mouth might stray in between.

Nevertheless, in one respect Sam was exactly like other stand-ups. He collected material every waking hour. Around Sam, your life was not quite your own. It was Sam's, to use in his act.

On November 14, 1985, three months after his breakthrough on HBO, Sam made his network debut on *Late Night with David Letterman*. A few weeks earlier, back in Los Angeles, he and I had gone shopping with my daughter, Ginger. Leaving a music store with a bag full of CDs, Sam saw me pushing Ginger around in her stroller. I must have seemed slightly dazed.

He said, "You look like Dawn of the Dead, man."

I laughed, then I didn't give it much thought. Until I watched him that afternoon in New York, taping the Letterman show.

"Any of you have kids?" Sam asked the studio audience.

"Have you seen those guys? Those guys in the malls with the strollers—have you seen them? With that look on their face like they envy the dead?" Pretending to be a zoned-out suburban father pushing a stroller, he suddenly started screaming: "SOME-BODY SHOOT ME! THIS ISN'T A MALL—I'M IN HELL! OH! OH! AUGGGHHH!"

After Sam's first network TV spot, David Letterman seemed to be tickled by him. Before introducing his next guest, Letterman yelled into the camera, *"Ahhhh! Shoot me! Ahhhh!"*

Sam flew back to New York three weeks later, to work on his first appearance on *Saturday Night Live.* Although he loved the cast, especially Dennis Miller and Dennis Quaid, by midweek Sam was irate at NBC. While promoting the upcoming show, NBC kept referring to him as "the Beast," a media tag he'd picked up along with "the Screamer." Sam already had designs on starring in feature films. Billed as the Beast or the Screamer, he feared he'd never transcend stand-up comedy. He wanted the public to just call him Sam Kinison.

When Sam found out *why* they kept pushing him as the Beast, he was no longer angry at NBC. He was now irked at APA, his new big-time Hollywood agency. APA had sent NBC a promotional photo of him. Under Sam's name it read in bold black letters: THE BEAST.

The Friday afternoon before the Saturday broadcast, Sam called his agent, Marty Klein, at his office on Sunset Strip. Sam had another Hollywood guy working with him, a temporary adviser named Bill Hand. On a coast-to-coast conference call, Sam complained about the headshots that called him the beast. Marty Klein managed to calm Sam down, but then Klein made a mistake. Klein told Sam not to wear his beret when he went on *SNL.*

Already self-conscious about his thinning hair, Sam told Marty, "Forget it." But Sam was too embarrassed to tell Marty why.

I don't know what Marty said next, but Sam went ballistic. "Fuck you!" he exploded. "I'm not asking you to change my image! I'm wearing the beret! And I don't want to be advertised as the Beast! If you can't handle that, I'll find someone else!"

Sam listened a moment or two, then he lost it again. "Obviously you're not getting the picture! When I get back on Monday, why don't you just have my papers ready for me! Fuck you, and fuck your agency!"

Sam asked Bill Hand, who apparently hadn't said much, "Are you jumping off the ship too?"

Hand said yeah, he and Sam were also through.

The purge unloosed, Sam slammed down the phone and called his attorney, Peter Paterno. "Hey, Peter, I just dumped Klein and Hand. Are *you* on the ship or not?"

Paterno told Sam he was sticking around.

After "waiting ten years" for the phone call from Marty Klein, Sam fired him in four months. In part, Sam felt only he had the right to monkey around with his image. In part, he still resented the show business establishment for taking so long to allow him into their club. In part, Sam only truly respected his fellow artists; he thought agents and managers came and went like busboys. Mostly, however, he left APA so fast because he had a war raging inside him. With Sam, the line between love and rage was very thin.

The night after firing Marty Klein, Sam made pop cultural history. While other comics had hosted *SNL*, none had come on just to do stand-up. Sam opened up with a bit on the twelve disciples: "I felt sorry for the disciples though, you know? Those guys had the toughest job in the world. They could never call in sick." Sam mimed a disciple making a phone call, faking a nasty cough so Jesus will buy his excuse. " 'Yeah, listen, Jesus? Four or five of us went fishing last night and we forgot our sweaters. We kind of got a cold and we're not gonna be able to walk with you to Jerusalem today.' " For a few beats, the disciple listens to Jesus. " 'Uh, what? We're healed? What do you mean, we're healed? You don't have to be here, you can send the word and we're healed? I didn't know that. All right, we'll see you in about ten minutes. Come on, guys, let's go, WE'RE HEALED!' "

Using Jesus Christ as his bridge, Sam lamented mankind's treatment of visionaries and prophets. "Seems like everybody who tries to help kind of goes that route. That's the wonderful thing about the planet Earth here: Anybody tries to change the world, we shoot 'im. He's trying to change the world—SHOOT 'IM! Every guy, I swear to God. Look at history. Gandhi. Abraham Lincoln. Sadat. It was like: 'Well, he was gonna bring peace to the Middle East.' Yeah, good luck, pal. Sadat, you did such a good job, we decided to have a parade for you. Make sure you wear something bright, and sit down in front, okay? This one's for you, pal.' "

After the show, Lorne Michaels invited us to a meal with the *SNL* cast. Riding with Lorne in the back of his limousine, Sam and I were impressed by his blunt but friendly manner. Sam said Robin Williams might be meeting us at the restaurant. Lorne told Sam not to bet on it—Robin was famous for not showing up where he said he would.

At the restaurant, just before Lorne stepped out of the limo before us, he praised Sam's performance that night and invited him back on the show.

"This is unreal," Sam whispered to me.

Once inside he paid his respects to the *SNL* cast, and to that week's guest host, John Lithgow. Then Sam took me into the bathroom and tried getting me to do blow.

I'd first done drugs in Houston, along with Sam, at the same time he discovered them. I was thirty by then. I'd been preaching since age nineteen. Doing drugs was fun and strange and rebellious. It was also something to share with Sam and Kevin.

In Houston I smoked pot and did an occasional Quaalude. Sam was already taking cocaine, but only rarely. I didn't use blow myself until three or four years later, and then mostly with

Sam once he moved to L.A. With cocaine, the innocence and fun went out of things quickly for me. Cocaine made me angry. Sometimes I used it because I was already angry. After a few years I quit, when my daughter Ginger turned one year old. I did it not so much for her, but because I wanted a cleaner life for myself. For one whole year after that, Sam made it a personal quest to get me to backslide.

"Just one little line," he'd say. "It ain't gonna hurt you, brother."

It was tempting. When Sam wanted a partying partner, he could be amazingly persuasive. But I never once let him draw me back in.

I also gave up liquor at the same time, since the only reason I drank was to take the edge off the blow. Besides, seeing Sam get drunk was the best advertisement for me to stay sober. When Sam got drunk he wasn't even worth talking to. He wouldn't be listening anyway. Sam was a loudmouth even when sober. Drunk, he turned into the great philosopher-king. Sam, the god of dysfunctional relationships, would even counsel his buddies on how to deal with their women!

But Sam was more than a talky, self-absorbed drunk. Alcohol often drove him to rage, and the rage killed all the tenderness inside him. Although few people knew it, cocaine was not the largest part of his problem. Alcohol was. Even when Sam went stretches without doing blow, the booze was still there. He favored hard drinks, particularly Jack Daniel's.

Now, at the New York restaurant, the bathroom was small, we were alone, and Sam locked the door behind us. Cutting lines on the counter in front of the mirror, Sam made two or three vanish and then nodded at me.

"Come on, dude, let's celebrate," he said, sniffing. "I just did *Saturday Night Live!*"

"No, Sam, I quit."

"Quit tomorrow, man."

"No. You can do whatever you want, but I'm not doing it with you."

Sam kept snorting and talking. He asked me, again, what I thought of his new manager, Elliot Abbott. Ever since's Sam move to L.A., he'd been pushing *me* to become his manager. Since I still wasn't prepared to, Sam had just hired Elliot, who came recommended to him by Lorne Michaels and Penny Marshall. After meeting one night at the Comedy Store, Penny and Sam had recently started dating.

"Elliot's fine for right now," I said. "But I'd dump him soon. Let him do what he can for you, then get rid of him. The guy's a phony."

I'd just met Elliot that week in New York. I said something mundane, and trying to kiss my ass so he could represent Sam, Elliot said, "Bill. What a perfect way to put that."

From that moment on, Elliot Abbott started to lose my trust.

Back in Los Angeles that winter, Sam ended his brief affair with Penny Marshall. In perfect Hollywood style, they broke up over a movie.

While preparing to direct her first feature film—*Jumpin' Jack Flash,* starring Whoopi Goldberg—Penny had offered Sam an important supporting role. Then Penny called us back while we were in Las Vegas. She told Sam that Whoopi Goldberg had nixed him from *Jumpin' Jack Flash.* When I took the phone, Penny told me the same thing. She seemed to be telling the truth, but I wasn't angry at Whoopi. I thought she'd simply made a smart business decision. She didn't want Sam to blow her off the big screen.

Sam took it personally. He felt backstabbed by Whoopi and never forgave her. Making it even more galling to him, Sam never thought Whoopi was even remotely funny. "Whoopi Goldberg," he told a reporter for *Rolling Stone.* "A nation decides not to hurt somebody's feelings." In the *Village Voice,* Sam flippantly said he'd slap her the next time he saw her.

"Tell him to bring his fat ass to the Comedy Store," Whoopi responded. "Let him try it there." On *The Howard Stern Show,* she called Sam an "illiterate, impossible, talentless turd."

Exacerbating it all was the flap over *Comic Relief.* Sam, one of America's most popular comedians, was never invited to the comedy event of the year. He never even got asked to sit in the audience. Sam mostly blamed Whoopi for this, but when he got drunk, or went on *The Howard Stern Show,* Sam castigated them all—Whoopi, Billy Crystal, even his friend Robin Williams. If Robin had said the word, *Comic Relief* czar Bob Zamuda would have invited Sam in a heartbeat. The comedy industry knew it. Sam knew it. Famously loyal to *his* friends, Sam never understood why Robin didn't go to bat for him. And even with all his other accolades, *Comic Relief* became a tremendous sore spot. Sam's fans would ask him on the street: "How come you're not on *Comic Relief?*"

After Sam split up with Penny Marshall, his next celebrity girlfriend was Beverly D'Angelo. Beverly was so strikingly pretty—without any Hollywood trickery—that Sam wasn't even depressed when their fling ended quickly too. He just seemed thankful it ever got started.

Sam's dating Beverly D'Angelo was a bold sign in itself that his fortunes had radically changed. Shortly before they broke up, he and I had both gotten another huge clue. One night in Las Vegas, while we were walking along the Strip to meet Beverly at her hotel room, people kept rushing up and shouting right in Sam's face, "Oh! *Oh! Aaaaugh!*" This took about two minutes to get unnerving. But people screamed in Sam's face his entire career.

As a child, Sam felt unliked and unwanted. Now that he had

people to talk to, a way to express himself, he never missed his old life. Still, he was starting to see that fame could feel lonely too.

"Being a celebrity is really strange," he told the *Los Angeles Reader* that winter. "People look at you like you descended from a saucer or something, and I'm just me—the same person I've always been. There are times when I need to just hide out. I'll go to a friend's place and we'll unplug the phone. It's only a couple of hours until someone tracks me down again. That's where I got my idea for my bit on Jesus in need of a vacation. You know . . . he's been the Messiah for a couple of years, day after day, and he just wants to get away, just be alone somewhere, and no matter where he goes a leper or some blind guy finds him, going, 'Heal me! *Heal me!*'

"What I keep in mind is, I'm doing this for a reason, a purpose: I want to say what I think."

On January 27, 1986, just ten weeks after Sam's first appearance, he played again on *Late Night with David Letterman.* That week he also debuted at Caroline's, a prestigious comedy club about eight blocks from Times Square. One night, when my mother and I were in the crowd, an electric-haired black man stood near the back of the room yelling at Sam, "You're a fighter! From the womb to the tomb! You're a fighter!"

With the spotlight blinding Sam to all but the first few rows, he could only hear the man's voice.

"From the womb to the tomb?" Sam said to the crowd. "Who is this fuckin' guy?"

The tall-haired guy was boxing promoter Don King, who I'd recently met while preaching in Atlanta. While introducing me to Muhammad Ali, one of my idols, King had inquired about managing Sam. I thought he was just talking, but there he stood now, at Caroline's in Manhattan, telling Sam he was a fighter, from the womb to the tomb! After the show, we told King we weren't interested. But if Don King wanted in, clearly Sam was happening.

Later that week in New York, the astronauts died in the *Challenger* explosion. The gruesome network footage depressed the entire nation, including Sam. He became melancholy that evening, and when Sam got melancholy he usually drank. This time the liquor led to cocaine. When the coke ran out, Sam wanted more. Getting desperate when he couldn't find it, he even asked our elevator operator. Then he asked our cabbie, who said he could help.

We rode in the cab to a neighborhood in the Bronx, but it looked so forbidding that Sam was scared to get out. Instead, he gave his cash to the cabbie, who quickly ran in and back out of a grimy two-story brick building. Sam hungrily opened the square of tinfoil. The stuff was white, but it didn't look like cocaine. To my horror and shock, Sam pulled out his coke spoon anyway.

"Hey!" I said. "Are you nuts? You don't even know what it is. You can drop dead back here."

Sam couldn't hear me. His demons were screaming at him.

He snorted all the shit by the time we drove a few miles.

Still in New York the next night, we had our first big fight about drugs at a small Chinese restaurant. I'd lent Sam some money a few days before, just until he got paid at the end of his week-long engagement at Caroline's. At dinner, I realized Sam had spent it all on cocaine. When I gave him a hard time, he thought I was getting religious on him. It wasn't that long ago that we'd snorted and drunk together.

I said, "You're doing too much cocaine, man."

Sam said, "I got it under control."

I said, "How do you figure? You con me outta money, you con your mother, how do you call that under control?"

Between 1980 and 1985—after Sam moved to L.A. but before he hit it big—our mom and A.D. sent him about $100,000. The consummate con man, only Sam knew how much went into his binging.

"I got it under control," he repeated. "I can quit whenever I want to."

"The other night—you had it under control? Cab drivers taking you places, you're afraid to get out of the cab? You got it under control, Sam?"

"You used to party with me. Now you're on my case. Fuck you, man."

That meant he wanted to fight, and once he got warmed up, Sam liked going all night. Normally, I'd just shut up, which would piss him off even more. This time, I tore back into him. We walked out of the restaurant barely speaking.

Later that week, a few minutes after Sam got paid by Caroline, we were parked in a limo outside her club. Sam was straight and relaxed. We hadn't forgotten the other night, but we'd forgiven.

Sam said, "Bill, this is amazing. I just made five grand in less than a week."

I said, "It is amazing. I know."

"Forget about doing crusades and everything. In church, what's the biggest week you ever had?"

I didn't respond. I was never quite sure what Sam might hold against me.

"Come on, man," he pushed. "How much?"

"In church? Well, I used to go down to Jacksonville, Florida. I could usually make about seven thousand a week there."

"Really? Do you know I never had a single year in the ministry where I made five thousand dollars? You made more in one week in a church than I made in any year."

"Well, Sam, things have turned around."

They might have been turning too fast. Our one week in New York had felt like a month.

And from that period on, New York was a hazard for Sam.

7
Movies, Albums, Howard Stern, and Seka

TEMPERAMENTALLY, SAM WAS BEST EQUIPPED FOR DOING LIVE stand-up in comedy clubs. There were no retakes, the way there are in movies and sitcoms. There were no film editors or directors to fix his mistakes. Sam went out alone, before a live audience, and he got it right the first time—or else he died up there.

It gave him such a rush—the risk of performing live—that Sam often talked about it in sexual terms. He said the greatest comedians, like Richard Pryor, stripped themselves naked emotionally. He said the sensation he felt performing live was "orgasmic." When an opening comic stayed out too long, Sam jokingly called them "stage whores."

Doing live stand-up in clubs was also about maintaining control. Sam created the material. He performed it. He had no censor to clear it with first. Up on the stage, *he* was omnipotent. "I may not be able to be the Comedy God," he kidded, "but I can always be comedy's Jesus Christ."

But Sam always dreamt big, and like Eddie Murphy, Steve Martin, and Robin Williams, he wanted to leap from stand-up to making movies. Still, at the same time he yearned to emulate

their success, he was also extremely aware of all the lousy movies that other comics were making.

"*Caddyshack II?*" Sam told *Rolling Stone.* "Dan Aykroyd's got
an arrow on his ass, going, 'Will you please suck out the poison?'
Oh, *man.* What the fuck is *that,* man?" Talking about Bob
Goldthwait, Sam said, "Watching somebody you hate in a bad
movie is such a high. You know they hate their lives. It's like
they're in gay porno!" Sometimes Sam and Sly Stallone would
rent movies starring Goldthwait, whom they both disliked, just
so they could sit around and howl.

Sam broke into feature films on Friday, June 11, 1986, when
Back to School opened at 1,605 theaters. Although excited about
its release and the good industry buzz, Sam had no inkling of
how it would strike the public. Nobody in Hollywood ever does.

Back to School came charging out of the gate, earning $8.8
million its opening weekend, making it the country's number-
one movie. When it went on to earn more than $90 million, it
became one of the summer's biggest hits. For his two days of
filming in Santa Monica, Sam had been paid union scale—about
$1,500. In the long run, however, we figured he made millions
from *Back to School.* His part was small, but it gave him tremendous exposure. Even after seeing him in the movie, some
still didn't know Sam by name. But the moment someone would
say "the history teacher who snaps," there would be immediate
recognition.

Rodney Dangerfield carried the picture as Thornton Melon, a
wealthy clothing magnate who goes back to college to help his
freshman son become a man. In his one extended cameo, Sam
appears in a classroom as Professor Turgeson, a history teacher
who seems initially sane. After earnestly telling the class how
"sacred" he holds history, he asks if anyone knows why the U.S.
finally pulled out of Vietnam. A prim coed answers, a bit too
politically correctly. Turgeson grins at his students through grit-
ted teeth.

"Is she right?" he asks the class.

Nobody says a word.

"Because I know that's the *popular* version of what went on there. I know a lot of people like to *believe* that. I wish I could, but I was *there*. I wasn't here in a classroom, hoping I was right, thinking about it, I WAS UP TO MY KNEES IN RICE PADDIES, WITH GUNS AND AMMO, GOING UP AGAINST CHARLIE, SLUGGING IT OUT WITH 'EM, WHILE PUSSIES LIKE YOU . . . WERE BACK HERE PARTYING, PUTTIN' HEADBANDS ON, DOING DRUGS, LISTENING TO GODDAM BEATLES ALBUMS! OHHH! AUGGHHHH!"

Rodney, playing the oldest student in class, tells Turgeson to calm down. So Turgeson poses his next question to him. Back in the Korean conflict, "How come we didn't cross the 38th parallel, and push those rice eaters back to the Great Wall of China . . . AND TAKE IT APART BRICK BY BRICK, AND NUKE THEM BACK INTO THE FUCKING STONE AGE FOREVER? HOW COME? TELL ME WHY! SAY IT! SAY IT!"

"All right!" Melon fires back. "I'll say it! Because Truman was too big of a *pussy*-wimp to let MacArthur go in there and *blow* out those Commie bastards!"

Turgeson suddenly mellows. "Good answer. Good answer. I like the way you think. I'm gonna be watching you."

That September in *Rolling Stone,* in a laudatory feature story on Sam, Joe Dalton described his four-minute classroom scene as "brilliant." The story was headlined "Primal Screamer," with the subheading "Sam Kinison, preacher turned comic, shrieks for our sins."

After introducing Sam as "one of America's hottest young comics," Dalton said, "Other comics love Kinison; the underground reputation precedes him. He's a risk taker, trying something new." He then quoted Sam: "I don't want to tell jokes like 'Two penguins walk into a bar.' I'm an average middle-class white guy that comes home from the job and sits there wondering why things are the way they are. I'm a product of the middle-class mediocrity, and I want to get people through it. If you think about Eddie Murphy, a black guy, or Rodney, a Jewish guy—they're very funny, but they're not the guy sitting there drinking a beer. I want to get to that guy."

"Which is aiming pretty high," Dalton observed. "The last person to realize that ambition was, of course, John Belushi."

He asked Sam about the "toughness" of his jokes.

"I guess they're tough jokes—Jesus using his hand as a whistle, Ethiopia. But there's lots of things you laugh or cry at. And you just can't cry."

Dalton also interviewed me, wanting to know more about Sam's unlikely segue from comic to preacher. I told him, "When two preachers get together for a cup of coffee, what do you think they talk about? They talk about what Sam talks about onstage—if Jesus came back to earth, would he really *want* to see a cross? Did the apostles have the worst job ever, because they could never call in sick? Sam's just opening new areas."

Dalton moved onto what he called "the voice, which is to your voice as Blaupunkt is to Delco. At times it can be downright pixieish, a five-year-old girl's voice. At other times, the Voice starts low in the diaphragm and swirls out hot at your feet, like someone just drained a crankcase. When Kinison screams, 'I live in *hell*,' you believe it because you're standing in it."

Robin Williams concurred. "The key thing I guess is the voice. The *voice*. He can just be spinning along up there and then out comes this great *expulsion* of air: the voice. Yes."

Sam was thrilled at all this praise in *Rolling Stone,* a magazine he grew up on. But as for his voice, Sam never gave it much consideration. Except for the fact that he never got hoarse, despite all the SCREAMING, Sam's voice didn't impress me much, either, because I had the same one. On the telephone, even people we knew for years couldn't tell us apart. And as Sam became more famous, as the media increased their demands on his time, I often did his phone interviews for him. Sam was so allergic to responsibility, I got sick and tired of trying to make him do interviews. Once Sam saw I could pull it off, he told me, "Hey, man, you do 'em."

So I did. During phone interviews with papers as large as the *L.A. Times* and *Chicago Tribune*, I answered their questions pretending that I was Sam. As we traveled on tour from city to city, I also did it on local radio shows, when the deejays called Sam's hotel to promote his concert that evening. It became a point of pride that I never got caught, until one night in Boston, when Sam stepped onstage and gleefully told his crowd, "I'll bet you thought that was me on Mark Parento's radio show this morning. That was my brother!" Mark Parento, Boston's top-rated radio jock, got extremely upset—at me—when he found out he'd been fooled.

"You keep doing that shit," I told Sam, "I'm not gonna do your interviews anymore."

So Sam would stop. For about a week.

With his first movie, *Back to School*, still in the theaters, Sam's first album came out that September on Warner Bros. Records. Earlier that year, as Sam launched his first road tour, he'd taped *Louder Than Hell* in small rock-and-roll clubs across the country. Essentially the best of Sam since he started doing comedy in L.A., it featured "Manson," "World Hunger," "Letter from Home," and "Alphabet." In a cut he called "Sexual Therapy," Sam also waylaid Dr. Ruth, who he happened to meet later on and who turned out to be a good sport.

"Dr. Ruth? Do you hate her fucking guts, or is it just me? What a psycho-bitch this woman is, I'm sorry. 'Take the man's penis and'—when was the last time you *saw* a man's penis, Dr. Ruth? Do you remember? Can we have some clues, who was president then? Did we have cars yet, or did you suck dick on horseback, Annie Oakley? Huh, TELL ME! TALK TO ME, DR. RUTH! Good sex with Dr. Ruth, huh? When I hear you *swallow,* Dr. Ruth, that's when I'll buy the good sex show, okay? I listen to her, I'm driving down the street, she goes: 'If the man's penis is too small to satisfy the woman, then it's perfectly acceptable for the woman to use a dildo or a vibrator, and pleasure herself later, after she has pleasured the man.' So I'm listening to this psycho-fuckin'-bullshit. Pleasure herself later after—yeah, thanks, Dr. Ruth, that's real smart fuckin' advice. That's gonna pump the guy full of sexual confidence, huh? Trying to make love to the woman he cares about, she's going: 'Listen, when you're through there, Mister Tonko Toy would like a shot at it, all right? You want to plug it in on the way out of the bedroom, thumb-dick? LET'S GO, MOVE IT! Hope the grinding noise doesn't disturb *Miami Vice* for ya.' Guy's in there going, 'Yeah, thanks, Dr. Ruth, thanks to you my wife's fuckin' a lawn mower. Why don't you go back to Häagen-Dazs's and make milkshakes where you belong?' "

Louder Than Hell! was such an instant smash, we were confident it would go gold by the Christmas shopping season. That would mean 500,000 in sales inside of three months, at a time when comedy albums were marketplace poison, and 50,000 sold was considered a winner.

With a hit movie in summer and a hit album that fall, Sam looked like a runaway comedy train. But in late September he took a professional setback. Several months earlier, he'd performed another cameo in the John Landis–directed *Three Amigos.* Sam played a lunatic who comes out of the mountains and attacks the Three Amigos—Steve Martin, Martin Short, and Chevy Chase. They shoot Sam and he doesn't die. He gets stabbed, drowned in a river, the wacko keeps coming. Since Landis wanted Sam, instead of a double, to come storming out of the river, Sam caught a nasty cold. He didn't dwell on it, though. Everyone on the set told Sam he was great.

In September Landis told Sam he was cutting his scene. He

didn't care for the way he shot it, Landis explained. Even though Sam was disappointed, he never got angry at Landis. He never got mad at Steve Martin or Martin Short. Sam thought those guys were all "cool." But he hated Chevy Chase. In his short time on the set, Sam found Chase arrogant, cold, and pompous. So Sam pinned the blame on him. He thought Chase had convinced Landis to cut Sam out of the movie. After all the attention he got for *Back to School,* Sam thought Chase feared he'd steal the spotlight on *Three Amigos.* It didn't really make sense, a director as strong as John Landis bowing like that to an actor. Sam, being Sam, went with it anyway.

The following month, on October 18, Sam made his fourth appearance on *Saturday Night Live.* This was the show for which he was censored on the West Coast, then apparently banned for life from NBC. When the network backed down, and Sam guest-hosted *SNL* just one month later, he demanded that Seka the porn star join him onstage for the opening bit. This would serve two purposes: On national television, it would underline Sam's image as an outlaw; and it might get Seka to sleep with him.

They'd met just a few weeks earlier, backstage at Sam's show at Chicago's Vic Theater. That night, they only traded phone numbers. But after their *SNL* gig, Sam invited her to meet us in southern Florida, where the next day we'd board a plane for a brief trip to the Bahamas. Once Seka accepted, Sam strutted around making jokes in a deep macho voice: "She's been with Johnny Wad Holmes, now she wants *me.*" Before leaving Florida, however, Sam bought some acid. Beneath his boasting and kidding, he was worried about having sex with the queen of porn. Seka *had* been with Johnny Holmes. To even remotely impress her, Sam felt he had only one chance: "Drop the acid and just go nuts."

From his one night spent with Seka in the Bahamas, Sam etched a routine. Without using her name, he warned his crowds of the perils of taking acid before making love. According to Sam, he and his partner were all alone on a pristine tropical beach. They kissed, they touched, they got all heated up. Just as Sam positioned himself to perform oral sex, the acid kicked in. And Sam started getting all spiritual.

"You're down there, you're staring right at it, and then you go . . . wait a minute . . . wait a minute! This is the center of all creation? This is the cradle of *life?* Man, it's not even a pussy anymore. This is where life begins! THIS IS WHERE LIFE BE-GINS! OH! OH! AAUGGH!"

Even had Sam made it up, I thought it would have been funny. But he swore it was all true. Sam took such a strange trip, he said he never had sex with Seka. He also said she got furious.

They were still fighting back at the airport in Florida, as we were continuing on to another show, and Seka was getting ready to step on a plane back home.

"Fuck you!" Seka shouted at Sam. "I don't ever wanna see you again!"

Sam said, "Yeah? When I wanna see you, I'll take a buncha quarters out to a peep show!"

One month after it started, the Seka era had ended.

One night that winter, I flew on a red-eye with Sam from L.A. to New York. The whole way across, Sam fretted about Howard Stern. About to debut on Howard's show in the morning, Sam thought it could be vital to his career. Already strong out West, Sam wanted to build his East Coast following. Howard, on his way to becoming a national star, was already huge in the East.

Sam and Howard had never met. All Sam knew about him was what other comedians told him: Barring a few exceptions, mostly Richard Belzer and David Brenner, Howard *disliked* having co-medians on his show. The few times he did, Howard said they just came on and did shtick. Also, if Howard considered his guest a jerk, he might go after him right over the airwaves.

Just before we landed at JFK, Sam finally made up his mind. "I'm gonna give it up to him," he said. "I'm gonna let Stern be the guy."

I was surprised. Around his comedy peers, Sam never shrank into the background. He was usually riffing the loudest.

He stuck with his plan, though. Sam schmoozed Howard that morning and let him maintain control. They instantly connected and turned into dear friends, and appearing on Howard's show became one of the joys of Sam's life. Sam considered Howard the "god of radio"—the best radio artist who ever lived. He also admired in Howard what Sam saw in himself: a quicksilver comic mind, a desire to walk the edge, a willingness to piss off both liberals and conservatives. Since Sam partied and Howard was straight, they didn't socialize much; their relationship was mostly on the air. But a few times Howard had Sam to his house on Long Island for dinner, with Howard's wife and daughters, and Sam really enjoyed that. In a business of phony friendships, Sam felt his and Howard's was set in stone.

On his radio show, Howard loved Sam's honesty and his openness. At the slightest prodding from Howard, Sam would talk about having sex with two women at once. Or else Howard, knowing that Sam was already feuding with them, would mention another comic like Goldthwait or Whoopi Goldberg. After Sam went off like a rocket, Howard would say, "Oh Sam! Sam, hey! Don't say that, man! You can't say that on radio." Then Sam would always tell Howard after the show, "Man, we have great radio."

Sometimes when Sam hadn't seen him in a while, he would drop to his knees in front of Howard. "I bow before you," he'd shout. "You're the comedy god, you're my hero, *I wanna suck your dick!*"

Sam was clever that way. Even while paying homage to Howard, Sam was the one on his knees, shouting "I wanna suck your dick!" and getting the laugh.

It wasn't just Howard, either. Sam dropped to his knees and shouted for anyone he thought was funny: Belzer, Rodney, Robin Williams, the list went on. One night I saw Sam do it to Dabney Coleman.

In October, feeling burned out after seventeen years in the ministry, I finally accepted Sam's offer to be his manager. Though my wife, Sherry, was pleased about leaving the Midwestern winters, she had mixed feelings about my working for Sam. Sherry met Sam and me when we were all teenagers. She knew how devoted we were to each other, even when we were fighting. But she also understood how starkly our roles had reversed. In sports, in school, in the evangelical field, Sam was always known as Bill Kinison's brother. I was walking in his shadow now.

Our latest conflict started that winter, as I traveled with Sam for the first time on a tour. In his first series of road shows back in the spring—before his first movie and album, his feature story in *Rolling Stone,* and his two ostentatious spots on *Saturday Night*—Sam had played mostly Ramada Inns and small rock-and-roll clubs. Some nights those crowds were as small as three hundred. By the time I joined him that winter, Sam's popularity had soared. He was now playing to crowds of up to two thousand. He'd just rented his first customized tour bus. He'd assembled a small entourage.

That's where we clashed: Rather than sticking to our agreement and making me his manager, Sam informed me that I would be his "adviser." This meant I ranked fourth in his chain of command, beneath his manager, Elliot Abbott, his booking agent, Liz Rush, and his thuggish head of security, Bob Suszynski. It also meant I got the task of unloading the tour bus. Elliot Abbott gave me the word, but I knew Sam must have okayed it. I felt humiliated. From preaching to thousands, I now made sure Team Kinison got all its luggage.

"I want you to learn the ropes," Sam told me when I confronted him. "Elliot says this stuff is complicated."

"The guy has you totally snowed. You think there's some magic to this business? You're on top, man. People will do whatever you want."

"Just give me some time," Sam said. "Then it'll be you and me. I promise, we'll be the guys. We're gonna run the fuckin' industry."

This usually pacified me, until Sam would start feeling entitled to boss me around. Though his entourage would keep swelling and swelling, he'd already surrounded himself with sycophants and toadies. Sam expected me, like Elliot, Liz, and Suszynski, to jump at his every command. But I didn't give a shit if I got fired, and when told to fulfill what I thought was a menial errand, I told Sam, "Get off your ass and do it yourself. That wasn't part of our deal."

As his ego grew, as people who once ignored him now lined up to kiss his ass, Sam got less and less used to being told no. When he heard it from me, he retaliated sometimes by embarrassing me during his show.

"My brother went to college," he'd tell his crowd from up on the stage, where Sam always had bigger balls. "I don't even have a high school education. Now my brother works for me."

When he performed sober and clean, I thought Sam was a comic genius. But even when he was high, he was still one of the funniest people around.

As hard as he tended to party in New York, he *seldom* showed up straight for *The Howard Stern Show*. He'd fly in the day before, stay out all night at his favorite bars and strip joints, then still be buzzing on Howard's show in the morning. Then again, David Letterman did his tapings at five in the afternoon, and Sam was often high on that show too. The peculiar thing was, Sam was always very funny on both Letterman and on

Stern. And that was part of the problem. Sam knew he could get away with it.

By December 1986, his *Louder Than Hell* tour had turned into one endless party. By then, he'd added "road manager" to my role as his "adviser." Though my salary didn't change, there were a few new positives. I no longer unloaded the tour bus. I didn't have to take orders from Bob Suszynski.

Before I joined the tour, Suszynski had been hired by Elliot Abbott as Sam's security man. But his drug problem was even bigger than Sam's. An ex-convict and a former member of Chicago's infamous Skunk Gang, he was out scoring drugs from the same dealers he was paid to fend off. He and Sam were binging so hard on our tour bus I fired him myself three different times. Each time he tracked us down at another stop on our tour. Each time Sam rehired him behind my back.

That first major tour was madness. Virtually every night, Sam performed drunk, coked up, or both. When he drank too much Jack, he sometimes snorted cocaine just to burn through his alcohol fog. He frequently took a blast just minutes before a show, and sometimes as he made his way to the stage. Some nights I almost hoped Sam would flop, so perhaps he'd stop and take stock. Instead, his adrenaline would pump when he got in front of a crowd, and he would go out there and kill.

A few weeks before Christmas, friends started calling us up while we were on tour. They wanted to buy Sam's album, but the stores in their cities were all out of stock. Released three months earlier, *Louder Than Hell* had already sold about 420,000 copies. Just 80,000 more and it would go gold.

As we traveled from show to show, Sam and I started hitting the malls, and we found the same thing. Although sales had not tapered off, most record stores were out of his album. I made some calls back to L.A. This is what I was told by record industry friends: At Warner Bros., gay employees resented having Sam

Kinison on their label. They had petitioned their bosses not to release the album in the first place. Once the album came out anyway, the internal strife mounted, until Warner stopped printing Sam's album a few weeks before it went gold.

It was only a rumor, but Sam and I found it semi-plausible. For one thing, even though organized gay groups were not yet protesting him, some people had already labeled him antigay. Secondly, Warner's main business was music albums, not comedy albums, and music albums often sold in the millions. A few thousand fewer sales on one comedy album? If it helped restore peace within the company, the top brass at Warner might think it was worth it.

Sam never considered himself antigay, just as he never perceived himself as anti-God, or antiwomen. Sam wasn't interested in political correctness. He wasn't running for office. Sam was a comic, and the bottom line in comedy is this: Somebody always gets hurt. This tenet went double for Sam, because he dealt in extremes. This was a guy who made jokes about Jesus Christ on the cross. Satan. Other comics. Right-wing televangelists. Rockers Against Drugs. The sexual foibles of straight men and women. His own sexual failings. In "Letter from Home," his own mother's conception of him.

Sam did not dislike gays as a group. He really didn't. But he did find parts of gay life to be comical, and puzzling. He did believe in freedom of expression, no matter how cutting. He did love to demystify, to stand on a stage and scream things that made people wince. And he did refuse to worship taboos. Any taboos. Liberal or conservative.

"Just because I do a few comedy bits about gay people," Sam told the *Los Angeles Times,* "that does not mean I'm out there promoting some antigay cause. It's acceptable to ridicule the Pope or the President of the United States, but God forbid you do a joke about gays. The gay community is the last sacred cow in this society."

*   *   *

Louder Than Hell never went gold, but it did become a "must-own" among other entertainers. Including Phil Collins, Randy Newman, Ted Nugent, David Lee Roth, John Entwistle, C. C. DeVille of Poison, Jon Bon Jovi, and the guys from Mötley Crüe, musicians in particular seemed to adore it. With all the hours they spent out on the road, they would play it and replay it on their tour buses. The first time they'd meet him, some rockers would come up to Sam and recite his entire routines.

Back when Sam lived in Houston, he'd once talked Carl LaBove and me into sitting with him for hours outside a barbecue place, because someone told Sam that Texas-based ZZ Top ate their barbecue there. Seven years later, in Los Angeles in 1986, Sam met ZZ Top guitarist Billy Gibbons. "I've played your album every night since I bought it," Billy told a flabbergasted Sam.

Cash, Fame, and Turmoil

"Thank you very much. Hello, London! How are you? I'm a little different than the other comics you're gonna see, the other comedy. The difference between them and me is that you might want to *see* them again. Because I don't have an act. I don't have a home. I don't have a *car,* I had to borrow these *clothes*—SHE TOOK IT ALL! I WAS MARRIED FOR TWO YEARS, AND ALL I HAVE LEFT IS A PRIMAL SCREAM! But I try not to have an attitude about it."
—Sam on *Saturday Live,* the English version of *SNL.*

Sam turned thirty-three on December 8, 1986. A few weeks later we met on Ventura Boulevard in Encino with his new show business accountant, Lester Nesbit. In his seven years in the ministry, Sam only earned about $35,000. Before hitting it big in comedy, he earned about $25,000 his first five years in L.A. In 1986 alone, Sam earned about $600,000. The projection for 1987 exceeded $1 million. Now Lester was telling Sam he should try and live on a budget.

"If you can live off twenty thousand dollars a month," Lester said, "I can make sure you still have a million left every year."

"Jesus!" Sam said. "Twenty grand a month? That ain't no problem, pal."

From that period on, Sam never had an American Express bill for less than $20,000 a month.

Believe me, I know. When AMEX took his card away, he rang up mine.

I always felt Sam's extravagant spending came from the same emotional place as his self-abusive intake of liquor and drugs: his poor self-esteem.

In public, Sam always came on strong. He never equivocated or doubted himself. But the private Sam, the Sam that I knew as a brother, was insecure. Despite all he accomplished, he couldn't shake off his childhood. On some level, he was still the poor, angry kid whose parents got a divorce when he was twelve—the same kid who wet his bed until age thirteen. I never thought money could heal those kinds of scars. That's why I felt Sam gave it such little regard.

Over and over and over, I tried getting him to hold on to some of his money. I did it for his sake but also for mine, since Sam frequently plowed through his cash before he could pay me. I wasn't alone. For all the money Sam earned, he was often in serious debt.

When we were kids, Sam used to rip holes in the clothes I handed him down. I was five years older, but he was already bigger. Once he became a star, Sam never looked at price tags. His favorite store was H. Lorenzo on Sunset. He sometimes spent $15,000 there during one spree. He'd buy their silk T-shirts for $150, rip them at the collar, wear them one time onstage, and throw them away.

At restaurants and bars, Sam picked up every check in sight. At Spago, Chasen's, Dan Tana's, the Palm, first he'd gorge his friends on huge meals. Then he'd ask the waiter or waitress, "What's the largest tip you ever had?" Then Sam would always double it.

He also spent a small fortune on transportation. Every commercial flight was first-class. When he partied too hard and missed a commercial flight, he'd just charter a private plane. He also spent thousands and thousands on limousines. Out on the road, if he played a small town, he'd rent a fully stocked limo and keep it for twenty-four hours. After the streets rolled up early, that way Sam and his gang could still party in comfort. They wouldn't even cruise around. They'd just sit, getting blitzed, in front of Sam's hotel.

At the Comedy Store, where he'd once ripped off tickets and sold them on the street, one night Sam ordered twenty large pizzas to feed the insolvent stand-ups. Without being asked to, he lent struggling comedians money and sometimes paid their rent. For all his anger and lashing out, Sam really did have a soft heart. One night we filled up a truck with half his furniture, then drove it to a small apartment in West Hollywood, where the Comedy Store piano player lived. Sam felt bad for the guy. His wife was pregnant and they didn't own any furniture.

He also loved spending money on cars. Shortly after his breakthrough on HBO—with his cash still trickling in while the offers all got sorted through—Sam leased a new black Corvette with a personalized license plate reading EX REV. Then he bought our mom a Mercedes-Benz 560 SL. One night, at a time he was nearly broke, Sam showed me the new Trans Am he'd brought home that afternoon. The special edition, it cost him $40,000. That didn't faze me much. Then Carl and Christy LaBove drove up in a new Bonneville.

"Did you buy them their car?" I asked Sam when we were alone.

"No."

"You sure?"

"I didn't buy them the car, man."

The next time I saw Sam's accountant, I asked him how many cars Sam had purchased that day. Lester said two. He said Sam had called his office that day from the car dealership, instructing Lester to messenger over a check.

"It'll wipe you out," Lester warned.

"Hey," Sam said, irate. "It's my fuckin' money. Send the goddam money here *now.*"

Many performers get famous and leave old friends behind. Sam kept his old friends and picked up new ones. For his ever-growing entourage, Sam bought round-trip airplane tickets, jewels, designer clothes, and designer furniture. When he escaped for a week to his favorite resort—the Mauna Kea Beach Hotel on Hawaii's Kona Coast—Sam often picked up the tab for ten or twelve people. Average traveler: $5,000 for the week.

Sam *was* exceedingly generous. Every year he donated thousands to charities, and to the church, without calling a press conference to announce it. But Sam also used money to buy people's friendship. He was so hungry for love and approval, he was scared to tell people no.

In January of 1987, after three years of refusing to visit doctors, Kevin inexplicably relented. I drove him to a clinic in Long Beach, where he was diagnosed as manic-depressive. I was saddened, and surprised, and yet relieved to know *something* about my brother's condition. For three years we had all been in the darkness.

As the psychiatrist explained it to me, most people with this disease are manic, or depressive, but rarely are they both. The doctor said Kevin was manic.

That made a lot of sense. Kevin had never sunk into black bouts of depression. His oddest behavior, instead, had been marked by euphoric highs and hyperactivity. I finally understood: That's why we'd never convinced him he had a problem. Kevin always felt "up."

I asked the doctor why Kevin at times could not carry on a coherent conversation. The doctor said his world had fallen apart, so he'd reconstructed a new world inside his own mind. Kevin no longer drew from a "normal" frame of reference.

I asked him what caused manic-depression. He said the disease was too complex to determine with any certainty. He did say it has a genetic predisposition, and that mental and physical trauma can produce it. I'd already told him what had happened three years earlier, at the onset of Kevin's mental disorder. Kevin had spent three days alone in a house. Already starving himself in the hopes of returning to modeling, he may not have eaten at all. He may have been using drugs at the same time.

The doctor said the mixture of drugs and not eating might have sparked a chemical imbalance, and this could have triggered the manic-depressive genes. Regardless, he said manic-depression was a more serious illness than most people realized. That week he started Kevin on lithium.

Sam reacted at first with angry denial, insisting the clinic was wrong. Kevin had problems, but he wasn't manic-depressive. The "trigger" theory was bullshit.

After his rage was spent, after he learned more about the disease, Sam was wracked by guilt. More than any other factor, Sam thought his own life-style made Kevin ill. Sam was Kevin's hero; Kevin did whatever Sam wanted him to. When Sam partied all night, Kevin did too. But very few people, including Kevin, had a constitution like Sam's. Sam thought he'd worn Kevin down—until he became sick.

Sam also felt shamed that he'd left Kevin alone those crucial three days, after telling him he'd be right back with some food. Then, when Kevin broke down, Sam had, in his own words, "shipped" him back to Tulsa the very next day.

I felt Sam was partly responsible too. Intellectually, I knew we would never learn why Kevin got ill. The doctor told me himself: Manic-depression is too unknowable.

But there is thought and there is feeling, and I couldn't help feeling resentment toward Sam. I never told this to Sam, or to anyone in our family, but when Sam blamed himself for Kevin's collapse, I made no real effort to ease his conscience. I still felt too bitter for that.

In the spring of 1987, even as Sam felt heartsick over Kevin, his career had never been stronger. While touring through the Midwest, where some people felt his humor might be too audacious, he frequently sold out venues of up to five thousand seats. On two consecutive nights at Chicago's State Theater, a total of ten thousand people saw him perform. At the Fox Theater in Detroit, Sam sold fifteen thousand tickets in three nights. A stand-up comedian, Sam was packing out halls that rock bands usually played in. At up to $25 a ticket, some nights he also charged rock concert prices.

In March, ABC's nightly news did a full-blown segment on Sam's improbable rise from preacher to star comedian. Judd Rose, taking his cue from Kathleen Sullivan, called Sam "the comedy equivalent of *The Texas Chainsaw Massacre.* Sam Kinison is gross and graphic, lewd and loud, and the hottest man in humor. On tour, he's playing to sold-out crowds across America."

"What are you doing up there?" Rose asked Sam after a concert.

"It's kind of like Jesus if he did performance art," Sam said. "It's a very evangelistic *style.* It's not really that different from the way I used to preach."

But now, Rose continued, "the gospel of Kinison is laced with acid comments on sex, love, and women." Rose then flagged down some of Sam's fans as they left Sam's show. He stopped one guy who looked to be about forty. He had glasses and a mustache and could pass for an accountant. Judd Rose asked him what he saw in Sam.

"He relates well and he's been there," the guy said. "Have you ever been divorced?"

Rose said he hadn't.

"Well . . . then you don't know what I'm talking about."

Back in late 1985, after his life-changing spot on Rodney's HBO special, HBO had signed Sam to one of his own. About one year later, in Hollywood, Sam had done two shows in one night at the Roxy. HBO filmed both performances live, then chose the sharpest routines from each. Four months later, in April 1987, HBO aired *Sam Kinison: Breaking the Rules.* As millions of viewers looked on, Sam was in total command, a wild man at the absolute peak of his powers.

Unwittingly, I had something to do with a bit Sam did on that show. Several monthes earlier, on a Sunday night at the Comedy Store, I'd asked him if he'd read that morning's *Los Angeles Times.* Sam said he hadn't.

"You're not gonna believe this," I said. "There were these gay guys who were going to Forest Lawn and spending, like, three thousand dollars an hour to fuck the freshest male corpses. There was a ring of these guys. They got busted by the police."

Sam's eyes started to shine. "That's funny, man. Give me the article."

"It's not a joke, Sam. It's just something I read."

"I know. Gimme the story the next time I see you."

Within a few weeks, at the Comedy Store, Sam was working out a routine on homosexual necrophiliacs. Taking the point of view of the startled corpses, he turned it into a riff on life's never-ending unfairness. On HBO, Sam first performed the bit for a national audience.

"Man, I read this thing and went, Oh! OH! AAAAUGH! Thanks for the VISUAL! I felt sorry for these corpses, man. You'd think death would be bad enough, wouldn't you? The one thing that scares the shit out of everybody is death. You don't wanna think about it, you don't *joke* about it, you put it out of your mind, but you figure if you *faced* it, that's it. What could be worse than fuckin' death? I mean, you hated it, but you got *past* it. I felt sorry for these corpses, because I knew these guys were laying down there on slabs."

Sam lay on the stage on his belly. He began speaking philosophically. "Well, my life was tough, it was pretty hard to live up to, but I faced death and I'm glad I went through it, and now I'm ready to spend eternity in heaven and be with Jesus."

Abruptly, his eyes opened wide. "Hey, hey . . . what's this shit? Oh, I don't *believe* this. This guy's got his *dick* in my ass? Oh, you mean life keeps fucking you in the ass even after you're dead? IT NEVER ENDS! IT NEVER ENDS!"

Sam also did several inflammatory minutes on Jesus Christ and the Bible. "I read the resurrection story, folks. I'm reading this, and it's an exciting story, but I read it and I thought, I know Jesus was never married. The guy never had a wife, was never married, because *no* wife . . . would buy this story in a hundred years. The disciples will, the believers will, but *no* wife would buy this fucking story. First of all, he leaves on a Friday afternoon with twelve other guys. He's gone for three days, no message, no way to get in touch with him. He comes home Monday afternoon looking like he hasn't slept, like he's partied out . . . and Mrs. Jesus is waiting on him: 'Well, I'm glad you could find your way home . . . *savior.* Where's your twelve friends who won't get a job—*huh?* Where they at? Yeah, the disciples my ass. They're *losers*!' "

Sam replied as a world-weary Jesus: " 'Ohhh, I don't need this shit. Not after what I been through this weekend. No, honey, it's okay, I'll tell you where I been. C'mere, I'll tell you. First of all, not that it ruined your weekend or anything, but I was *dead*! Do you understand that, you fuckin' bitch? I was *dead*! While you were *sitting* here on your ass, *having* a drink, *out* on the town, I'm fighting *death, hell, de*-composure, I'm about to come into a spiritual form and go into the Kingdom of God, and I'm going, Wait a *second*! I gotta go back because *she* doesn't know where

I been! So now I gotta *find* the angel of death, *get* my fuckin' soul back, *crawl* outta the grave, go through *all* this shit—because I missed you, HONEYYYYY!"

Still on religion, Sam also observed, "Jesus is up in heaven right now. They're going: 'Why don't you go back down to earth, be a symbol of peace and love to the world.' And he's going: 'Yeah, sure, sure, I'd like to help. Tell 'em I'll be there. *Soon as I can play the piano again!* THANKS A LOT! I'LL BE THE ONLY SAVIOR THAT CAN USE HIS HAND AS A FUCKIN' WHISTLE!"

This was not just Sam being shocking. Like our father, Sam didn't believe in the physical return of Jesus Christ.

Moving to a piano, he performed his "Love Song" as an encore. I was with Sam when he created it, in 1980. Just after he and Kate Connelly split up, we went for a drink at a piano bar in New York, where John Lennon used to hang out. The bar owner asked Sam if he'd play a little something. Sam sat down, opened his mouth, and "Love Song" came out. It blew me away, because Sam wrote it all in his head.

On HBO, as Sam gently "spoke" the introduction, he played the piano beneath his words. "I wrote this about this girl that I met about five years ago. I was gonna come out here with some money, try and live out here for a while. I met this girl and I wanted to impress her, so we went through all my cash in about a year. Then one day she said, 'You know, Sam, there's something missing from our relationship.' I said, 'That wouldn't be the *cash,* by any chance, would it, honey?' She said, 'Nooo . . . we found so many special things about each other, I hate to see it all go to waste. Can't we still, like, see each other once in a while . . . and uh, have lunch, or see a movie, or . . . just be friends?' I said: 'Yeah, friends, I think I know what you mean. I become some kind of emotional tampon that you need for four or five days a month, because no one else will take your fuckin' bullshit. But we don't *fuck.* Isn't that about right, honey? That's what friends is—we don't *fuck,* right?' She said, 'Well, yeah, that's kind of it.' I wrote her this song. It goes like this: 'YOU FUCKIN' WHORE! YOU USED ME! YOU NEVER LOVED ME! I HOPE YOU SLIDE UNDER A GAS TRUCK AND TASTE YOUR OWN FUCKIN' BLOOD! DIE! DIE! DIE! I WANT MY RECORDS BACK! I WANT MY RECORDS BACK!'

"I APPRECIATE YOU COMING OUT, HOLLYWOOD! I LOVE YOU! GOOD NIGHT!"

As Sam left the Roxy stage to a standing ovation, HBO's camera followed him out a side door. The camera then moved to his black Corvette, zooming in on his license plate reading EX REV. When the screen faded to black, the very first credit was mine. In large white letters, America saw: BILL KINISON, EXECUTIVE PRODUCER.

At that precise moment, I burned my final bridges back to the ministry.

Of the millions watching Sam on HBO, several thousand people belonged to the church.

And Sam had just done routines about Jesus Christ saying "fuck."

I first learned there was a problem a few weeks later, while attending a preachers' convention in the Southwest. Despite having preached at this church on several occasions, I still hadn't been asked to speak by the final night of the week. Evidently, people were talking. The convention-hosting pastor said from his pulpit, "I know we have one of the best preachers in the United States who's been here at this convention. We haven't used him. Right or wrong, it's been my decision."

The congregation went silent. The silence turned to a low, rumbling murmur. I tried looking calm, even as I felt the stares of hundreds of people who knew me.

I spotted the pastor mingling after the service. I told him we needed to talk, went into his office, and sat behind his desk, a little something I'd learned about who would intimidate who. The pastor came in shortly with two traveling preachers. I knew both these guys too.

"You loaded me up out there," I said. "What's going on?"

"Well," the pastor said, "I just wanna say right now that I'm no prude. I'll say fuck and shit and damn, but the boy hates God!"

"What do you mean, he hates God?"

"I didn't see that show, but everyone told me about it. They told me! He hates God!"

Sam loved God. He never lost his faith. What he doubted was religious organizations. Furthermore, I'd known this particular pastor for many years. Nights when he wasn't preaching, the guy liked to drink. He also fooled around on his wife. In fact, he once fucked his dentist's receptionist. At his dentist's office. In his dentist's chair.

Now he felt the moral right to pass judgment on me and Sam? Sam for telling jokes? For making people laugh, feel good, forget their cares for a while? Me for producing my brother's TV show?

The two traveling preachers said they hadn't seen Sam on HBO, either, but they both agreed that he must hate God. Then the pastor mentioned our mother. At the beginning of the special, before Sam came onstage, she'd been shown saying how much she loved her kid, how proud she felt of him.

"Your mother was on it too," the pastor said, turning the sentence into an accusation.

I cut him off there. "Hey! Sam doesn't hate God. He hates the *system* of religion. He hates the hypocritical shit you got goin' on right here. *That's* what he hates. You say you haven't seen the tape. You should watch the tape. Then, if you come here and tell me he hates God, you can kiss my ass. Because that's not what any of that was about."

I stared straight at the pastor. "Out of everyone, man, in this group, I could expect this stuff out of them. But *you? You?*"

Things deteriorated rapidly. The dialogue grew so heated I mentioned the woman he'd fucked in his dentist's chair. That quieted him, but it didn't end there. Within a few months of

Sam's first HBO special, I found myself banned from most Pentecostal churches. If I preached at all after that, it was for family or very close friends.

That spring, the fallout from Sam's HBO special gave me a glimpse of my future. As he became a greater figure of controversy, people were always asking me about him. Is he that wild in real life? He is? Really? Was he *always* that way? I met women who flirted with me because they'd just seen Sam on *Letterman,* or on *Saturday Night.* Other women grimaced when they heard my last name, taking umbrage at Sam's routines about women and men and sex. I met both men and women who loved to party, and assumed that I did too: "You must get down pretty good. Your brother's Sam Kinison."

It got very old very fast, so I stopped telling people I met that Sam was my brother. Of course, there were many people who already knew. One morning in Colorado Springs, while driving to breakfast with a minister and his wife who I'd known for years, I felt a familiar tension starting to build. Sam had recently played at a club called the Comedy Corner. I knew "the speech" was coming.

The minister's wife said, "You know, your brother was just here at some club."

I told her yes, I knew. I was Sam's road manager.

"We have this backslider in our church," she said. "Well, this backslider went down and saw your brother's show. He came back and told me, 'Maybe I backslid, but I tell ya what, I'm better off than that guy! He's filthy!' "

"Folks," I said, "why don't we stop this conversation right here."

"And why is that?" she said.

"Let me ask you a question. When Sam was in the ministry, did you ever invite him to preach for you? When he was broke, he had nothing, did you ever send him so much as five dollars, to help him pay for his car, or his rent? When he needed help, did you support him in any way?"

The minister, a thoughtful man, finally spoke. "No. I suppose we never did give Sam any help back then."

"Well, then I don't think he cares about what you all think. I don't mean to sound hard, but that's probably the truth."

The minister said, "Yes, I think you're absolutely right. There is no reason for us to talk about this."

He looked at his wife and smiled. She seemed angry.

Women

"I love women, I swear to God. It may not seem like it, but I do. It's so funny, women are always out there in the audience, going: 'How come you don't talk about men? How come you don't say what's wrong with men? How come you only talk about what women do?' Well, THERE'S A REASON! THERE'S A FUCKIN' REASON! BECAUSE A MAN NEVER BROKE MY FUCKIN' HEART! A MAN NEVER LIED TO ME IN LOVE! A MAN DIDN'T MAKE ME WANNA DRIVE MY CAR INTO A FUCKIN' WALL! So, when I talk about love, when I talk about relationships, I'm gonna take the man's viewpoint. It's all I have to work with."

—Sam at Dangerfield's in New York

Sam and Tamayo Otsuki, a stand-up comedienne, were winding down their relationship by that summer. It lasted on and off for almost a year, making it one of Sam's longer romances. A native of Japan, Tamayo barely spoke English when she came here, but she nevertheless carved out a modest career. Sam, eager to help, asked several times if she wanted to open for him during his concerts. I asked Tamayo too. She'd make more money that way. She could test herself on a larger stage.

Tamayo seemed too proud. "I have own career," she'd say, turning us down. "I have career too."

Although Sam never understood Tamayo's attitude, he loved what he called her "little tits." One night I was staying with Sam and Tamayo at his rented house in the Hollywood Hills. They walked into my room as I struggled to sleep.

"Show him," Sam said. "I wanna show him your little tits."

Tamayo lifted her nightgown, revealing her breasts. I said something stupid like "Ah." Sam grinned at me and kissed Tamayo's cheek. They let me go back to sleep, but I suddenly wasn't sleepy.

Shortly before they split up, Tamayo made a mistake. She told Sam she'd once slept with a comic he knew named Angel. Tamayo said it had happened before she met Sam, but he threw a jealous tantrum anyway. Once he and Tamayo broke up, Sam vowed to steal Angel's girlfriend, Malika Souiri. She and Sam had already met at the Comedy Store, flirting a couple of nights when Angel wasn't around. The next time Sam saw her at the club, he told Malika that Angel had slept with Tamayo. He also suggested a way for Malika to even the score. Dump Angel and start seeing Sam.

By then, Sam was renting a beautiful house owned by Elliot Abbott. High in the Hollywood Hills, it had a pool and a sweeping, stunning view of the city below. One morning that summer I answered the telephone there. It was Malika's teenage sister, Sabrina, pretending to be Malika and asking for Sam. With Sam still asleep, I took a message and told him later that morning.

"Who's this Malika?" I asked.

Sam said, "Oh, man! That's Angel's girlfriend! What did she say?"

"She wants you to call her and meet her today for lunch."

Malika and Sabrina were already at the restaurant when Sam

arrived. It must have been some lunch. Within two weeks, Malika moved out of the small apartment she shared with Angel. Both she and Sabrina moved into Sam's house in the hills.

Malika was about twenty-one when she met Sam, who was thirty-four. Sabrina was fifteen or sixteen. They'd grown up in Las Vegas, where their childhoods had been hard. Their parents divorced when they were small, their mother was alcoholic, their father mostly raised them single-handedly. Malika loved to party, Sabrina was pretty much straight. Malika worked in Las Vegas as a show girl, dancing topless at the Sahara. A bisexual, dark-haired beauty, she sometimes indulged Sam in his passion for three-way sex. Malika wasn't shy about it, either. One morning we all went to New York, where they candidly talked about it on *The Howard Stern Show*.

Sam said to Malika, "Should I tell them about how you bring women to me sometimes? No, never mind, never mind."

Howard said, "Malika, that's true, I know that, I've heard that."

"You heard what?" Malika said.

Sam interrupted. "What? Is that the *worst* gift that can be given?"

"Let me tell you something," Howard agreed. "You are the luckiest man alive. If my wife would once bring home a woman, I would be so thrilled. No, that she can't do. But really, Malika, how do you make that happen?"

Laughing, Malika tried evading the subject. But Howard knew great radio. He asked, "How many women at once could Malika bring home, on a good night?"

Malika said, "I don't know, we never tried that. But there's still the future."

Sam said happily, "There's still the future! That's my girl!" Then he started singing, "I want a girl, just like the girl, that married dear old Dad."

Howard intended to stick to the subject. He asked Malika,

"Would you pick out a good-looking woman, or a, uh, uh . . . ?"

"Yes, I would have to like her too," Malika said.

"So it's up to you, who you choose," Howard said. "In other words, it's up to you, not up to Sam."

"Yeah, that's true," Sam said.

"And how do you make that move?" Howard asked Malika. "What's the move? So the girls at home can do this too."

Sam interrupted again. "*My* attitude has to be: Honey, this is a little dark. It's a little nasty, but if it's what *you* want, I'm willing to lend my services."

They went on in a similar vein, then Howard asked Malika, again, how she made that last, critical move, once she and Sam and their partner all got back to Sam's house. Malika said it was a mutual kind of group thing.

Howard said, "Oh, this is straining the little Cub Scout in my shorts. Oh, man!"

A few minutes later, Howard asked Malika if Sam ever brought home men to her. "Will he go to a bar and pick up a nice guy?"

Sam jumped in before Malika could speak. "No! Homey don't play that."

Along with their mutual fondness for threesomes, liquor, and drugs, Sam and Malika shared a vindictive streak. Early in their affair, they sometimes called Angel while having sex at Sam's house. Sam would say, "Hey, Angel, I'm banging your girl-friend." Malika would take the phone and tell Angel how good Sam was. Laughing, Sam and Malika told me this together. They said they got pretty graphic.

One night at the Comedy Store, Angel tried getting Malika back. Showing up drunk while Sam and Malika were there, Angel tried talking to her, and Sam told him to beat it. Angel reached past Sam, grabbing Malika's arm and squeezing a little too hard. Rick Jones, Sam's huge security guy, was all over Angel

Our new baby Sam in my arms in late 1953.

Sam and cousin Brenda, growing up in Peoria.

Sam at age three, shortly before the traumatic truck accident.

Sam at age seven, a year or so after our family moved into a church.

Our last family picture before our parents split up. Sam is twelve.

Sam and his girlfriend Sonia at the Pinecrest Bible Academy in upstate New York.

Sam, sixteen, shortly before he ran
away from home.

Sam's first year in the ministry at age
eighteen.

Sam, eighteen, plays guitar at my wedding.

Sam gets married to Gail at age twenty-one.

Sam, Gail, and
preacher Louise
Copeland. Notice
Sam has his hand full.

Sam and Kevin—buddies
and brothers.

Sam, twenty-five, just a few weeks before leaving the ministry.

Sam down in Houston, the first night he performed after being banned.

Sam performing in Houston. The content will get deeper, but the style's already dynamic.

In Houston, the original
Outlaws of Comedy:
from left to right, Carl
LaBove, Bob Barber, Bill
Hicks, and Sam.

Before hitting the big time,
Sam shares a stage with Robin
Williams at the Comedy Store.

In 1985, Sam's life-changing,
breakthrough performance
on HBO.

Kevin and Mom and Sam in 1985,
Sam's first year as a star.

The promotional shot that caused Sam to
fire his first prominent agent. Sam liked
the pose, but he didn't want to be
known as The Beast.

AGENCY FOR THE PERFORMING ARTS

Sam and Whoopi Goldberg before
their ongoing feud.

GEORGE GARCIA

Chilling out at the Comedy Store: Sam, Ted Nugent,
and Robin Williams.

Bob Seger, Sam, and Randy Quaid at
post—*Saturday Night Live* party in
Manhattan.

Sam and Beverly D'Angelo during their
brief romance.

in seconds. Rick lifted him off the floor and drove him into a wall. Rick was twice Angel's size—I told him to let Angel go and to leave us alone. With Sam due onstage any minute, I told him and Malika to get lost too.

"I feel bad for you, Angel," I said when the others left. "I know you still like Malika. But she doesn't want anything to do with you. That's how it is—you should accept it. Otherwise you're gonna end up getting hurt. No one here's gonna hurt you because they're too big. But I'm more your height. You show up again like this, I'm gonna kick your ass. You're getting to be a problem."

Angel stalked out of the club, swearing at me in Spanish. About ten minutes later, after Sam went up to the Main Room, Mitzi Shore told me and Carl LaBove, "Angel is back. He's looking for Sam and he's got a giant with him."

First telling Mitzi to call the police, I poked my head inside the Main Room. I saw Sam but no Angel, or his apparently giant friend. I looked all over the building, then stepped outside onto Sunset and glanced up and down the street. As I turned back to walk in the front door, Angel came flying out it. He stumbled over the sidewalk and over the curb, smashing finally into a car parked on Sunset.

Rushing out next came Carl LaBove, Sam's best friend. He'd just literally punched Angel out the front door.

More people piled outside pushing and shouting, getting excited, anticipating a brawl. Rick Jones came out entangled with Angel's massive partner. About six feet seven and four hundred pounds, he made Rick look like a baby. Fortunately, he instantly recognized me. He knew Sam and me from the Rainbow Bar and Grill, a trendy West Hollywood nightclub a mile or so down on Sunset. Sam called it the bar where the "possessed go to mingle."

"Bill," the big guy said, surprised. "What are you doing out here?"

"I'm gonna beat Angel's ass, like I said!"

"Is Sam in this?"

"Yeah. That's who Angel wants, he wants to get Sam."

"I got no problem with Sam. Angel didn't tell me it was Kinison."

The first police car rolled up and everybody feigned innocence. Sam was inside the entire time, telling jokes.

Sam surprised me that summer and fall by his faithfulness to Malika, since he normally demanded total fidelity, while *he* pretty much slept around. Even with Malika, after one of their serious fights, Sam would sometimes spend the night with an old stripper girlfriend of his. But other than that, he rarely brought other women into his bed. Unless, that is, Malika was with him, too.

Sam was insanely jealous of her, because he was insecure, and because he'd return home some nights to find Malika with another young woman. One night in L.A., while our aunt was in town, she and Sam drove back to his house after Sam's show. Just as they walked in, another girl and Malika strolled out of the bedroom in panties. "Well," Sam told Malika, "I see you enjoyed yourself while I was gone."

Sam was embarrassed but kept his cool, because he was with his aunt. Another time, in Las Vegas, he went ballistic. After playing the Dunes Hotel, Sam and Malika went nightclubbing with some friends. Sam invited me but I told him no, figuring he and Malika would only end up fighting. Later that night, feeling antsy and changing my mind, I met up with them at Sam's favorite strip joint. All the guys ended up in a private VIP room, while Malika and two of her girlfriends went up to the Main Room to watch the male strippers. The VIP room had a closed-circuit TV. Watching it, we all saw Malika start grabbing the stripper's crotch and rubbing his balls. I don't think she knew Sam was watching her on TV.

Sam got so red in the face, he looked like a cartoon character. "Oh, oh, that fuckin' bitch! Oh, that whore!"

Later, back at the Dunes, Sam said they fought until sunrise.

Malika, from my point of view, was like most of the women Sam dated—emotionally unhealthy. Even after he was famous, his women of choice were strippers and topless dancers. Sam liked their wildness, but it also reflected his own poor self-image. These were the only women Sam felt he could get.

"Why can't I find a good woman like Sherry?" he would ask me in frustration.

I'd tell him, "Even if you did you'd turn her into a whore."

Sam would laugh. He knew it was true. If his women didn't dress like hookers already, Sam talked them into it. Then he got mad when any guy looked at his date.

Knowing all this about Sam, I still never understood why he stayed with Malika. They fought constantly and explosively. I don't know how they treated each other when they were alone, but most of the fights I saw were precipitated by Malika. She seemed to get some perverse thrill from belittling Sam in public. She embarrassed Sam in front of our family, his friends, his favorite publicist Florence Troutman, his fans, and even powerful people in show business. "You're not anything," she'd tell him in front of others. "You're not a man." Or else she'd complain to his friends: "He doesn't like to have sex anymore. I wish he'd do me once in a while."

If several of us went out for a meal in public, and a woman came to our table wanting Sam's autograph, she'd frequently get a drink spilled on her by Malika. Malika always pretended she didn't mean it, but it must have happened a dozen times.

"Don't embarrass me," Sam would hiss under his breath. "Because if you embarrass me, I'll embarrass *you* in front of everyone here."

Usually, that would ignite them. Then they'd get loud and profane. Later that night, when they were alone, sometimes they got physical. Malika knew how to fight—she punched like a man. Sam was willing to hit her, too. A few stormy nights, they blackened each other's eyes.

From the time Malika first moved in with Sam, I was concerned. To me, they seemed trapped in something ugly and loveless, with a heavy, heavy emphasis on booze. Sam owned several hundred home videos, and one of their all-time favorites was *Days of Wine and Roses.* They usually drank while they watched it, and sometimes Sam got choked up. One night I heard him say, "Look, honey, that's us."

"I was married twice. Then I said, Hey, you know, I bet if I become more sensitive, and a better fuck, I won't have to give away everything I own *every five fucking years*! Oh, women. We love you, ladies. You have the pussy. You *have* the pussy, do you understand that? It's not the only reason we love ya, but it's on the top fuckin' five. So we're fucked, they got us, man. You might as well have a trigger on it, because we *do* what you say. 'Is *this* what you wanted? Let's go, come on. I think this is what we were talking about, right? The pussy? Let's go. It's time to go home, say good night to your friends—*come on!* Get your *fat* fucking ass out in the car, or you will not get *this!*' The guy's going, 'SHE'S GOT THE PUSSY! I GOTTA GO HOME, GUYS, I'D LIKE TO STAY AND PARTY LIKE A REAL MAN, BUT SHE'S GOT THE PUSSY!' It's true, you know it. Every one of us, every guy in this room, has been at a party that was just a party for guys . . . and *they* wanted to go home: 'Can we go home, please? I'm bored, my eyes hurt from all the smoke in the room, all your friends want to do is drink and get high.' 'All right, honey, just let me go into the bathroom and

change into a fuckin' *dress* in front of all my guys. You got
a skirt out in the trunk I can wear out? Because that's what
I'm gonna look like—a big fuckin' pussy, who doesn't have
any control over his own life. All right, honey?' And then
they try to hurt you: 'Well, why don't you just go ahead and
get high *again?* 'Well, as a matter of fact, honey, I am gonna
go get high again, because that's what you DO AT A
FUCKIN' PARTY! YOU GET TOO HIGH, YOU GET TOO
DRUNK, YOU STAY TOO FUCKIN' LONG! THAT'S WHY
THEY CALL IT A PARTY!' "

—Sam in concert in Orlando

One fall afternoon in 1987, I went looking for Sam at Mitzi
Shore's pink mansion, just a few hundred yards uphill from her
Comedy Store on Sunset. Sam tended to binge there for days at
a time. We needed to handle some business, and he hadn't returned my phone calls all week.

I walked into the mansion a little after 3:00 P.M. Except for a
few unknown comics who lived there rent-free, the party had
died and the mansion looked deserted. I found Sam, alone, in
the dining room, slouched in a chair in a barely conscious stupor. Snot dripped from his nose. His pants pockets looked to be
rifled. His clothes stank of liquor and smoke and perspiration.
So did the filthy pigsty of a room.

I helped Sam out of his chair. He never spoke but acknowledged me with his eyes. I drove him in silence to the house he
rented from Elliot Abbott. I put Sam in his bed, took a cab back
to the mansion, then drove his Corvette back to his place.

I drove out to his house again the next afternoon. I wanted to
see how he felt, and we still had some business pending. By then
he'd slept for almost twenty-four hours. Sober and showered, he
seemed embarrassed. Though he'd barely been coherent, he remembered me dragging him home from Mitzi's mansion. Sam

also confirmed my suspicion. Someone had gone through his pockets and stolen his wad of bills.

I didn't stay long. Sam didn't seem to want me around, or to talk about what happened. My presence alone seemed to reprimand him.

The rest of that day I felt depressed and distracted. Sam and I didn't relate the way we used to. A wall had gone up between us: Sam wan't ready to straighten up, I refused to return to alcohol and cocaine. Sometimes I found myself wishing we were still kids. I was my brother's keeper then too, but Sam and I were closer. And the issues seemed less complex.

As for the mansion, Sam rarely returned there. One of the few times he did, he showed up roaring drunk and went straight out to Mitzi's balcony. Grabbing her old, battered furniture, he began throwing it over her ledge, down the side of the hill. Several other comics stood cheering and egging him on.

Though the other comics were more discreet, Sam was hardly alone in his enmity for Mitzi. Ever since opening her club, she had been famous for playing favorites among the stand-ups, for creating tension and jealousies. And even now, after all these years, she still barely paid them. To get paid by her at all, several comics had gone out on strike in 1979. Some crossed the picket line; the strike turned bitter and ugly. That same hot-blooded year, comedian Steve Lubetkin jumped to his death from the roof of the Hyatt Hotel, which stands next to the Comedy Store on Sunset. Rightly or wrongly, some of the comics blamed Mitzi. They said Lubetkin killed himself right after she told him he wasn't funny. Sam knew what it meant to feel like a loser; he was badly shaken when he heard about Lubetkin. Sam would talk about him sometimes when he railed against Mitzi.

In October of 1987, *Esquire* magazine did a cover story on the state of American comedy. Its author, Tom Shales, concluded that

for all the pretenders out there, American stand-ups were still setting high standards. According to Shales, one of the very freshest
comics was Sam. Shales even compared him to Lenny Bruce,
one of Sam's gods. Without Lenny Bruce, Sam felt, there'd
never have been room for a biting social comedian like himself.

Shales wrote: "Kinison is the most lacerating new comic, the
dean of the screamers, whose ranks also include the rather
meaningless Bobcat Goldthwait. He follows in the hobnailed
bootsteps of the great Don Rickles, high lama of the confronta-
tional comics. He rages against heaven like a Russian novelist,
storming onstage in a dirty old-man's Goodwill overcoat and
beret. No longer is comedy just not pretty. Comedy is not nice.
This is Lenny Bruce at ramming speed. . . . Kinison is not only
beyond hip, he's beyond gonzo. He runs riot. It's refreshing,
even when it's offensive, because it seems an antidote to com-
placent Reaganism instead of just another exploitation of 'the
mood of the country.' Kinison is a harbinger of doom. He doesn't
stop at harbingering. He, like, *is* doom."

Compared to Sam, Shales concluded, "most comics in the
clubs are just trying to be like each other."

The previous year, in *GQ*, Robin Williams had called Sam a
"kind of white Richard Pryor." Richard Pryor and Lenny Bruce
were Sam's two greatest inspirations. To be identified with both?
In two respected national magazines? Both times, Sam was de-
lirious with happiness. He was also slightly stunned. Sam knew
how close he'd come to not being heard of at all.

By that fall, Sam had signed with Creative Artists Agency for
representation in feature films. Since breaking through as a
comic, he'd been passed over for *Jumpin' Jack Flash,* lauded for
his small but dynamic part in *Back to School,* and cut out of
Three Amigos. In his hope to become a star in feature films, Sam
now had heavy artillery on his side. Headed by Mike Ovitz, the
most powerful man in show business, CAA had remarkably deep

penetration throughout the motion picture industry.

Sam's agent at CAA was Todd Smith, who told Sam's manager, Elliot Abbott, about an available movie property called *Atuk*. Purportedly based on a story by Mordecai Richler, it was first conceived as a vehicle for John Belushi. When Belushi passed, the property languished in Hollywood for almost a decade. In its latest incarnation, *Atuk* was standard fish-out-of-water Hollywood fare. An Eskimo goes to Manhattan and gets exploited by a ruthless, Trumplike tycoon, but the Eskimo wins in the end.

CAA resurrected *Atuk* by turning it into a "package." Producer Fred Roos, director Alan Metter, and costars Christopher Walken and Harry Dean Stanton all came attached to *Atuk* when it first got pitched around town. All were CAA clients. So now was Sam, the film's star. Using Sam's "heat" as its major selling point, CAA set up *Atuk* at United Artists. It was slated to shoot in New York and Toronto in February of 1988.

In return for "delivering" Sam, Elliot Abbott was named executive producer. Later, Sam and I were told that Elliot passed on at least one other major movie project—without even running it by us—because that deal didn't include Elliot as a producer. We were told this by Alan Rich, the president of Guber-Peters and a big fan of Sam's. According to Alan, Guber-Peters intended for Sam to star in its comedy *Beetlejuice*. He said the title role, played by Michael Keaton, had been written with Sam in mind. "We wouldn't make Elliot Abbott executive producer," Alan told us in Atlantic City. "That's why you never knew about it."

But that was later. In 1987, when *Atuk* surfaced, Elliot still managed Sam and Sam still trusted him. As a result, Sam never met with anyone from CAA or United Artists. Instead, Elliot dealt with both companies directly. This is what he reported back to us:

Sam could rewrite the script of *Atuk*. UA wanted him to, because it wanted a "Sam Kinison picture." That's why they'd gone into business with him in the first place.

There were several major problems from the beginning. Sam agreed to star in *Atuk* before there was any script. Once a screenplay was written, it was read and accepted by Elliot—not by Sam. When Sam finally read the *Atuk* script himself, much later than he should have, he thought it was awful.

With what amounted to a seventh-grade education, Sam was never much of a reader, and that included screenplays. Still, he *should* have made it his business to read that script more promptly. It was partly Sam's irresponsible nature, partly his naivety toward the world of feature films. Since CAA and UA were both on board—and since Elliot Abbott kept saying, "This thing is great."—Sam thought it *must* be a quality project. He didn't understand yet: Even at its highest levels, Hollywood doesn't operate that way. In truth, Hollywood cares as much about making great deals as it does great movies. And once certain people in Hollywood sniff a deal, they'll convince even themselves that a lame project is strong. If they can snow themselves, they can possibly snow the next person, and the next, all the way up the Hollywood food chain, until somebody in authority says, "Green light."

To my later regret, I had very little involvement with *Atuk*. It was a CAA package, I was still only Sam's road manager, and Elliot was serving as our liaison with both CAA and UA. I asked Sam several times anyway: "Hey, did you read the script yet?" Sam kept saying he was waiting for the other comedians' comments. Told by Elliot that he had UA's permission, Sam had brought in some comedian friends to punch up the screenplay with him. After reading it, they returned to Sam with a frightening consensus: The script wasn't funny. The story was also weak and lacking in logic.

Unfortunately, Sam never read the script himself until January, about six weeks before it was slated to shoot. He not only agreed with his friends, Sam said the plot reminded him of *Crocodile Dundee.* Sam's reputation was based on being *different.* He now feared being accused of making a retread. With a nervous edge to his voice, Sam started calling his movie *Eskimo Dundee.*

The first week of February, Sam convened with his writers at the Regency Hotel in New York City. From there he flew to Toronto, where he learned how to drive a dogsled. Sam called me several times from both locations, sounding alternately stressed and optimistic. One night he told me Fred Roos had dropped off the project. Roos, a colleague of Francis Ford Coppola, had produced *Apocalypse Now* and *The Outsiders,* two movies Sam admired. Roos was one of the reasons why Sam had signed on.

Charles Roven replaced Roos, and Sam said they started fighting the moment they got to New York. They fought about casting, the script, how much Sam's friends would be paid for their work on the rewrite. Sam's clashing with Roven didn't surprise me. Like most famous comedians, Sam had eaten a lot of shit on his way to the big time. He'd built his career by himself, with virtually no connections. Roven, in contrast, was married to Dawn Steel, the first female studio head in Hollywood history. Sam thought Dawn Steel got Roven the job on *Atuk,* because that was the word on the set among Roven's other detractors. When Sam looked at Roven, he thought he was seeing a guy who paid no dues.

Sam also kept telling me that Roven had a "people problem."

"This guy doesn't like anyone," Sam said. "I don't think he likes human beings. It's affecting the set. Me and Metter are going to get him fired."

Atuk's director, Alan Metter, had also directed Sam on *Back to School.* Now Metter was collaborating on the rewrite with Sam and his writers. More than ever, Sam thought he had UA's blessing to rewrite *Atuk.* The movie's *director* was working with him.

There was more to the story, though. Sam also said he and Metter were binging together, hitting the New York clubs at the end of the workday, and then partying into the morning in Sam's hotel suite. I asked Sam if he'd missed any read-throughs or meetings or shown up late. Sam admitted he had, and that he and Roven were fighting about that too.

Pressure built on the set. Rumors flew that *Atuk* was already in trouble. Along with a few others, Sam and Metter kept vowing to get Roven fired. And yet, as filming approached, Sam still sounded excited about his first movie. Sam was used to dissension. He thought things would work out once filming began.

The first day of shooting arrived on February 15. Sam surprised me that night when he didn't call. When he still hadn't phoned the next day, I figured the first few shots in New York were in the can, and that Sam and everyone else had flown back up to Toronto. Sam finally called me at home the following morning.

"How's it going out there?" I said.

"I'm home."

"What do you mean? Where's home?"

"I'm here in L.A," Sam said.

"You *can't* be in L.A.!"

"They pulled the plug, Bill. They canceled the movie."

Sam said he'd flown all night on a red-eye. Sounding drowsy but calm, his main emotion seemed to be one of relief.

"If I did it the way they wanted me to," he said, "I could be working Laff Stops the rest of my life."

Sam told me it fell apart like this:

The night before shooting was meant to begin, a crucial meeting was called for late the next afternoon. UA chairman Tony Thomopoulus and head of production Roger Birnbaum would by flying in from Hollywood. All week long, Sam and Metter had told each other that Roven needed to go. When they heard that the UA bosses were coming out, they assured each other they'd both speak out at the meeting.

The next day Sam delivered about one-third of the script he'd rewritten with his friends and Metter. This included the first few scenes to be shot in New York. Sam was not blowing off the rest of the script. He thought they would have ten more days to rewrite it, while production stopped before everyone left New York for Toronto. Furthermore, on *Back to School,* Rodney and Harold Ramis had been writing new pages throughout the production.

Sam put on his full Eskimo costume and makeup, thinking, We'll have to shoot *something.* But shooting never started. Sam sat around, then went to the meeting late that afternoon. Entering the room, he saw several people lined up on one side of a table, and one chair on the other side waiting for him.

Dressed like an Eskimo, Sam felt like an ass.

He also understood he was totally on his own: Along with Roven, Thomopoulos, and Birnbaum, Alan Metter sat on the other side of the table. So did Elliot Abbott.

One of the studio heads asked why no one could get along. Sam, alone, said the problem was Roven. One of the studio heads cut to the chase—the script for *Atuk* would be shot in original form. Sam said that script wasn't funny. UA should use his rewrite.

"What rewrite?" one studio head asked Sam. He told Sam that UA had no knowledge of one.

Intuitively, Sam believed him. He glared at Elliot, who'd been telling Sam for months that the studio *welcomed* a rewrite. He glared at Metter, who'd been *working* with Sam on one.

The meeting degenerated, and Sam lost his temper. He told the UA executives, "You think it's a funny script? Let's do it the way it's written. I'm in costume, let's do it right now! But I promise you one thing. I'll walk through this fuckin' movie!"

Metter got nervous and finally spoke up. He'd just directed Richard Pryor in *Moving.* The film wasn't released yet, but word had spread that it reeked, and that Pryor had walked through his role. Metter said he couldn't direct another movie like *Moving.*

Sam chimed back in. "I'll do this movie, because I have a contract. But after it's out I won't promote it. I will not promote a bad movie."

One of the studio heads said he'd heard enough. *Atuk* had too many problems. UA was pulling the plug.

Sam said, "Okay, I'm going back to L.A." He stood up and walked out the door.

After I heard Sam out, I formed this opinion:

Thomopoulus and Birnbaum had not planned on killing *Atuk* when they flew to New York that morning. If the matter was closed, why even step on a plane? Even during the meeting, when they said they were closing it down, they were just trying to frighten Sam into compliance. Powerful men, they expected Sam to beg for another chance. But they ran into a guy as stubborn as they were.

Although nobody won on *Atuk*, Sam took the hardest hit. UA probably spared itself the embarrassment of releasing a flop. In fact, before it shut down operations, UA briefly shopped *Atuk* to other comedians, but nobody wanted in. As for the $5 million UA announced it had already spent in preproduction, studios often make entire movies which are never released to the theaters. On a film that was looking increasingly like a dog, UA might have saved itself millions by cutting its losses early.

When the news first got out, the entertainment media smelled blood. Unsurprisingly, it was Sam who got eaten alive. Why tell a complicated story, where everyone shares some guilt, featuring unknown names like Roven and Metter and Abbott, when the public might find that boring? Why risk upsetting the Hollywood power structure when Sam's "self-destruction" made such an appealing target? Keep it sexy, keep it simple. Bury the mouthy comic.

Before *Atuk*, Sam had been labeled "colorful" by the media. He was mostly seen as a guy who raised some Cain, a guy whose black humor you might not get, or approve of, but a guy who was easy to like if you met him face to face. After *Atuk,* Sam was "out of control."

In Hollywood, I never saw a quicker retreat from somebody in trouble. EVERYONE turned their back on him. Todd Smith, his agent at CAA, didn't return Sam's calls. I tried calling Smith too; he wouldn't talk to me, either. Sam had to hear through the grapevine that CAA had dumped him.

Elliot Abbott jumped ship before even leaving New York. He sent a note to Sam's hotel.

As for Alan Metter, Sam's partying partner out in New York, he escaped quietly. "The guy was in a coke stupor every night," Sam told me, "but now I have all the problems." Several of Sam's writers, including one who was totally clean and sober, confirmed that Metter and Sam were binging together.

By the time Sam flew home from New York, only his accountant was still part of his team, and even Lester was getting worried. He kept calling all week, saying, "Bill, it's getting worse. He trashed a hotel suite up there. It's in the news."

I called Sam and he told me, "I never trashed any suite. They're nuts."

I think Sam would have told me. He'd have said, "Fuck 'em." Also, I paid the credit card bill, and I was never charged for a trashed hotel room.

As UA and CAA cranked up their PR machines, all kinds of rumors began making the rounds. One of the wildest ones we read was that Sam "had shown up late for the meeting with UA, drug-crazed, clutching a wad of loose notebook pages." Other stories floated that he'd stormed off the set in the middle of a scene, while the cameras were already rolling.

The cameras had never rolled.

The rumors grated on him, but Sam was much more upset by United Artists' next salvo. On February 25, it hit Sam with a $5.5 million breach-of-contract lawsuit. Although Sam was concerned about legal fees, I thought we should fight it. So did Sam's attorneys. Sam was in costume that day, ready to work. He never left the set until *they* plugged the plug. Not that Sam was blameless. He should have read the script before signing on. He should have dealt directly with UA and CAA, instead of relying on Elliot. He *was* getting high in New York. But to pin the collapse of an entire movie on him? A movie that never had an *idea* behind it in the first place? I thought that was bullshit. I thought they wanted to teach him a lesson, because Sam had refused to back down.

His contract with UA promised him $350,000, but it was supposed to be paid in weekly installments, beginning at the end of the first week of production. When UA pulled the plug, Sam never got paid at all (except for a few thousand dollars in expense money). His attorneys suggested we countersue UA, to collect the $350,000. While we mulled this over, we learned that UA had also sued Elliot Abbott for breach of contract. Apparently UA agreed with Sam on that much: Elliot had misrepresented both sides.

In the following weeks, Sam did nothing to mend his rift with Hollywood. He tore it wider, in fact. During his concerts and on *The Howard Stern Show,* Sam blasted away at the whole industry. He even ripped Mike Ovitz. The funny thing was, Sam and I didn't think Ovitz was even involved. We thought he was too big a player to spend his time damaging Sam.

Sam being Sam, though, he aimed for the top. "They're business people, not artists," he fumed to *Rolling Stone.* "I'm not going to be their fucking bitch, man. Let them get that from the other pussies. I know Mike Ovitz and all those guys think they're such big fucking bad-asses. Well, my message to them is, *Fuck you,* I don't need any of you. . . ."

I couldn't quite believe what was going on. One night I sardonically told Sam: "Ovitz? Why don't you stop messing around with these little guys? Why not just take on the biggest fuckin' guy in the business?"

Sam vented some steam. He proved he would not be broken, bullied, or compromised. As he told *Rolling Stone,* "I'd rather have *five* lawsuits like this than be in one *Twins.*" He also said, seething, "When you hang a man, you better be sure he's dead. I'm not going away. We're coming after your fucking asses, you losers, to show you what comedy's all about. Taking all your fucking money and offices, and you can park our cars."

But Sam, in the end, was his own fiercest enemy. Hollywood doesn't like that kind of talk, especially not from "talent." Hollywood also lives on the telephone, and it's really a very small town. Enrage a few top executives at one company, and a week or so later you can't make a deal with three others. In no time at all, Sam found himself blackballed from feature films.

He couldn't understand what was happening to him. He'd see Goldthwait and Howie Mandel making terrible pictures, he'd see Dice doing *Ford Fairlane,* Roseanne doing *She Devil,* and it made Sam insane.

He'd say, "They make *that* stuff and they can still get work? I get kicked out for *not* making a piece of shit like *Atuk?*"

I tried telling Sam that this whole sorry mess was about more than just *Atuk.* "You can't make movies because of *Atuk,* but also because of your overall reputation. And most of your reputation, most of your *problems,* come from your life-style."

Sam wouldn't accept this—yet. Although he was down, he still hadn't hit rock bottom.

Sam had always been angry, but his first three years in the big time had also been fun and exciting. But after *Atuk,* Sam's anger was shot through with bitterness. He *loved* being a part of *Back to School.* And with Rodney as his godfather on that set, everything had gone smoothly. Then the movie earned $90 million, and everyone told Sam that he just about jumped off the screen.

Why couldn't he parlay it?

Sam would say to me, "Bill, I wanna make movies! I know

there's someone out there who will take a chance with me!"

After *Atuk,* for a long time nobody risked it.

With *Atuk* canceled, Sam was out his $350,000 salary. UA also stuck him with the bill for his pricy stay in New York at the Regency Hotel. Sam had never saved his money. He owned no property, had no investments. Money came in, money went out.

Sam returned from New York with $300 in his savings account. It gave him a shock. For the first time since Sam became a star, he seemed to understand he could blow the whole thing.

Eighteen months after I moved to Los Angeles, Sam asked me again to manage his career. This time he meant it, and I said yes. Sure, Sam was a screwup. He did everything the hard way. But he was my brother.

Sam told me that winter, "I'm never getting in that position again. This is the reason I asked you out here. Fuck Hollywood. Maybe we'll hook up with some rock-and-roll management, but you'll still make all the decisions if we do. It's just gonna be me and you now."

Kevin

SHOW BUSINESS CAREERS MOVE IN REPEATING CYCLES. PERFORMERS are golden, then they're finished, then they're golden again. As hot as Sam had been, as controversial, he was due to take a fall. Given time, I thought we could even get him back into the movies. In the short term, Sam needed cash. Expecting to work on *Atuk* for the next four months, he had no concert dates booked.

The first deal I struck was with Mitzi Shore. For the next ten weeks, Sam would play Thursday through Saturday nights at the Comedy Store in La Jolla. Sunday nights, he'd play the Comedy Store on Sunset Strip. Each Monday morning he'd fly to New Jersey, where he'd perform shows at Rascals Monday through Wednesday.

Sam was used to a grueling pace: He averaged more than two hundred dates a year, mostly to finance his high-end life-style. But even Sam needed a break by early May. He took it in Tulsa, where it was time for our annual preachers' convention, held at our mother and stepfather's church. Sam seemed anxious and pressured when he arrived. He was out of debt but exhausted, and *Atuk* was still eating at him. Almost instantly, though, he relaxed. Tulsa always did that to Sam. He especially loved to sit in our mother's church, among family and friends, and replenish his spiritual side. I always said that Sam was two different people. The Hollywood Sam and the Tulsa Sam.

The first night I preached the convention, I saw him slip out of his seat in the front row. Hearing me preach always moved Sam. I figured he wanted to cry where no one could see him.

Our mom saw him leave too. She followed him and found him inside her office, going through one of my notebooks. Unlike Sam when he was a preacher, I was a great believer in preparation. Over the years, I filled dozens of notebooks with thoughts and pieces of scripture and threads of my future sermons.

"What's wrong, honey?" our mother asked Sam. He was crying while he was reading.

"The guy's a professional," he said.

"What are you talking about?"

"Look at these thoughts the guy gets. The guy's a pro. He's the best."

I was in tears that night too when my mom told me what happened. The way that Sam and I were raised to believe, a person preached because he'd been chosen by God. By persuading me to leave the ministry and start managing him, Sam probably felt he'd robbed me of my true calling.

Although he invited some stand-up friends to see the preachers' convention, Sam stayed mellow all week and barely partied. Kevin seemed unusually peaceful too. Up until then he'd been drinking a lot, and several months earlier, in November, he'd been arrested for drunken driving. I'd convinced him, again, to seek treatment in Long Beach. This time, he spent thirty days in the rehab clinic there.

When Kevin came out, I had to keep harping at him to continue taking his lithium. I would remind him, he would pretend to take it, we would go through our routine. Twice during this time, Kevin talked to my daughter of killing himself. Ginger was only five and adored her Uncle Kevin. Both times she ran into my bedroom crying and screaming.

I knew he was in pain. I even went so far as to lock up all my guns. But I never thought Kevin would kill himself.

"Kevin," I told him, "Ginger believes what you tell her. You tell her you're going to do something to yourself, she *believes* you."

"I know," Kevin said. "I don't know why I said that to her. I shouldn't have said that."

In Tulsa that week, for the first time in seven years, all four Kinison boys were under one roof. Kevin seemed lucid and happy. One morning we played golf and he played his ass off. He shot an eighty, I shot eighty-three, we kicked a few other guys' butts. We laughed and needled each other and had a wonderful morning.

That evening I preached again, and Kevin came down to the front at the end of my message. "I'm free," he told me, weeping. "I'm really free."

At our service the following morning, Kevin sat in the front the entire time, enjoying the different preachers. We all ate lunch at the church, then I needed to Fed Ex a package by two that afternoon. I drove to my mother's house to pick it up, but the front door was locked and no one was back from the church yet. To my great surprise, I went around the side and the patio door was open. That was very unlike my mother. Her house had been burglarized twice and looked like Fort Knox.

I went inside, grabbed my package, came rushing back out the front door, and almost ran straight into Kevin. He said Sam had just dropped him off and was coming back in ten minutes, so they could go to the mall. I told him I'd see him later that afternoon, after he and Sam came back to Mom's.

"Hey, Bill," Kevin called out as I walked to my car. "You were really high-energy last night."

Those are kind words to a preacher, and coming from Kevin they meant a lot. I told him so and thanked him.

While pulling away from the house, I passed my mom and A.D. driving home from the other direction. They went inside just minutes later, going straight into their bedroom to get some rest. With his eyes closed, Kevin was lying on top of their bed. Our stepfather, A.D., kicked his leg gently. "Son," A.D. said, "get up and go on into your own room. I've gotta lay down here awhile."

Kevin didn't stir. My mother looked at his face and noticed its whiteness.

"I think he's passed out," she said.

She went to touch Kevin's face and spotted the blood. She staggered backward, screaming. She thought someone had broken into her house and struck her child in the head.

My in-laws were home by then; they rushed in at the sound of my mother's screams. Sherry's father smelled gunpowder. They found a .38 under the bed. Someone called 911 and reported a suicide attempt. From that moment on, that's how the Tulsa police handled the case.

About thirty minutes later, I came back to the house from the Federal Express office. I saw three police cars and two paramedic vans. I thought A.D. suffered a heart attack.

In front of the house, past the vans and police cars, I saw Sam and my mother sobbing.

"What happened?" I asked.

"He shot himself," Sam said.

"What?"

"Kevin shot himself."

My throat closed tight. I could not take a good breath.

When I ran inside the house, the police said he was unconscious but still alive. They carried him out on a gurney. In our shock and our dread, we all told Kevin to keep hanging on.

I kept saying, "Talk to his spirit, talk to his spirit. Please tell it to hang on."

Later that day a surgeon showed me the X-ray. A .38 hollow-point, after hitting bone, had exploded into fragments. Kevin was brain-dead, the surgeon said. He did not have much time to live.

Kevin was twenty-eight.

I went back to my mom's and told Sam. He went reeling all over the kitchen, smashing things and shouting. Then Sam lowered his voice.

"Why?" he said. "Why now? Why are you doing this to me?"

For a moment I thought he was talking to Kevin. Then I realized Sam was talking to God.

Kevin died the next day at two in the afternoon. By then, after several emotional hours by Kevin's bedside, Sam had returned to his hotel room, unable to watch the end of his brother's life. I walked in and found him alone, lying facedown on the bed. At first, I mistakenly thought he was drunk. I tried to raise him, but Sam was too big and he wouldn't let me. He wouldn't open his eyes. For a long time nobody spoke.

I finally said, "He's gone, Sam . . . Kevin is gone."

"I know he is," Sam said. "I know."

That was all he said. Then I left him alone.

The question kept coming up: Why did Kevin do it?

Our mother never, ever thought that he did. She always felt Kevin was murdered. Though I didn't agree, I also couldn't deny how puzzling some of the circumstances were. The police said people who kill themselves almost always use their dominant hand. Kevin golfed, played basketball, and did everything else right-handed. Yet he'd been shot behind the left ear, at a very peculiar angle for someone right-handed. The gun had been found *well* under the bed. How could Kevin have pushed it there? The gun had no fingerprints on it, and a rag was found

near the wall smeared with cleaning solution. Outside, in a small
guest house behind my parents' main house, the doorknob was
jerked completely off the door. Footprints were found running
up the back fence.

Unfortunately, the police didn't discover most of these facts.
Our family did, and in some instances not for two or three days.
When I went back to the police, they said they'd come to the
house expecting a suicide, because that's what they'd been told
when they got the call. They admitted they'd botched the crime-
scene investigation. If it was murder, they said, it was difficult
finding a killer once forty-eight hours had passed. They reopened
the case but had no suspects.

When I called Kevin's psychiatrist in Long Beach, he seemed
astonished. "That's impossible," he said. "He was not capable
of hurting himself or anyone else."

"Well, he may not have been capable, but he shot himself."

"I'm telling you, he wasn't capable of doing that."

Sam and I both believed that Kevin had killed himself. Then
again, maybe we only willed ourselves into this. Just as some
people never accept that a loved one committed suicide, we
were unnerved by the thought of a killer, filling our brother with
terror before he shot him.

In public, Sam blamed the rehab doctors, charging that they'd
given Kevin too quick a fix. In particular, Sam condemned the
lithium they'd prescribed. He told *Rolling Stone,* "They dealt
with Kevin chemically instead of dealing with his inner pain.
Now people will never know what it was. I don't even know if
he knew." The *Los Angeles Times* quoted Sam: "Great cure,
huh? They get you addicted to something else and now the guy's
dead and still no one knows what was beneath all the pain."

Privately, Sam castigated himself. More than any other factor,
he blamed his own life-style for Kevin's death. Sam felt all the
liquor and drugs they'd done together, all the sleepless, cranked-
up nights of going too far, had pushed Kevin over the edge into

mental illness. And Sam thought the illness made Kevin lose his will to live.

I had my own guilty feelings.

Had I taken greater precautions . . . had I believed Kevin when he tried telling my daughter . . .

Another part of me, hostile and bitter, felt Sam was right. He *had* infected Kevin with all his dangerous habits. He *had* helped trigger his mental collapse.

I never said this to Sam. But I never really soothed him.

When Sam blamed himself, I'd only say, "Kevin is gone. Nothing we can do now. We all feel responsible, like there's something we could have done."

Sam would say softly, "Yeah, but we know. We know it's my life-style that did it."

After Kevin's death, Sam couldn't get on with living his own life. Even though Kevin was an adult, we all thought of him as the baby. Losing him was like losing a child. Sam cried for Kevin every day. One night, Sam called a friend and said, "God chose the wrong one. It should've been me." Then he hung up the phone, weeping.

Sam talked about Kevin compulsively. On our tour bus one evening, Sam said to me, "I want you to tell me everything you remember about his last minutes. Please?"

I took a deep breath, and I told Sam about seeing Kevin's monitors, seeing his pulse and blood pressure drop, until he was gone. Then I broke into tears. Sam came after me as I walked away. In the back of the bus we hugged and cried together. Then I told him, "I can't keep reliving this, Sam."

"I know," Sam said. "I won't keep bringing it up."

"You *can* bring it up. Just not every hour. I can't keep running it down. I can't take this much of it, man."

It was no use. Sam couldn't not talk about Kevin. Sam couldn't stop drinking and using. Alcohol in the past was Sam's biggest problem, but now he used more cocaine than I'd ever seen him.

I asked Sam to stop. I asked him to slow down. I told him he needed to sleep.

This time, Sam didn't resent my efforts to corral him. But he also made no attempt to get more sleep. When he did sleep at all, Sam said he kept dreaming of Kevin, then waking up and thinking he was alive.

Even after the news came out in the press, the public never learned the entire truth. How could anyone know how crazy Sam felt with guilt? How could they know he felt responsible? People saw only his rage.

The trouble started fast, when Sam took no time off to try and steady himself. Instead, he went straight back to work the day after Kevin's funeral. After performing all week at Rascals in New Jersey, Sam came back to L.A. and went on a tear. His first Sunday night back, blasted on liquor and coke, Sam went to the Comedy Store looking for Mitzi Shore's latest comedian boyfriend. According to what several comics told Sam, the guy had joked in his act while Sam was in Jersey: "If I was Sam Kinison's brother, I'd have killed myself a long time ago." The guy wasn't there that night, but Sam saw a friend of the guy's outside the building. Angry words were exchanged. Sam started throwing punches.

Mitzi told one of Sam's friends that she wanted him to come in. She wanted to talk things out. When Sam walked into the club one day that week, he found Mitzi standing with two plainclothes narcs. Unless Sam underwent rehab, Mitzi told him, he was banned from the Store. He stalked outside the club and never came back.

At some level, Sam may have understood he needed help. But he didn't think rehab programs had done much for Kevin. He also felt Mitzi had set him up. The day she invited him in, Sam thought she was hoping he'd cause a scene, so the two narcs would arrest him. That way, Sam couldn't beat the crap out of her boyfriend.

I agreed with Sam. Mitzi was never known for her compassion, or for taking a hard line on drugs.

One afternoon, Sam's second week back in L.A. after Kevin's death, I heard a shotgun blast in Sam's front hall. No matter where he lived, Sam normally kept several pistols, an Uzi, and three or four shotguns. Some people own guns because it's second nature, because they grew up around them. Sam wasn't one of those people; our family had never had guns when he was a child. Sam owned guns as an adult because he was drawn to danger.

I ran into the front hall and found Sam clutching his new shotgun. He had been moving it out of his closet and hadn't known it was loaded. It discharged in his hand, blasting a gaping hole in his closet wall.

Sam put down the gun and we both sat on his couch. I noticed his hands were shaking.

"Jesus Christ, Sam," I said. "You gotta be careful, man. We just lost Kevin. We don't need to lose another one."

Rock-and-Roll Comedian

"The number one form of music is rap music? I know, I know—I love rock and roll, but I'm telling you what's selling. Come on, man, I was fifteen in 1969. I was raised on the Beatles, Rolling Stones, Allman Brothers, Pink Floyd, Led Zeppelin, ZZ Top. I was raised on fucking *bands.* Rock and roll! I thought rap would go away by now, like disco. I bought one rap tape, because I wanted to be fair. I bought 2 Live Crew's *Nasty as We Wanna Be.* Yeah, I heard these guys were the outlaws of rap, they were on the cutting edge, they took on the First Amendment, the free-speech amendment. If you *haven't* bought the tape, take about seven dollars out of your wallet, and wipe your *ass* with it. It's about the same feeling. Aw, man, it's the worst fuckin' music. One song was 'Suck My Dick.' That's the song. 'Suck My Dick.' Not 'please.' Not 'Honey, do you have a minute?' 'Suck My Dick.' Like the Beatles would have wrote that one." Sam, speaking "British" like Paul McCartney: " 'Hey, John, would you like to write "Suck My Dick"?' " Sam as John Lennon: " 'Well, I don't know, do we have time? Sounds

like such a hard song to write.' 'Suck My Dick!' That was
the song. Like the guy got up one morning and went, 'Today, I wanna write a song. Today, I wanna write a love song.
I want to write a song that tells how a woman and a man
feel when they meet each other for the first time, and they
fall in love. I want to put into *words* the feelings that men
have always had but they've never been able to express. I
think I'll call this song . . . "Suck My Dick." ' Yeah, that's
gonna be the song on that K-Tel Goldie Oldie rap album.
Where were you when you heard 'Suck My Dick'? Remember those old days?"

—Sam in concert in Houston

Like many of Sam's routines, this one had a glint of truth behind it. Not only did rap leave him cold, Sam really was a die-
hard rock-and-roll fan. And, like most troubled kids who pick
up a guitar, for years he'd dreamt of becoming a rocker himself.

"What originally inspired you to play guitar?" Sam was once
asked by *Guitar World* magazine.

"Well, someone gave me a tape with three tracks from the
Best of Cream album. I heard 'Crossroads,' 'Badge,' and 'Sun-
shine of Your Love' in a row, and that's all the guy had. I thought
Clapton's guitar was a saxophone or a horn or something. But
the guy who gave me a tape said it was a guitar. I said, 'Shit,
man, I've got to learn how to do this.' And I just fell in love right
there. I got on my knees and began to pray and bow to the
guitar."

In the summer of 1988, Sam was approaching two milestones:
his thirty-fifth birthday and ten years of doing stand-up. Sam still
loved comedy, but he wanted a change in his life. With Hollywood still freezing him out of feature films, he wanted into rock
and roll.

Sam was already there in his personal life. Throwing wild parties up in the Hollywood Hills, spending a fortune on limousines,

tweaking the establishment—Sam already lived more like a rock star than like a comic. To help make the transition in his career, we signed with Front Line Management, the top management firm in the history of rock. At one time or the other, Front Line represented Janet Jackson, the Eagles, Don Henley, Steely Dan, Boz Scaggs, Jimmy Buffett, Heart, Warren Zevon, and Jackson Browne. Front Line was owned by Irving Azoff, the most powerful executive in the record industry. Brutally hard on record companies, Azoff was therefore beloved by his rock-star clients. Most artists want a hard-ass for a manager.

At a time when Hollywood shunned him, Sam considered Irving Azoff a godsend.

"He's not so crazy," Azoff told the *Los Angeles Times* after signing Sam. "Compared to the people I deal with in the record business, he's like Mother Teresa. I can really identify with his material, especially his rap on marriage. One day he was over at my office and all I could think of was—'I've got to get him to call my wife and have him yell at her.' "

With Front Line behind Sam now, MTV began using him as a guest emcee and veejay. At the China Club, or at Spice, or after doing his stand-up act in concert, Sam started playing in "all-star jams" with Slash, Ozzy Osbourne, Joe Walsh, C. C. DeVille, Steven Tyler, Jon Bon Jovi and Richie Sambora, John Entwistle of the Who, Robin Zander of Cheap Trick, Mötley Crüe, Poison, and Ratt. A guitarist since age fifteen, Sam wanted his rocker buddies to take his music seriously. Although they pretended to, I think they enjoyed Sam's anarchistic spirit more than his playing.

On July 13 and 14, Sam had two sold-out shows coming up at the Universal Amphitheater, and Front Line arranged to have several rockers join him for a musical encore. The impromptu band included Ted Nugent, Billy Idol, Leslie West of Mountain, Rudy Sarzo of Whitesnake, and Vince Neil and Tommy Lee from Mötley Crüe.

Before his first show on Wednesday night, Sam never made it to his own sound check. The all-star band, planning on performing "Jailhouse Rock," said they could run through it with me standing in for Sam. Since Mötley Crüe had sung "Jailhouse Rock" for years, I asked their lead singer, Vince Neil, to tell me the words.

"I don't know the words," Vince said.

I thought he was ribbing me. "How can you not know the words?"

"He doesn't," his bandmate Tommy Lee said. "I keep telling the guy to learn the fuckin' words."

Nobody else knew the lyrics, either.

"You gotta be kidding!" I said. "We got an all-star band here, and nobody knows the words to 'Jailhouse Rock'? Sam's planning on doing this. How are we gonna do this?"

"Just tell Sam to mumble the words," Vince Neil said. "That's what I always do."

"You're kidding!" I said again.

Tommie Lee said, "No, he's not."

In that night's musical encore, Billy Idol completely butchered "Jailhouse Rock." Sam kept cursing him in the dressing room after the show, even though Sam liked Billy. "Fuckin' Idol," Sam kept saying. "Fuckin' Idol messed it all up."

"Forget it," I said to Sam. "But you guys can't do 'Jailhouse Rock' again tomorrow night."

Leslie West suggested "Wild Thing," the classic rock-and-roll anthem by the Troggs. Great idea, everyone told Leslie.

On Thursday morning, the *Los Angeles Times* crucified the musical part of Sam's show. The writer saved most of his venom for Billy Idol. Out of embarrassment, perhaps, Billy never showed up that night for Sam's second gig.

This time Sam did attend his own sound check, but a moment before it started he pulled me off to the side.

"I have someone backstage I want you to meet," Sam said.

I stepped backstage with Sam and saw Jessica Hahn.

Sam introduced us, and Jessica gave me a hug.

"Oh, excuse me, they're hard," she said.

"Pardon me?"

"My tits. I just got 'em done and they're still hard."

Sam had invited Jessica there that evening, after meeting her one night before at the Playboy Mansion, where they'd done a little flirting. It was obvious to me now that Sam was in serious heat. I excused myself so they could be alone, but Sam was back five minutes later to do his sound check. It happened again for the second straight night: A few lines into "Wild Thing," none of the heavy metalists knew the words. Sam just slashed away at his guitar. "Let them deal with it," he said, since he wasn't the singer.

After Sam introduced Jessica to the packed house, after he did his comedy, the all-star band ran out for the musical encore. When Vince Neil came to the part where he stopped knowing the lyrics, he surprised Sam by sticking the mike in his hand. Sam hesitated for only a moment. Then, in his own maniacal style, he improvised new words as they flashed through his brain: "Wild Thing . . . I think you move me . . . but I wanna know for sure . . . EVERY TIME I KISS YOU I TASTE WHAT OTHER MEN HAD FOR LUNCH . . . THE ONLY THING THAT COULD GET YOU OFF IS TO SEE ME IN PAIN—BUT I THINK I LOVE YOU!"

The metal sound kept building. Sam kept remaking "Wild Thing" on the spot. "YOU MADE ME TRUST YA . . . THEN STUCK A KNIFE IN MY HEART! YOU'RE A LYING, UNFAITH-FUL, UNTRUSTABLE TRAMP, AND I THINK I LOVE YOU!"

The crowd at Universal was on its feet laughing and cheering. I told Sam in our dressing room after the show, "I don't know how you did that, but you gotta record that song. It'll be a great video!"

When he followed my advice, "Wild Thing" became a bona fide hit, both on MTV and radio. People began calling Sam "the rock-and-roll comic." That it happened so fast was a monumental fluke. If Billy Idol hadn't screwed up "Jailhouse Rock" the first night in L.A., the band would never have switched to "Wild Thing." If Vince Neil had known the words to "Wild Thing," Sam would never have made them up.

But Sam never told anyone that. In interviews, he pretended that making "Wild Thing" was carefully plotted. Sam always wanted people to think he was in charge. In truth, he rarely calculated anything—not even controversy. Controversy came naturally to Sam, because of his reckless mouth and his reckless life-style.

After his two big shows at the Universal, Sam had a concert later that week outside San Jose. He still hadn't slept with Jessica Hahn, so he flew her up to the gig on a chartered Learjet. As he had at Universal, Sam brought Jessica onstage and announced her to the crowd. Back in L.A. that same night, after the show, Jessica, Sam, and Malika all partied together. But rather than even suggest having a threesome, Sam sent Malika home. He ended up with Jessica in a hotel room.

When I had dinner with Sam the following evening, he told me what had happened before we opened our menus.

"I did her," he said matter-of-factly.

"How did it go?"

"It was the worst pussy I have ever been with."

"What?"

"Granted, man, I was out of it. I was drunk and I fell asleep in her."

"What do you mean?"

"With my dick in her, I fell asleep."

Minus the sexual details, the media promptly found out about their improbable "romance." As the story took on a life of its own, both in the tabloids and in the legitimate press, the behind-the-scenes truth was even more peculiar. After sleeping with her one time, Sam wanted nothing more from Jessica than her friendship. But whatever happened that boozy night in their hotel room, Jessica Hahn had fallen in love with Sam.

Smitten by him, she kept popping up without warning at show after show. Malika tried becoming Jessica's friend, as Malika tended to do with women she perceived as genuine threats. But when Jessica would leave at the end of an evening, Malika and Sam would have screaming matches about her. "She's coming around on her own," he'd swear to Malika. Malika thought Sam was lying, even though he wasn't.

Malika got even angrier that summer, when Sam cast Jessica in his video for "Wild Thing." Also making cameos were several members of Aerosmith, Guns N' Roses, and Bon Jovi, in return for Sam's having appeared in videos of their own. I was present the day they taped. Except for Slash and Billy Idol, all the hard rockers acted like gentlemen. Slash, so high he could barely stand up, tried breaking his guitar at the end of the song, but instead plunged head over heels into a box. It looked so goofy it wound up staying in. Billy Idol, drunk and coked up and obnoxious by nature, kept spitting down at Jessica while she and Sam wrestled around in a pit.

I never cared much for Billy Idol. He was one of those guys who hits on his own friends' dates, then acts surprised when they want to punch him out. When I told Sam I didn't like Billy, Sam laughed and said he was harmless. Then came the infamous night at Bally's in Vegas.

By then, both Malika and Sabrina were part of Sam's road shows. Scantily dressed, they'd escort him onstage at the start of his stand-up routine, then rejoin him later on for his musical encore. On this night at Bally's, Sam had two consecutive shows with a short break in between. Billy came out the first encore to join Sam on "Wild Thing." Strutting up behind Malika and Sabrina, Billy pressed his fingers up into their G-strings. Sam turned at just that instant and saw Billy do it. Murder came into Sam's eyes, and Billy ducked offstage before the song ended.

In between shows, Sam told me his plan for his second musical encore: He would beat Billy's ass onstage in front of three thousand people. But Billy probably knew it and never showed up. Billy's guitarist friend Art did, however. As Sam broke into "Wild Thing," he turned his back to the crowd and riffed with his drummer. Art slid over toward Sam to join him.

"What happened to Billy?" Sam shouted over the music.

"He's too out of it," Art shouted back. *"He couldn't make it this show."*

"When you see him," Sam yelled, *"Give him this."*

Right on the beat, Sam popped Art in the mouth. Then, screaming, "WILD THING," Sam turned back to face his astonished crowd.

The second week of November, to coincide with the start of Sam's next major tour, Warner Bros. released his second comedy album. Poking fun at his blackballing in Hollywood, Sam titled it *Have You Seen Me Lately?* Once he gave Warner Bros. the title, they created the concept for the front cover—a spoof of a missing-child milk carton. Above all his vital statistics, there was a photo of Sam as a smiling teenage boy in a white shirt and tie. Everyone said how gentle Sam looked back then. And it was a good picture of him. He also ran away from home a few weeks after it was taken.

Nominated for a Grammy, *Have You Seen Me Lately* included:

His doubts about MTV's Rock Against Drugs campaign. "Everyone's trying to be straight now. Doesn't that piss you off, these fucking rock-and-roll pussies? I watch MTV all the time, they have these Rock Against Drugs commercials. These guys have, like, slid into school buses and killed twenty children. 'Rather than face a life sentence, they made a *public* service announcement.' Yeah, no shit. I love these guys." Sam, like a British rocker: " 'Hello, listen, don't get caught with drugs, or you'll have to do a commercial just like this one.' I think I found the message—the message is don't get caught. Rock Against Drugs, what a name. Somebody was high when they came up with this title. It's like Christians Against Christ. Rock *created* drugs."

His angst-filled second marriage. "There were times I just wanted to stop at a red light, just get out of the car and fuckin' *run*. Just leave the engine going and go: 'OH FUCK, I HATE YOU! I JUST WANNA LIVE! AAAUGHH!' So I finally got a divorce and let her have everything. I just wanted out. Jesus. And I was bitter for a while, but I'm over that now."

His lack of remorse for TV preacher Jim Bakker. "This guy deserved *everything* he got. Hypocritical, self-righteous bastard. Guy used to be on the air: 'I know God personally, no one will get in without my little seal.' Jerk! Jesus is up in heaven right now, he's going through the Bible going: 'Where the fuck did I say build a water slide? How did they get that out of this? I never said build an old folks' home and use it as a tax write-off—oh, you dick, you fuckin' dick!' God kicked his ass, though, man. He's lost everything, he's ruined. And the worst thing of all, he still has to wake up to *her*! OH! AAAAUGH!"

His disdain for Oral Roberts. "I don't know how we got stuck with all these wacko preachers, folks. We got, like, God's special education team here in America. Oral Roberts? 'I saw a nine-hundred-foot Jesus in Tulsa, Oklahoma.' Yeah, great, Oral, great. Take your fuckin' medicine, will ya? And you'll stop seeing these nine-hundred-foot Jesuses. 'He won't take the medicine, doctor. I keep telling him.' What a dick!"

Sam's fantasy about the Pope, while touring America, watching late-night porno in his hotel room. "I'm a nasty Pope, I'm a nasty Pope."

His roof-raising remake of "Wild Thing," featuring Rudy Sarzo of Whitesnake, C.C. DeVille of Poison, and Vince Neil of Mötley Crüe. "YOU USED ME! YOU NEVER LOVED ME! WHY DIDN'T YOU TELL ME YOU WERE A DEMON FROM HELL? YOU DESERVE THE MEN YOU'RE GONNA BE WITH! RAILROAD

BUMS! TRANSIENTS! OUT-OF-WORK GUYS! GUYS THAT ARE GONNA USE YOU LIKE YOU USED ME! GUYS THAT ARE GONNA TAKE MONEY OUT OF YOUR PURSE AND THROW IT OUT A WINDOW! WILD THING—I THINK I LOVE YOU!"

Friends who egg you on at parties once you get wasted. "You can't blame your friends, you gotta take a little bit of responsibility, but you gotta watch friends, man, they're fuckin' out of their minds. They'll let you piss in your fuckin' suitcase in front of people. 'Don't you remember when you pissed in your suitcase last night, man? You were so drunk?' No, no, I don't fuckin' *remember* that. But I wanna thank you guys for letting me *do* it. Thanks, buddies! I'm glad I could be the fuckin' home entertainment center for everybody! I'm glad you let me show everybody my dick and piss in my suitcase. Thanks, buddies!"

His riff on Jesus Christ's followers exploiting his generosity. "Jesus had it tough. People took advantage of him. They found out he could do miracles, do wonders, you know. So he'd be, like, healing the blind, and healing lepers and shit, five thousand people would show up with no fuckin' *food*. They weren't sick, they didn't need healing, they were too fuckin' lazy to make a sandwich for the day. 'I know, let's let Jesus get it.' He's trying to preach, he's trying to share all this information, he goes, 'What? *What?* Five thousand of you, and not one of you brought a sandwich? Ohhhh, I guess you expect *me* to get it, huh? That's no pressure, I'll just create *food* out of the fuckin' *air*. Thanks!' 'Well, you said you were Son of God.' He's like, 'I DON'T THINK YOU'RE GETTING THE FUCKIN' POINT HERE—YOU FUCKIN' JERKS! I DIDN'T COME TO BE JESUS THE MIRACLE CATERER!' He had a tough gig, he had a fuckin' tough gig."

"Rubber Love" was the cut that caused the commotion. Complaining in general about the overrighteous, Sam segued into a discourse on safe sex. "Goddam these fuckin' bastards—*get off of our back!* Because a few fags fucked some monkeys . . . they got so bored that their own assholes weren't enough, they had to go in the fuckin' jungle, grab some fuckin' monkey and fuck *him* in the ass . . . and bring us back the Black Plague of the fuckin' eighties. Thanks, guys! Because of this shit, they want us to wear fuckin' rubbers. . . . Do we like to wear rubbers, guys? WE HATE RUBBERS! WE FUCKIN' HATE 'EM!''

It was crude, brutal humor—I know. But I have to say it again: Sam *never* hated gays as a group of people. He hated being told what he could and could not say. And once certain gays tried legislating his humor, well, then it was war.

Something else about Sam's battles with gays: Many people felt it was political—Sam was a former preacher who grew up in the conservative Midwest—but I thought it was more psychological. Sam had an inferiority complex, so he lashed out at everyone else. Most of his targets shrugged it off: He's just a stand-up, they're only jokes, he *is* funny up there.

The gay community didn't shrug it off. It battled back, it took him on, and that's why Sam was so hard on them. Once a fight started, Sam couldn't back off. It would make him look "soft" to the public, and that would inflame his own insecurities.

All of that said, I thought Sam should stop doing that bit about AIDS. I wanted it out of his act, and off of his second album.

"Those jokes are cold," I told him. "These people are victims of a horrible disease. I think you're over the line here."

Sam said, "They're only jokes. And where *is* the fuckin' line? Who gets to draw it?"

When I persisted, Sam said exactly what he would say when my brother Kevin or I tried telling a joke: "Hey. Leave the comedy to the experts."

Even before its release, the album made headlines. Under pressure from gay activists, and some of its own employees, Warner Bros. placed two stickers on the front jacket. One read, EXPLICIT LANGUAGE AND MATERIAL, PARENTAL ADVISORY. The other was much more unusual: OPINIONS EXPRESSED IN THIS RECORDING DO NOT REFLECT THE VIEWS OF WARNER BROS. RECORDS.

I heard about the stickers on the radio, and Sam learned about them from me. Feeling that Warner Bros. should have told him directly, Sam seemed more put out by them than he was by the protesting gays. As Sam told Joan Rivers on her talk show, "I mean, I didn't surprise them. They knew when they signed me what I do. They knew what the content of the album would be. And they were excited, and they were behind the album, until they got all this flak from these groups, and then of course there were all the stickers and denials . . . 'Yeah, we help him take his money to the bank, but these are not our views.' "

Ultimately, Sam excised all his AIDS remarks from his act. He came to regret ever making them. Through the T. J. Martell Foundation and MTV, Sam and other entertainers helped raise $3 million for the cure and research of AIDS. But Sam took these positions willingly, because he had a change of heart, and not because any interest groups bullied him into it.

On November 10, at the Celebrity Theater in Anaheim, Sam launched the most ambitious concert tour of his career. In the next four months he was booked into forty cities. With "Wild Thing" in heavy rotation on MTV, with his album selling briskly despite/because of the tumult, he was now playing venues of up to six thousand seats. To go barnstorming with him across the country, Sam invited: Malika and Sabrina. A full professional rock band to jam with him during finales. A group of opening stand-ups he dubbed the Comedy Outlaws—Carl LaBove, Alan Stephan, Mitchell Walters, and Jimmy Shubert.

Our very first show in Anaheim, Sam picked up three more roadie/comedians. "Where are we gonna put them?" I asked Sam. Our tour bus slept twelve, but his entourage had now swelled to an all-time-high seventeen.

"I don't know, man, but we'll fit them in somewhere," Sam said. "I wanna give these guys a break."

From that first concert on, Sam and I fought about carrying so many people. Paying hotel and travel expenses for seventeen people, how did he expect to turn a profit? There would also be thousands of hours spent on the road, and our tour bus was overjammed in every direction. There were too many bodies and moods, too much liquor and drugs. In selecting his entourage, Sam had encircled himself with fellow drinkers and dopers, a few of whom were true friends, but most of whom had no real feelings for him, and were only leeching along so they could get blasted for free. They didn't give a shit if Sam did his show each night. They didn't care about his physical well-being. Either Sam couldn't see this or it didn't matter to him. The tour kept on. The madness continued.

In the midst of it all, Sam was falling in love with his girlfriend's teenage sister. He told me flat out at the start of the tour: "Man, I think I'm in love with Sabrina."

"She's just a kid, Sam," I said. "She's seventeen."

"I know," Sam said, "but she reminds me of Gail. She has that innocent thing about her."

Sabrina did seem innocent, particularly when compared to her older sister. Traveling from gig to gig, Malika wore skintight shorts and plunging blouses. Sabrina liked jogging outfits. On tour, when we arrived at hotels in the late afternoon, Sam and Malika usually went to their room and opened the bar. Sabrina would call my room to see if I wanted to jog, or else pump iron downstairs in the hotel gym. I found this a great release from our traveling zoo, but then Sam went and ruined it. Every time I exercised with Sabrina, he seemed resentful and touchy. I had enough aggravation with him. Without explaining why, I started telling Sabrina I liked to work out on my own.

One afternoon in Maui, on a short break from the western leg of our tour, Sam first glimpsed Sabrina's bare breasts when she leaned over in her swimsuit.

All that night, reliving the moment, Sam kept saying, "Oh, man!"

One of his buddies told him, "You're acting like *you're* seventeen!"

Sam lusted for Sabrina, there was no question of that. But Sam was also in love. It didn't make sense, he *knew* it didn't make sense, but there it was. Sam wanted to spend the rest of his life with Sabrina. If he had to, Sam told me, he'd even marry her. I couldn't believe it. This was a guy who made a career out of skewering the institution. The guy who said marriage made "hell seem like Club Med." Before Sam met Sabrina, I used to kid him: "You better not meet a woman you wanna marry. Your career will be over tomorrow."

Sam was thinking about his heart, not his career. Sabrina was all he wanted to talk about anymore. How much he yearned for her. How frustrated he felt with her right there on the tour bus. How crazy it drove him back in L.A., with her sleeping next door in the house the three of them shared. I never minded Sam's obsessing about Sabrina. She was a bright, likable person, she didn't party, and she kept Sam's mind off of Kevin. But I did think at some point Sam should come clean.

I told him one night on the tour bus: "If you really love her, then one day you just have to tell her: 'Either I'm the one you want, or else I'm not. If I am, it's gotta be just me and you. I can't put up with Malika here anymore.' "

Sam wasn't prepared for that yet. "They're still a package deal," he said. "I'm not gonna marry Malika—I'm not in love with her. But if I make her leave, Sabrina would leave me too."

"You gotta believe in love. What else you gonna do? Give sheep the vote? I've been in love about eight times now. And I buy it every time. Every single time, I buy it. Love comes into my life and goes: 'Come on. This is love. No, this is real love. Not like the others—this is *real love*. I wouldn't lie to you nine times in a row, you *ass*. OPEN THE DOOR!' " Sam opens a door—and the devil is there to rip out his heart and eat it. "OH! AAAAUGGH! YOU LIED TO ME AGAIN!"

—Sam in London on *Saturday Live,* the English equivalent of *SNL.*

The Tour from Hell

"Even when Sam Kinison is happy, his language is rough. Now Sam Kinison is angry and the words he says cannot be used on television. The latest uproar over the controversial comedian stems from this cover story in the upcoming issue of *Rolling Stone*. When the magazine sent Kinison's publicist an advance copy of the article, he got hold of it and promptly called up the reporter to complain."
—John Tesh, *Entertainment Tonight*, February 1, 1989

"I said: 'If you're unhappy, write a letter, you know, we'll publish your response.' He said: 'I don't write letters, I kick ass.' "
—David Handelman, the *Rolling Stone* writer, on the same
Entertainment Tonight

What made our Februarys so toxic? One year earlier, when *Atuk* fell apart, the stigma shoved Sam out of feature films. In February of 1989, he seemed to average a crisis a week.

The year itself started out on a high. At a special price of $50 a ticket, Sam sold out the Universal Amphitheater on New Year's

Eve. About halfway through his performance, I picked up a check backstage for $154,000, the largest single payday of Sam's career. With the audience still cheering after his encore, we rushed outside the building and into a waiting limo, rode fifteen minutes to Burbank Airport, then were whisked by a Learjet to Las Vegas, where Sam played the Sahara at 4:00 A.M. After another sold-out concert, we flew back home to L.A. with the rising desert sun.

After that heady New Year's Eve, Sam spent most of January at home, seeking some respite before he went back on the road. Instead, he got hammered by *Rolling Stone.*

Although *Rolling Stone*'s readers never found out, there was a story behind the story. The real trouble between Sam and David Handelman started in San Diego on December 17. Sam had a gig that Saturday night at Golden Hall, concluding the western leg of our forty-city tour. After the show, to celebrate, our promoter Bill Silva planned on having a wrap party. He hired a local stripper with an unusual specialty. While wearing asbestos panties, she'd pretend to set fire to her vagina.

The moment Sam ended his show, I settled with Silva back in his office. By the time I came out, Sam and the tour bus had already left for L.A. It didn't matter to me—I was driving my own car—but it was still unlike Sam to split so quickly. He usually stuck around to see how much we'd taken in.

I'd forgotten, for a moment, about the writer from *Rolling Stone.* On and off for the last few weeks, he'd been riding with us on our tour bus. Sam had even invited him into his home, which Sam never did with the press. It was part of an informal deal we'd struck. In exchange for our allowing him excellent access, Handelman said he would write a "positive piece." Sam and I had no interest in puff. That would be dull, and no one would buy it anyway about Sam. We did hope for some balance. "It'll be a positive piece," Handelman kept reassuring us.

Then San Diego happened. When I gave Handelman the

news—Sam and the tour bus were already gone—his eyes filled up with tears.

"He left me," Handelman said. "I can't believe he took off without me."

"Dave, it's not a big problem," I said. "I've got my own car and I have to drive back to L.A. You can ride with me if you want. If you want a hotel room, we can do that, and you can take Amtrak tomorrow. There's flights that run this late too. I can take you right now to San Diego Airport. Whatever you want to do."

Nothing could pacify him. "He left me, man," he said. "I can't believe he did that to me."

I thought: This guy works for *Rolling Stone*? I thought these guys have all been through the wars.

Back in Los Angeles the next day, I called Sam and asked him what had happened. "I didn't wanna hang around there all night," he said. "With Malika and Sabrina, there with the stripper? It's not worth the fuckin' headache."

I told him how freaked out the writer was. Sam said he'd just wanted to leave; he'd forgotten the guy was traveling with us. Sam did find it comical, though, a writer for *Rolling Stone* getting teary-eyed over missing a ride to L.A.

When the cover story came out, Sam wasn't laughing. What might have been a professional highlight, a once-in-a-lifetime thrill, turned into a major embarrassment. Bad enough that Handelman did a number on him. Bad enough that he did it in *Rolling Stone,* a magazine Sam had grown up on. But the cover photo they chose made Sam look like an animal. It showed him roaring, enraged, with his wrists locked in manacles and chains. No one had put a gun to Sam's head. But they'd also taken dozens of other photographs. We were hoping they'd run one that showed his softer side.

I'd been sitting close by during many of their interviews. When I saw Sam's printed quotes, I thought, *Wait a minute!* Because

Sam had said certain things with a twinkle in his eye. He was trying to get a reaction, both from Handelman and from the people sitting around them. None of that subtext made it into the story. Handelman left it out.

By printing them in a national magazine, the story also gave creedence to what Handelman called "vicious rumors." Attributed to Sam's "detractors," two of the rumors were semitruthful: "That he keeps a gun in every room of his house; that his women of choice are strippers and young girls." But the paragraph full of rumors also included these beauties: " . . . he views himself as a savior figure and leads a cult of comics in satanic rituals atop the Sunset Hyatt; before going onstage at the Comedy Store, he kills a cat for good luck."

Sam found a way to have fun with this in public. If one of his concerts started late, he'd apologize because he was "out looking for cats." Or as he told Joan Rivers on her afternoon talk show: "Like I really got time to go out and find a cat: 'You're on in five minutes. Five minutes, please, Mr. Kinison.' 'Wait, wait! Here, kitty, kitty.'

"Not that I'm *against* cat death," Sam added.

Privately, he was pissed off. "No one reads the word 'rumors' " Sam said. "All anyone reads is 'He kills cats before every performance.' "

What most enraged him, what made him pick up the phone and call the writer, was the quote about our stepfather, A.D. Handelman quoted Steve Epstein, a comedian who knew Sam back in Houston, saying, "The key to Sam's personality is that his real dad was into Jesus, his adopted dad looked at preaching as more of a business and that God didn't seem to reward people for doing it just for love."

The key to Sam? Nobody knows the key to anyone, let alone to a complex person like Sam. More to the point, Steve Epstein never met our father. He never met A.D. Neither did Handelman. Yet reading between the lines of this psychobabble—one father preached from goodness, one wanted the cash—some people took it as fact. In truth, A.D. was one of the straightest, kindest, most devout men I ever knew. Even though we didn't like it, our family could handle the criticism of Sam. He was a public figure, and he wasn't exactly shy in expressing his own opinions. But A.D. was eighty years old, and he still pastored a church. Without a legitimate reason, why shame and embarrass him?

Sam was never sophisticated enough—or phony enough—to pretend that he wasn't bothered by lousy press. When he called to complain, Handelman told him to write a letter, as if that could negate anything. The smugness of the remark set Sam off like a rocket. Really, Sam said, he'd rather kick Handelman's ass.

Had he not been left behind in San Diego, would Handelman have written a more evenhanded story? We never knew. All we saw was what ran: a very well-written piece, but a caricature, a cartoon. Except for a few perfunctory "positive" paragraphs, the story showed only Sam's darkness.

It radically changed his attitude toward the press. Sam had never been one of those stars who shun reporters all year, then suddenly pop up all over to hawk a new project. If you could get Sam to sit still, then you could get your interview. You could pretty much bank on getting good copy, too.

Now he became wary, almost paranoid toward the press. I had the same reaction. Unless it was someone we already knew—not somebody soft but somebody objective—a reporter would have no chance of talking to Sam.

On the night of February 2, I pulled into LAX in a van packed with luggage for seventeen people. Our tour bus and driver were already in Cincinnati. We'd fly there on a red-eye, play Cleveland the following night, and kick off another series of road shows.

When I parked at the Delta curb and asked the skycap for help, he just shook his head no and kept moving. That's pretty strange, I thought.

I stepped out of the van and noticed a second skycap. He leaned against the building, apparently staying dry. A light, cold rain was falling.

"Excuse me," I said. "Can you give me some help here?"

"You want some help?" he said, striding quickly toward me.

"Yeah."

He whistled loudly, shooting his right hand into the air. I saw guys rushing toward me from every direction. They were all in law enforcement—LAPD, FBI, DEA. There seemed to be about thirty. A few police dogs appeared suddenly too.

After getting a tip, a team of local and federal officers had been following Sam for three days and tapping his phone lines. Sam and his entourage, the police suspected, would be selling and transporting drugs on the next phase of our tour. The cops didn't care much about Sam's entourage, though. They wanted Sam Kinison, the outrageous comic who still told prodrug jokes.

I found all this out later. All I knew now was that we had another predicament.

"What is the problem?" I asked Sergeant Ricky Ross of the LAPD. Ross seemed to be running the show. He was the guy disguised as the second skycap.

"If you're carrying anything in that luggage," Ross told me, "let me know now. It'll be easier on you."

"Nobody's carrying anything," I said, hoping that I was telling the truth. Sam and his boys were buyers, not dealers, and they usually scored when they got on the road. But with seventeen people traveling, you never know.

As Sam's entourage began pulling up to the curb, the officers herded them in. Sam arrived next in a stretch limousine, accompanied by Malika and Sabrina, both young and beautiful. I could practically see the officers thinking, We're gonna nail this Hollywood bastard. Sam then managed to make matters even worse: He walked from the limo on rubbery legs. Fearful of airplanes, he'd taken a couple of Quaaludes to try to sleep.

Sergeant Ross told me again, "If we're gonna find anything, you should tell us right now."

I said there was nothing to find.

"Maybe you wanna talk to your buddies," Ross said.

I huddled with Sam and the others. "If any of you are carrying," I said, "let me know right this second. We'll get our lawyers down here, do this the way it's supposed to be done."

They assured me they were all clean.

I told Ross, but he looked doubtful. We had two options, he said. If we signed releases to let them search our luggage, he'd allow Malika and Sabrina to go wait in the park. Otherwise, we could stand in the rain for two hours while they tracked down a court order. Then they'd go through our luggage anyway.

We signed the releases. The police dogs frantically sniffed out nine pieces of luggage. My computer case and Sam's black traveling bag were among them. Sam said, looking directly at me, "Looks like they wanna check your case and your black bag."

"Just a second," I said to the cops. Then I pulled Sam to the side.

"What's in the fuckin' bag?" I asked.

"I got a little pot in there," Sam said.

"Jesus! You idiot!"

I asked Sergeant Ross if we could speak in private, away from his colleagues. "I'm gonna be straight with you," I lied. "That black bag there is mine. There's a little pot inside it."

"Is it for you?" Ross said. "The pot?"

"Yeah. I have trouble sleeping on the tour bus. I take a few hits, it mellows me out and I sleep."

"But it's just a small amount?"

"Yeah."

"Don't worry about it. It's a hundred-dollar fine and a misdemeanor."

They opened my computer case and found nothing odd. Unzipping Sam's black bag, they discovered two ounces of marijuana. I felt my stomach knot. When Sam said "a little pot," I'd thought he meant a few joints. I figured I'd get a ticket. Now, if things broke the wrong way, I could be facing felonies.

I tried not to glance at Sam, but I couldn't help it. It didn't matter—the police knew the pot was his anyway. They'd found extra-large clothes in the black bag it came out of. Sam's clothes.

One of the officers got in Sam's face. "Mr. fuckin' Big Shot," he said. "Mr. Celebrity, huh? Gonna screw your own brother, push it off on him? You know he's going to jail? You know he's facing three felonies? You're gonna let him do it, huh? Empty your fuckin' pockets."

Sam never spoke. Humiliated, frightened, and weak-kneed from the Quaaludes in his bloodstream, Sam pulled out the only thing in his pockets: a tightly rolled $100 bill he'd been tooting cocaine with.

"Aw, Sam," the same officer sneered. "You're *still* gonna stick your brother? Even after this bill? You know we can nail you just with this?'

That's when I lost my temper. Tired of seeing my younger brother degraded, tired of me being made to look like a saint, I said, "Guys! I told you it's my bag! I smoke some pot so I can sleep on the bus! You gonna arrest me? *Arrest me!*"

"All right, cool down," a different officer said. "We're going though every piece of this luggage. Hey, Sam? We find one more thing in *anyone's* bag, we're nailing you for the stuff that's on this bill."

After they hadn't found any more drugs, Sergeant Ross addressed me again. "Listen to me, Bill. I'm not gonna arrest you. And I'll recommend to the D.A. that they don't press charges.

We haven't found anything hard, and I know it's your brother's shit. Right?"

"No," I said, getting testy again. "It's *not* my brother's shit."

Ross said, "Yeah, okay, whatever."

The moment it ended, everyone left the airport quickly. Driving alone back to my house, I felt my hostility building toward Sam. He had pushed this on me because he knew he could. Out of everyone there, Sam knew his big brother would cover for him.

Too wired to stay in my bed, I hardly slept that night. Back at LAX the next morning—we still had the Cleveland show—I stayed off to myself for a while, not talking to anyone. Then I started feeling the rage, all the bullshit he'd put me through over the years. Little brother my ass.

I rushed up and physically pulled Sam aside. "How the fuck could you pull that shit?" I said.

"It's not a big deal, man. The cop said they're not pressing the charges."

"That's not the point! It *is* a big deal! I preached for seventeen years! I had people that respected me! Now they'll read in the paper that I've been detained for drugs! I might've taken the heat if you'd given me a chance. You just took it for granted!"

Sam never admitted that. He showed no contrition. Maybe I shouldn't have been surprised. Both of us had been caught in this cycle since childhood. Sam would screw up. I'd assume the role of his savior. We'd both resent each other.

But I *was* surprised when Sam didn't seem grateful. I just stood there at LAX, glaring at him, feeling the heat spreading through me again. So I turned and walked away. I thought if I didn't I might punch him out.

Three days later, on our way to a gig in Milwaukee, our tour bus pulled into our hometown of Peoria. We almost always stopped there when we had a Midwestern day off.

After visiting old friends and relatives all day, Sam partied all that evening with Carl LaBove. They never made it back to their hotel rooms, even though Carl's wife, Christi, was traveling with him. Still furious in the morning, Christi went to Sam's room to see if they'd staggered in yet. The only one there was Malika, and the two women had always hated each other. Things were especially touchy right now, after Christi's just-printed comments in *Rolling Stone.*

"Sam likes a certain type," Christi was quoted. "A light-headed, fluffy girl whose last job was, like, dancing topless. He likes them not to have much at stake so he can completely consume them with things he wants to do, because they're well kept." She was talking about Malika, and all of us knew it.

In Sam's hotel room, she asked Malika where Sam and Carl had been all night. They bickered. They fistfought. Sabrina came in and tried to protect her sister. Even though Christi stood five foot tall and weighed ninety pounds, she beat the crap out of both sisters at once.

When Sam finally appeared that afternoon, Malika's eye had turned black. Sam talked to everybody involved and sided with Christi. With the tour about to get hectic, Sam wanted to fly both sisters back to L.A., but Malika and Sabrina refused to go. Sam simmered down by that night, and Christi and Sabrina made amends too. But Malika and Christi had too much ill will. As we left for Milwaukee, we made sure they sat at different ends of the tour bus.

In Chicago later that week, Sam's ex-bodyguard resurfaced. The last time I'd seen Bob Suszynski, I'd fired him for scoring drugs for him and Sam. Sam put him back on the payroll in Chicago.

Chicago always loved Sam, and as usual he sold out the Chicago Theater. He needed to be up early to fly to New York, to tape the Letterman show, but he stayed up all night anyway in his hotel suite, partying hard with Malika and Suszynski. Sherry and I had a room in the same hotel. I called Sam's room in the morning and nobody answered. When I ran down the hall and knocked on his door, Sam could barely open it: Malika was lying unconscious in front of the doorway. Sam was wasted too. Suszynski was already gone.

I looked at Malika's eyes, rolled back in her head. Alarmed, I said to Sam, "What the hell is this? What happened to her?"

"She's not feeling good," he said feebly. "I think she's sick."

In fact, Malika's heart was failing. I checked for a pulse at her wrist and it seemed faint. I called my room and told Sherry to get an ambulance.

"She had a close call," the paramedic told us when he arrived within minutes. "If they'd waited much longer to call, she'd probably be dead."

Sabrina and Sherry stayed with Malika, while Sam and I took a cab ride to O'Hare. Sam barely spoke on the flight to New York. I wondered if he felt guilty about leaving Malika. She always came second to his career, it was never even close, but now she was hospitalized. I looked at Sam, still blitzed, and then it struck me: He probably can't feel anything. He's too fucked up to.

After our limousine ride to Rockefeller Center, Sam taped his stand-up spot on the Letterman show. When Sam sat down for the couch session, Letterman asked him about his love life. Sam said he lived with two sisters, his crooked smile implying he slept with them both. Letterman kidded him: You can't be too safe these days with all the diseases. "Yeah," Sam replied, off the top of his head. "They say heterosexuals die of AIDS too. Name one."

He'd said this before in concert. It was on his controversial second album. But he'd never said it before on national television.

I was watching the show being taped from the NBC green room. "That was a big mistake," I said out loud to myself.

"I wish you hadn't said that," I told Sam as he came backstage.

"Said what?"

" 'They say heterosexuals die of AIDS too. Name one.' "

"Don't worry about it. It's just a joke. Nobody's paying attention to this stuff."

"Yeah, well, we'll see."

Two days later in Philadelphia, before Sam's packed-out show at the Spectrum Showcase, Malika and Sabrina flew in from Chicago. As Sam and Malika rehashed her near-tragic evening, one moment they'd vow to get clean and stop living in turmoil. But the next moment they'd blame it all on Suszynski, for giving them "bad cocaine." I'd heard it all before, and it depressed me. They talked about getting straight but never made any real move to.

Still in Philly, before Sam's Friday-night show, I got a phone call from Trudy Green of Front Line Management. She was calling about Sam's gig on Tuesday night. At the Felt Forum in Madison Square Garden, he would headline a benefit concert for Lenny Bruce's mother, Sally Marr. Sam first got hip to Lenny Bruce by watching Dustin Hoffman portray him on film, and then Sam tracked down and bought some of Lenny's old tapes. Sam instantly saw they had something important in common: They talked about things in public—like sexual roles and the sanctity of religion—that most people only thought about. Without Lenny Bruce's breaking that ground, Sam felt there'd never have been room for a comic like himself. "I know one thing for sure," Sam always said. "Without Lenny Bruce I'd never be this popular, or making this kind of money."

Since Lenny was dead, Sam wanted to honor his mother. From his concert proceeds, Sam promised to give Sally Marr $100,000. I felt this was excessive, but Sam was intent. I also thought the show would be financed by HBO, which would then turn it into Sam's second special for HBO. I expected HBO to kick in $400,000.

Trudy Green gave me the awful news. "HBO's pulling out," she said. "They said Dice Clay's first special just bombed. It was so dirty they had to air it after midnight."

"That's tough. Sam isn't Dice, and we have contracts."

"No, Bill. We never got around to signing them."

"*What?* We're on our way back to New York, and we had no deal? We're booked at the Felt Forum?"

"Well . . . we had a verbal deal."

"Oh, shit!"

Calling HBO myself, I told them their comparison didn't stand up. Dice, not yet a star, was still playing comedy clubs. Sam was selling out venues that rock bands usually played in. At the Felt Forum show Tuesday night, all 4,100 seats were already sold. All the tickets were gone for his Wednesday-night concert too, and the Nassau Coliseum held eight thousand seats. In two straight nights, in New York, with all its competition for box-office dollars, twelve thousand people would pay to see Sam. What other comic could put up those numbers?

HBO politely countered, We just don't want to take the chance now. Tell Sam we'll do his next special down the road.

I was largely to blame—I should've made sure the contracts were signed and the deal was closed, instead of relying on Trudy—but Sam surprised me by letting me off the hook. "Forget HBO," he said. "We'll just sell it to Showtime."

I tried explaining to Sam that we couldn't do that. HBO's option on him didn't allow it. Sam, hearing my voice but not my words, kept talking up Showtime. Even though our financing had just fallen through, he kept spending his own money on showy, extravagant gestures. First he flew everyone into New York: Lenny Bruce's old buddies Pat McCormack, Sammy Shore, Jackie Gale, and Chuck McCann. Assorted rockers to play in an all-star band. An industry-famous film crew to shoot the concert.

Then Sam put them all up at costly Manhattan hotels.

To lessen the hit I knew he would take, I told him to donate less money to Sally Marr. I also thought that in the wake of his getting slammed in *Rolling Stone,* he might be trying to buy good PR.

But Sam was sincere. "Nah, man," he said. "I want to do this for Sally. She's broke."

"How do you know that? Because she told you? She's Lenny Bruce's mother. You told me yourself—he was the greatest con man on earth. Where do you think he got it from?"

Sam's voice stiffened. "I said I'm gonna do it."

I tried a different tack. "Why don't you give her thirty thousand, then? That's still a lot of money to give one person."

"I *promised* a hundred grand. If it was my mother, I'd want someone to do it for her."

"Yeah, but nobody would. Lenny Bruce's own friends haven't put up a dime!"

Back in New York on Sunday, we still hadn't heard a word about Sam's "name one" remark on the Letterman show. The backlash started on Tuesday morning, Valentine's Day. Outside his office, our promoter was telling me over the phone, several angry gay men were protesting Sam's concert. If they were protesting the *promoter,* I knew this wasn't the end of it. I decided we needed metal detectors at that night's show.

The first death threats of Sam's career came in that afternoon. Before the concert that night, police arrested gay protesters outside the Garden. Closer in, at the metal detectors, sixteen more people were busted for carrying knives and guns. Sam and I had no idea if they were gay. They could just be New Yorkers.

After all the headaches and planning, all Sam's showboating and spending, the Felt Forum show was a failure. Before Sam ever performed, the New York crowd sat through three opening stand-ups, the spotlighted entrance of Sly Stallone and Morton

Downey, Jr., a musical set by the all-star band, and Sally Marr, on a big screen, addressing the crowd from her home in California. Rather than attend her own benefit, she videotaped her comments and mailed them in.

When Sam finally went up, he seemed physically burned out. We'd been in New York three days, and for Sam three days in New York was like three days in Vegas: Hit every old haunt. Party like there's no tomorrow. Pass out and start over.

To my amazement—and to his loyal crowd's—Sam walked off the Felt Forum stage after just forty-two minutes.

I suggested we edit the hell out of the show and sell it straight to home video, which our HBO contract permitted. Sam over-rode me, thinking HBO might still change its mind, thinking Showtime, even thinking a possible feature film. As his yes-men kept bullshitting him about all his options, the project went nowhere. Later, Sam and Trudy Green wound up doing what I'd suggested from the beginning. They sold the home video rights. But they didn't tell me until the deal was closed, they waited too long, and they gave it away for $60,000.

But we had immediate worries. Without the money from HBO, Sam was about to take a crushing loss. To try to soften the blow, almost everyone waived their fees and worked for free: the promoter, the other comics, myself, the people at Front Line, and most of the all-star band. Only Leslie West, the guitarist, demanded his fee.

Despite everyone's help, Sam still got buried. With the New York unions' exorbitant prices, the stagehand bill alone came to $32,000. All in all, Sam spent $300,000 of his own money.

This included the $100,000 he promptly gave Sally Marr. But even after he did, we could not shake ourselves loose of Lenny's mom. Sam would play Las Vegas, Sally would see the ads in the *L.A. Times,* and she'd coax him into flying in her and her girl-friends. Because Sam couldn't tell people "No," he'd also pick up their hotel tab.

"Congratulations," I told Sam. "You just adopted an eighty-year-old woman."

When tax time rolled around, Sally called Sam's accountant, Lester, with one more tiny request. On that $100,000 he'd given her, could Sam pay the taxes? Lester told Sally, No deal—Sam doesn't have anything left.

He didn't. A few weeks before the benefit, Sam put down $150,000 to purchase his first home, a one-bedroom house with a loft on Pacific Coast Highway in Malibu. On top of that was the $300,000. The difference was, that cash was gone forever.

When *Atuk* got canceled in 1988, Sam had $300 in his bank account. After he had worked feverishly for one year, the Sally Marr concert wiped him out a second time. Emotionally, Sam never quite recovered from Kevin's death. He never rebounded financially from this.

Three days after the Sally Marr benefit, Bob Suszynski showed up in Detroit, where Sam had two weekend gigs at the legendary Fox Theater. After the show Friday night, about twelve of us went out to eat at a raucous Greek restaurant. I tried to tune out Suszynski and his deadly-dull rap. I tried reminding myself that Sam was an adult; I couldn't run his life, and I couldn't shut him off from all the dealers and creeps and parasites in the world. I was his manager and his brother and that's where it ended. I wasn't his parent. I wasn't his cop.

Once I got out from inside my own head, I had a good time. The restaurant was jumping, the Greek food superb, and the waiters entertaining. With every new course they all shouted, *"Oom fah!"*

Afterward, Sam and Suszysnki went prowling around Detroit with several more guys. They partied straight through until early Saturday night. Around 7:00 P.M., I stopped by Sam's suite to get him and the other stand-ups off their rear ends. Everyone still seemed high, but at least the other comedians were awake. Sam had just lain down on his bed after twenty-four sleepless hours. When I managed to rouse him, he kept mumbling, "Five more minutes. Just gimme five more minutes." Sam had been saying this since he was a kid.

Since he still had two hours before the show, I returned to the Fox with the other comics. Our tour bus driver Gene Holmes dropped Sam off at 8:45 P.M., just fifteen minutes before he was due to go on. Still roaring drunk, Sam didn't tell a single story or joke his first ten minutes onstage. Throwing both his hands up over his head, he kept shouting, "*Oom fah! Oom fahhh!*"

He was still thinking about the Greek restaurant from the night before.

As Sam shouted gibberish at 4,600 people, I rushed backstage to placate the promoter. Our two-night take at the Fox was $98,000, but we wouldn't collect until after tonight's show. If Sam didn't get it together, if the fans complained, the promoter might have to give refunds, and then we might have trouble collecting at all. Also, if Sam blew this show, the story would surely get out to other promoters. With his already fragile reputation, it might complicate our efforts to get future bookings. Promoters, as a rule, will forgive their headlining acts virtually anything—drugging, drinking, bringing in hookers backstage. But promoters *never* forgive issuing refunds.

I didn't think he could do it this time, but Sam pulled a Sam. His adrenaline started flowing in front of the crowd. It burned through the fog in his brain. After ten minutes of *Oom fah!* he managed to start being funny.

Once I saw the promoter relax, I went looking backstage for Suszynski. If Sam wanted to use, I knew that he'd find a way. But I couldn't stomach Suszynski any longer. Every time he surfaced, we had a calamity. The last time we'd seen him, Malika had wound up unconscious on the floor of her hotel room.

I found him in the backstage area, telling another pointless story and pounding a bottle of beer. I stood five feet four and weighed 145. About six feet five and 320, Suszynski fixed me with his stupid hard-guy grin. My heart pumped and I stepped directly in front of him. The people around us moved out of our way.

I said, "I'm gonna tell you something, you piece of fuck. If anything happens to Sam, I'm gonna make Cathy Smith look like an angel compared to you." I meant the woman with John Belushi, the night he overdosed at the Chateau Marmont.

"If the government doesn't get you," I went on, "then I'll get you myself. I'll make you disappear."

"You threatening me?" he said.

"No. Forget about threat. You ain't nothing to me. You're the biggest drink of water I ever seen. You got exactly five minutes to leave. Then I'm throwing you out."

Suszynski, to my surprise, left on his own. We never saw him again. Later, he was found dead of a drug overdose.

A routine had set in since the Sally Marr show at the Garden: death threats from militant gays each afternoon, beefed-up security and demonstrations at that night's concert. The death threats didn't alarm us until we left Detroit. Then several times each day, for the next three or four days, the same guy kept calling both my office and Front Line's. Sam had a gig coming up just outside Boston. He wouldn't leave Boston alive, the caller said.

For the first two days I brooded alone, thinking, This is another crank. The third day I told Sam.

"What should we do?" he said, seeming shaken for the first time since the threats had begun.

"I checked around," I said, "and the best guy for this job is Lonnie Brown. He coordinated George Bush's security when Bush ran for president. If you want, we can get Lonnie Brown in here."

On February 25, Lonnie Brown flew into Poughkeepsie, New

York. The next night Sam played the Worcester Centrum, a few miles from Boston. At Lonnie Brown's suggestion, we tripled our security force. We also pulled the tour bus inside the building, about ten feet behind the stage. Encircled by bodies, Sam hustled straight from the bus to the stage.

Nothing ugly happened that night, and we never canceled a show because of a death threat. But from Worcester on, gay groups protested every concert the rest of our tour. Except for three cities, they expressed their outrage at Sam without any violence. But in Seattle, they busted in a side door and threw acid on people inside watching the show. In Portland, they maced people standing in line to enter our show. In Minneapolis, they learned what hotel we were at and vandalized our tour bus.

Sam was now getting irritated on two counts. He felt he was being censored, and he thought his *fans* getting attacked was misguided and senseless. Still, in private, he managed to find some humor. Actually, Sam said, Queer Nation wasn't mad at him or his fans, they just used his concerts to meet other guys. Sam said there'd *be* no Queer Nation if not for him. Every time he came into a city, a new chapter opened.

In public, onstage, Sam responded characteristically. Rather than turn down the volume, he cranked it up. "I want to apologize to the gay community," he started telling his crowds. "No, no, don't boo. They're right. They say I'm not sensitive. Of course, this comes from guys who lick each other's *assholes* after a date! These guys tape up *gerbils* and shove them up their *ass!* Yeah, yeah, but *my* act is in bad taste!"

As the tour bus rolled on inexorably, as the road took its toll, Sam worried me more than usual that winter. There were more booze-soaked nights like those in Detroit, when he stammered and stumbled his first several minutes onstage. Sam was also short on new material. Among other comics, he was known and respected for creating a whole new act about every six months. In fact, Sam rarely performed a bit once he had recorded it for an album. Now he was still doing bits from his second record, which had already been out for several months. Though his venues were still large, and his fans still roared when he vented his famous anger, I thought Sam's anger seemed feigned, something he conjured up before each performance. Beneath it, I saw a deep sadness.

Ten months after Kevin's death, Sam was still shattered by guilt and grief. He still shed tears every day. He still told me and close friends he felt responsible. In public, Sam still swaggered. But when we were alone he was often subdued. Before Kevin's death, Sam had always bounced back up when life turned cruel. Now he was staying down for longer stretches of time.

He was drinking and doping so hard, I didn't know how to behave around him anymore. When I stopped intervening, Sam often went on a tear for days at a time. If I told him that he had a problem, that he needed some help, he became sullen and defensive. Our mother also spoke to him, but Sam told her what he always told me: "I got it under control. I can quit whenever I want to."

Sadly, without us ever discussing it, Sam and I stopped socializing together. Sam wanted to anesthetize his bad feelings, not be hounded by his older brother. For my part, I did not want to hang out with Sam and his blitzed-out army of yes-men.

I still saw him all the time, since I was his manager, but I stopped attending his parties, especially those where people were using cocaine. Sam, in turn, tried not to do blow around me. A few nights, when I entered his hotel room unannounced, I saw him shuffle the coke under the bed. Sam didn't like drinking around me, either. Rather than risk a confrontation, he'd usually just hold off until I was gone.

*   *   *

March 7. Kalamazoo, Michigan. About six in the morning. After driving all night from another gig, our tour bus pulled up to Wings Stadium, an ice hockey arena where Sam would perform that night. Livid and wide awake, Sam woke me up and told me to look outside. The arena marquee read: SAM KINISON AND JESSICA HAHN.

That afternoon we took Jessica's name off the marquee. We also learned how it had gotten up there. To boost their ratings, a local radio station was flying her out first-class, meeting her in a limo, and paying for her hotel. All Jessica had to do was wear the station's T-shirt, join Sam onstage during his show, and plug the station. But the plan had two serious flaws. This radio station competed with our sponsoring station, and Sam wanted Jessica Hahn out of his life.

When Jessica arrived, Sam wouldn't speak to her. I told Jessica and her group to forget their scheme. They'd spent a lot of money on this, the radio people complained. I told them tough shit, they were out of their minds for putting her name next to Sam's without our permission. As words flew back and forth, Jessica interrupted us.

She said, "I didn't know this was all going on, Bill. I didn't know there were two stations here. If you don't want me to go on, I won't go on."

She was the only one keeping her cool, and she had come a long way, so I compromised with them. Jessica could introduce Sam to the crowd, but not while wearing the radio station's T-shirt. She couldn't even mention its call letters. She would have to be back offstage before Sam ever walked out. In the morning, she and the radio guys could say whatever they wanted: "Jessica Hahn appeared last night with Sam Kinison, and here she is to tell you all about it."

When everybody agreed, I asked Jessica if we could speak alone. We sat in a small cluttered office on metal chairs. From the moment I saw her that night, I suspected she'd been using a lot of cocaine. She had all the obvious signs. Staccato bursts of speech. Shortness of breath. Blue, receding gums. A hard shiny mask instead of a face.

I'd seen it all in Sam.

"Jessica, you look like shit," I said.

"I do? Because I've really cleaned up."

"I hope so, because you need to. It's starting to show."

Before that night, I'd thought Jessica was still in love with Sam. After he refused to even talk to her, she started behaving as if she felt spurned. She kept calling in to radio shows Sam was on, picking fights on the air. Sam, of course, was no angel. One night, on CNN, he was the featured guest on *Live with Larry King,* being broadcast all that week from a studio in L.A.

"Are you still in love with Jessica Hahn?" King asked Sam toward the end of the show. "Were you ever in love with Jessica Hahn?"

"I was never in love with her," Sam said. "We had a short affair, because checkout time was at two."

King couldn't suppress a smile.

Sam said, "She's, uh, she's an interesting person."

"She's not dull," King said.

"She's not dull," Sam agreed.

"We'll return in a moment with Sam Kinison."

But Sam couldn't behave. "She is a little wide," he stuck in, just before the commercial. Then he held his hands about shoulder width apart, making it clear that he didn't mean she was fat.

After the break, a call came in from L.A.

"Hi, Larry, it's Jessica Hahn. You want to talk about who's wide, Sam?"

"Nobody said I was thin," Sam said, looking pissed off. "Look, I don't even want to talk to you. Why don't we just agree never to speak to each other again?"

After King jumped in for an instant, Jessica called Sam "a spineless, talentless has-been. You talk about Dice. Dice will make it way before you do, Sam."

"What happened?" Larry said, refereeing. "What went wrong between you two?"

"His big mouth," Jessica snapped.

Sam said, "Well, let's not talk about big orifices in the body."

King smiled again, then caught himself.

Sam and Jessica argued some more, until King had to sign off.

"Thank you, Jessica," King said.

Sam said, "Yeah, thank you, Jessica . . . for all the memories."

Laughing, Larry King said he was going back to Washington, "where nobody ever fights."

In early March, with Sam performing in Atlantic City, Alan Rich flew in from Hollywood to meet us. The president of Guber-Peters Productions, Alan admired a feature-film treatment we'd recently sent him. With Hollywood no longer sending him any scripts, Sam and Dan Barton—a talented novelist and comic and one of Sam's few sober friends—created their own original premise. Drawn partly from Sam's own life, *Stranger in Town* was the story of a troubled rock-and-roll singer who suffers the death of someone dear, retreats to a small town, and finds solace in its simplicity. Alan Rich, a longtime fan of Sam's and a major industry player, said he wanted to put the idea into development. Sam and I were grateful. The movie might never be made—that's why people called it "development hell"—but at least a quality company wanted Sam. Thirteen months after *Atuk,* we thought his blackballing might be over.

Mercifully, we had a break the next week from our interminable tour. Alan said he'd send out a writer to Sam's house. They could discuss the movie there.

By the time the writer showed up, Sam hadn't slept for two days, he'd forgotten the writer was coming, and he was drunk. Even under the best circumstances—since *Stranger in Town* was based on Kevin and Sam—Sam might have rejected the writer's input. Now the writer had no chance. Sam chased him out of his house. Then he called Alan Rich and physically threatened him too.

In minutes my cellular phone rang.

"Your brother just called me and threatened me," Alan said. "Something happened out at his house. I haven't been able to contact the writer to see if Sam did anything physical. I hope he hasn't, because if he did we'll take action."

I exhaled but didn't speak. When dealing with Hollywood, I normally downplayed Sam's drunken, destructive side. There was no room for that now.

"The deal is dead," Alan told me. "I'm not making this movie."

I called Sam and he rambled, so I waited until the next day when he'd slept it off.

"Man," he plunged in, "they sent this shitty writer, I didn't know he was coming. He had these shit-ass ideas. I told him I'd beat his ass. I told Alan Rich too! Fuck their bullshit, man!"

"Sam! You cannot call Hollywood executives motherfuckers. *Maybe* they'll take it from a manager. They'll *never* take it from an artist. I've told you this twenty times: I have to be the buffer. Then you can say, Yeah, well, that's my older brother. That's how he gets sometimes."

"Aw, man, they wanted to change the entire movie."

"*Sam!* There is no movie! Alan Rich said the deal is dead!"

Sam didn't give up. If he had a completed screenplay instead of a treatment, he thought *Stranger in Town* might still find a buyer. Without development money, he paid out of his own pocket to have one written. When the screenplay was done, I told Sam the truth: I thought it was funny and poignant. The story seemed to come straight from his heart.

We shopped it around. A few executives talked. Nobody pulled the trigger.

The Alan Rich story had already made the rounds.

Sam's demons were winning again.

Sex, Love, Divorce, and Show Biz

"People are going: 'Man, aren't you *afraid* to tell jokes like that? Don't you get just a small chill that runs through your blood when you tell a joke like that? Aren't you afraid of going to hell?' No, I'm not worried about hell. Because I WAS MARRIED FOR TWO FUCKING YEARS! HELL WOULD BE LIKE CLUB MED! Hell would be like a fuckin' *resort,* man. Matter of fact, if you been married? It ruins the devil's whole job. He's blown out, he's pissed off. You make him look a Ronald McDonald with big feet and orange hair. He doesn't know. You're walking down the hall, you're going to hell, he sees you coming, he goes: 'Yeah, here's somebody. Here's somebody I'm gonna scare the *shit* out of and torment. What? You been married? All right, let me take this shit off. Hold on. No, they didn't tell me. Well, come on in, I'll give you the tour anyway. There won't be any surprises here for you, but I'll show you around, come on in. Let's see, over here's where we torment the soul. Oooh, oooh. Well, shit, man, if you been married, there's not much I can scare you with down here. What? What? You been married twice? Would you like a *job* down here?

Because if you've been married twice, you qualify for our
job employment program here in hell.' Anyone who's been
married twice, you can be a tour guide in hell. You can take
your own groups: 'Folks, stick with me, I been married
twice, I know this place *pretty* fuckin' well. I won't lose you
on this one, all right?' "

—Sam in concert at the Roxy

Sam first did that bit in the early eighties, about a year after
splitting up with his second wife, Terry Marrs. There was no talk
of divorce until several years later, in 1987. Even then, although
Sam was making big money, Terry told me herself, "All I want
from Sam is out of this marriage." Terry made the legal arrange-
ments, and Sam and I flew to Houston. But they ended up sleeping together instead of divorcing.

One year after that, in 1988, Terry called my wife, Sherry, out
of the blue. In a casual tone, Terry said she and her daughter
had just moved back to L.A. Sam and I and Sherry all knew at
once: Terry had come out to file California residency.

In April of 1989, before his concert in Jacksonville, Florida,
Sam was signing autographs for his fans. One of the men standing in line handed Sam a sheet of paper.

"Here," he told Sam. "You're served for divorce."

The news got worse. Representing Terry was Marvin Mitchelson.

"What happened?" Sam said. "Satan was busy?"

Initially, he intended to fight it. Seven years had passed since
their separation, and Sam was flat broke at the time. Then, in a
courthouse meeting of Mitchelson, Sam, and Sam's lawyer,
Mitchelson frightened Sam into settling. After floating some fatter
numbers, Mitchelson came to his bottom line of $200,000. Sam
balked, until Mitchelson said he could pay it in four yearly in-
stallments. Sam seemed to take it all benignly—it was just more
money in, more money out. At $50,000 a pop, he told me and

his friends, "I can play one extra date a year for the next four years, and just pay Terry from that."

Just one month after Sam got served for divorce, he turned around and gave romance another chance. When Sabrina turned eighteen, Sam finally revealed his true feelings to her. She must have felt something too. Their affair started almost immediately.

So did the sneaking around. In Los Angeles, Sam would tell Malika, "I'm going to buy a video." Then he and Sabrina would meet at the Hyatt Hotel on Sunset. Out on the road, at Sam's request, I began buying one extra room in every hotel we checked into. Sam would come to me for the keys and return them a few hours later. This way, he explained, Malika could never bust him by rifling his pockets.

Despite the precautions, I felt we were all acting out a charade. How could Malika not know? On almost every talk show he went on, Sam made sly remarks about living with two sisters. Suddenly, the presents he bought Sabrina were nicer than Malika's. Malika was even telling my mother, "Sam wants to sleep with my sister." My mother would then call me, saying, "These people are *sick*."

Sam didn't see it that way. Once he and Sabrina began sleeping together, he fell harder for her than ever. "I've only loved three women my whole life," he told me one night that spring. "Gail, Kate Connelly, and Sabrina."

If Sam felt any remorse over any of this, he never revealed it to me. If Sabrina slept with Sam as a way of hurting Malika, I missed that too. And while I knew the situation was peculiar, I thought Sabrina was good for Sam. She was mellow and smart. Unlike Malika, she treated Sam with warmth and compassion. Since Sabrina didn't party, Sam tried his best to stay straight around her, and when Sam stayed clean his tenderness came back out. When I was alone with them, he was constantly touching her arm or kissing her cheek. Sabrina seemed happy too. I thought she might even love him.

But I did warn Sam to be careful. So did his friends Jimmy Shubert and Carl LaBove. If Malika was being ingenuous, if she honestly didn't know, we all thought Sam might be flirting with danger. Sam owned several guns, and Malika was prone to violent mood swings. Once, when Jimmy Shubert enraged her, Malika aimed a loaded shotgun at him—and Jimmy wasn't sleeping with her little sister. As for Sam? After Malika fell asleep in their bedroom, sometimes he and Sabrina made love in the bedroom next door.

"You're rolling the dice, pal," I told Sam. "That's all you're doing."

Sam was worried too that Malika might shoot him, but he couldn't. He couldn't stop himself from sleeping with Sabrina. Sam thought she might be his last chance to be loved.

"When I first became aware of you, you were the most outrageous thing. Everyone said: 'He's brilliant, he's brilliant, he's brilliant,' but the usual stuff: "He can't do television. What are we gonna do with him?' Did you find that at the start of your career? Did you ever try and change?"

—Joan Rivers, interviewing Sam on her TV show

"At one point I was gonna try and do the Carson show. This was back at the beginning of 1985. I was going to clean up, because I was really desperate—I was starting to get scared. I'd been out there for five years, I couldn't get a break. And, uh, I slicked up, I cleaned up my act, and I felt really *bad* about it. And the guy—can we say 'jerked'? The guy jerked me around a little bit. He'd come to see my showcase, and he'd go: 'Yeah, I think Johnny's gonna like you.' Then he'd call me the next day and go: 'No, I gotta see it again.' He did that to me six times."

—Sam answering Joan's question

The story Sam told was true. He was talking about Jim McCawley, the booker for *The Tonight Show*, who frequently came to watch Sam at the Comedy Store. One night in 1988, at the Palm restaurant on Sunset, Sam and I even ran into Johnny himself.

"I've been a fan of yours for years," said Johnny, who Sam thought was the absolute coolest. "I'd like you on the show. Call Jim McCawley."

They shook hands and Johnny walked out the door.

"A fan for years?" Sam said, flattered and irked simultaneously. "What the fuck is going on over there?"

Sam called McCawley the following workday. Nothing happened. Again.

"This guy's got a hard-on for me," Sam fumed.

It took another year, until May 24, 1989, for Sam to get booked on *The Tonight Show*. We were never quite sure what turned the tide, but we thought it had something to do with our signing with Irving Azoff. With Front Line's powerful roster of musical clients, Azoff could pressure even *The Tonight Show.*

For his debut, Sam wanted to sing his own version of "Are You Lonesome Tonight?" He and our mother were big fans of Elvis. When Sam was a kid and our parents divorced, he had sung her the song when he thought she felt blue.

Sam's new rendition was comic. Carson's producers agreed to it after they heard it, then they lined up professional singers to accompany him onstage. But Sam threw them a curveball the day of the taping. Arriving at NBC with the Comedy Outlaws— Carl LaBove, Mitchell Walters, and Alan Stephan—Sam insisted that *they* join him onstage. Since none of them could sing, Sam wanted them to lip-synch, while the real singers stood hidden behind the curtain. This way, Sam figured, NBC would have to pay *everyone.*

Sam had two motivations for this: to give his friends a thrill, and to take his revenge on McCawley.

Carson's producers weren't pleased, but Sam threatened to walk and they finally gave in.

Setting up the bit, Johnny Carson told his viewers that evening: "The first time I saw Sam Kinison perform, somebody brought a tape into my office. I laughed so hard, I was hysterical. Because he was absolutely outrageous. But Sam, believe it or not, has undergone a transformation. Because someone brought in another tape the other day and said, 'I want you to hear this.' And I didn't know who was singing, it was that good. He's a fine singer. He's got a new single coming out. Would you welcome please, Sam Kinison."

The curtain rose on Sam and the Comedy Outlaws, everyone looking deeply sincere. In a voice surprisingly sweet, Sam started off by singing the original lyrics: "Are you lonesome tonight . . . do you miss me tonight . . . are you sorry we drifted apart? Is your heart filled with pain . . . shall I callll back agaaain . . . tell me, dear, are you lonesome tonight?"

With the singers behind the curtain humming the melody, Sam started talking the words. "You know, I wonder if you're lonesome tonight. I wonder a lot of things. Like are you human? How do you live with yourself? Are you a reptile with a nice *hairdo?* YOU SNEAKY TRAMP! YOU LIED TO ME! WHEN YOU TOLD ME YOU LOVED ME—YOU NEVER LOVED ME! YOU SAID FOREVER, REMEMBER THAT ONE? OH, THAT WAS A JOKE! FOREVER! AH HAH HAH HAH HAH—FOREVER, HONEYYYY! Yeah, what does forever mean to you? Until another guy comes into your life with more money and a better car? 'Oh, I'm sorry, we better break up, I'm not growing as a person.' OH, THAT WAS A GREAT IDEA! YEAH, LET'S BREAK UP, HONEY! DID YOU GROW ANY, HUH? ARE YOU ANY TALLER? I'LL TELL

YOU WHAT YOU LEARNED, YOU LEARNED HOW TO BREAK MY HEART. Ohhh, but I'd rather go on hearing your lies, than to go and live without you—that's how sick I am. Now I'm standing here, the stage is bare, oh I can't say it—YOU KNOW WHAT YOU DID! YOU WERE WRONG! SAY IT, YOU STUPID, STUBBORN PIG: 'I WAS WRONG!' OH! OH! AAAUGH!''

Sam calmed back down. He resumed singing softly on key. "Is your heart filled with pain . . . should I call back agaaaain. . . . tell me dearrrr . . . are you lonesome . . . toooooonight?''

In a whisper: "I hope you die.''

The *Tonight Show* audience whistled and cheered. This was unexpected humor for network television, which tends to homogenize anyone it touches.

For the interview, Sam sat between Johnny and Robert Townsend. "Is that romantic?'' Sam said to Johnny.

"That really brings a tear to your eye,'' Johnny said. "That's what love is all about.''

"You know what the funny thing is? There's about seven girls out there who think I'm talking directly to them.''

"Sam, you are deeply disturbed. You know that.''

The subject turned to Sam's first failed marriage, at age twenty-one.

"That was pretty young to get married,'' Johnny said. "Things just didn't work out?''

"No, no . . . I know that's a strange thing to you, but it didn't work out.''

"*Yeah,*'' Johnny said, laughing.

Sam said, "I feel like I'm sitting with Yoda. 'You will learn great, Sam, you will learn.' ''

"Did you try marriage again?''

"Oh, I knew you were gonna ask that one. Yeah, I did.''

"So you're married now?''

"No, I just got divorced. She hired Marvin Mitchelson.''

"Woe,'' Johnny said, drumming his pencil.

Sam said, "You never had to go up against him, did you?"

"No, I don't think so."

"You would have remembered! You would have remembered!"

Sam told Johnny his second wife had waited seven years to divorce him—until Sam was on the cover of *Rolling Stone*.

"I gotta say," Sam said, "the best thing about marriage is that it keeps you from getting married."

"That's true, that's true. So, you're gonna wait until you try this again?"

"Yeah, I'm gonna wait awhile. I'm living with two sisters now."

"Well, *that's* good."

It was a magical moment for Sam—his first time on *The Tonight Show*, and Johnny Carson was clearly tickled by him.

I guess you could say Sam was versatile. Three weeks after winning over Johnny Carson, he partied out with two lesbian strippers after a show in Seattle. The next morning, Sam came down alone to our hotel lobby. "We need two more plane tickets," he said.

"We don't have time," I said. "We're running late right now."

"I don't care, man. You gotta do it."

That's when I spotted the strippers, stepping out of elevator. I said, "Aw, Sam, don't tell me."

"Yeah, dude, they're doing the show in the Meadowlands. I'll take 'em onstage with Malika and Sabrina."

Next Sunday at Giants Stadium, Sam was opening up for the rock band Bon Jovi. They were his pals, and Sam had jumped at their offer to be on the same ticket with them. For one thing, it proved he really was "the rock-and-roll comic." For another, 82,000 tickets were already sold. It'd be the largest life performance of Sam's career.

On our plane flight east, I had to explain to the strippers that lunch and soft drinks were free. Until I did, they kept turning everything down because neither one had brought any money. I'd seen Sam with unpolished women before, but this time he set a new standard.

On Sunday at Giants Stadium, all of us sitting backstage before the concert, Sam persuaded the band to stop feuding with Howard Stern. Early in their career, Howard gave them exposure by bringing them on his show and playing their music. When the band grew wealthy and famous, it neglected to do Howard's show on a promo tour through New York. Howard got angry. The band said it wasn't their fault; their itinerary had been made by Polygram Records, and Howard was not on the list. A band as big as Bon Jovi, Howard said, should call its own shots. While broadcasting his show, he started calling Bon Jovi "pussies" and "punks."

Backstage at Giants Stadium, Sam urged the band to join him on Howard's show that upcoming week. "You guys used to be friends," Sam said. "Let's go in there and patch it up." When the rockers agreed, Sam said he'd tell Stern himself.

After Sam and Bon Jovi performed their separate sets, they all congregated onstage for the evening's final encore—the hard-rocking, comedic version of "Wild Thing." Sam strutted out surrounded by women: Malika, Sabrina, and two lesbian strippers. Exhibitionists by trade—and drunk off their asses—the strippers went berserk when they saw the enormous crowd. They kissed. They rubbed each other's breasts. They wrestled around on the stage in their flimsy outfits. With 82,000 people looking on, they simulated going down on each other.

Jon Bon Jovi looked physically stricken. His parents were watching the show from a special box.

When the concert ended, Sam came off yelling at *me*.

"I want 'em out of here!" he said, yanking off his guitar. "Get 'em back on the first plane you can!"

"Are you nuts?" I shouted back. "I didn't want 'em here in the first place!"

I didn't want any more scenes, so I rode in a cab with the strippers to our hotel. They wanted to stick around until Tuesday night, so they could attend the party at Richie Sambora's. I told them I didn't think Bon Jovi would like that, not after what had just happened out on the stage. Inside their hotel room, they explained that they *couldn't* go home. They'd both lost their plane tickets somewhere. I said I had their tickets, remember? They kept horsing around until I lost my patience. So I packed their luggage myself, watched them climb into a limo, and handed the limo driver an extra hundred. "Make sure they get on the plane," I said. "Watch them get on it, and watch it take off."

On Tuesday morning, Sam called Howard Stern during his broadcast. Tomorrow, Sam told Howard, he wanted to bring Bon Jovi into the studio. Howard agreed and told his listeners all morning: Sam Kinison's coming in with Bon Jovi. Sam says they want to make up.

Sam and I went to the party at Richie Sambora's that night. By six in the morning, no one had slept, and the guys in the band told Sam they weren't doing the Stern show. If they did go in, they told Sam, Howard would only blast them.

"You guys can't do this!" Sam said. "He thinks we're coming. We gotta go in there."

Outnumbered, Sam couldn't dissuade them. Reluctant to call up Howard and tell him the bad news, Sam was also afraid to show up there without Bon Jovi. "Shit, man," Sam said. "I can't go in there alone. I'm not going in unless you guys do."

The Stern show, in the meantime, had crammed its Manhattan studio with camera crews and reporters. From CNN to the *New York Times,* they expected to file reports on the big reconciliation. But the hours continued to pass, and still Sam and Bon Jovi never appeared. They never even called in. Severely embarrassed, Howard went off on Sam. Howard said he expected this from the "punks in Bon Jovi," but not from his own close friend. Thinking that Sam had willfully screwed him, Howard lambasted him for almost an hour. "Kinison's dead," he told his listeners. "His career is over. From now on I'm gonna push Dice. Kinison is dead. Long live Dice Clay."

In New Jersey that night, Sam was playing at Rascals comedy club. Howard urged people with tickets to start chanting "Dice" during Sam's show.

When that's exactly what happened, Sam appeared stunned. Ordinarily, Sam annihilated hecklers. This time he merely pretended not to hear them.

Sam called Stern the next day to apologize, but they ended up fighting. In part out of stubborn ego, in part out of not wanting to rat out Bon Jovi, Sam never told Howard the truth: He had had every intention of coming on yesterday's show. It was the band that backed out.

Instead, Sam told Howard he'd simply pulled a "prank." Howard believed him and didn't think it was funny. The war still raged when they hung up the phone, and Howard ended up banning Sam from his show. Sam felt miserable during this time. He loved Howard Stern. He loved their adventurous times on Howard's radio show. Sam feared he'd lost both, forever.

Blood Brothers

"**I** KNOW IT'S YOUR BROTHER'S SHIT. I'M GONNA RECOMMEND TO the D.A. that we don't file charges."

Four months earlier, the night I took the heat for Sam at LAX, I'd been told this by Sergeant Ross of the LAPD. I thought it was over then.

The next morning, Sam and I had gone on tour for the next seven weeks. When we returned home, a stunning certified letter was waiting for me. It said I was charged with three felonies: possession of drugs, intent to transport, and intent to distribute. If I failed to appear in court, a warrant would be issued for my arrest.

While Sam and I had been touring, the district attorney had launched a "war against drugs." There would be "no tolerance" now on any drug case.

And my case was already on the books.

"You fuck!" I hollered at Sam when I read the letter. "They charged me with three felonies!"

"Don't worry, man. I'm gonna get you the best attorney there is."

My court date came up in June, the same week as Sam's falling out with Howard Stern. Sam hired a lawyer he knew to represent me. He paid her $10,000 as a retainer, so I figured she must be semidecent. At her counsel, I intended to plead guilty, in return for one year probation.

While waiting in court for the baliff to call my name, I glanced at my attorney. She was grinning.

"I guess you probably enjoy this," I said.

"I really do. I love it when I get to go to court."

"Whaddya mean, when you get to go to court?"

"I don't get into court much. I usually do music contracts."

"You've never handled something like this?"

"No.

"Oh, shit!"

About one minute later, the bailiff announced: "Bill Kinison."

On my lawyer's assurance that I'd receive probation, I waived all my rights and pled guilty on all three counts.

The judge seemed surprised. "Do you know you're going straight to jail?"

I said, "What?"

"You're going straight to county jail for thirty days. Then I'm going to bring you back and sentence you."

"Then I wanna change my plea!"

The judge said I could. Then, rather than jail, he sentenced me to a drug intervention program. He scribbled down the name of a probation officer in Santa Monica, and told me to go there straight from the courthouse.

In Santa Monica, I approached a tough-looking black guy sitting behind a government-issue desk. I didn't know it yet, but he was a former drug addict and convict. He'd done so well in rehab the probate court had made him an officer.

His desk had a homemade sign reading AMERICA FOR AFRICA. With my blond hair and blue eyes, my expensive suit, I looked like David Duke.

"Hello, Bill," he said. "When's the last time you had a drink, or got drunk?"

"I dunno. Maybe five or six years ago."

"When's the last time you did a line?"

"Six years."

He thought I was lying. "We ain't gettin' nowhere," he said. "You gotta level now with me, brother."

"I am leveling with you."

"Come on. Talk to me, man."

"I tell you what. Every week, I probably go through maybe half a gram of blow. I only drink to take the edge off the blow. I might also smoke half an ounce of pot every week."

"All right. Now I'm hearing some things."

"I'm *fucking* with you. I told you, I'm clean. When you get back the test, you're gonna find out I'm spic-and-span."

"Then why did you have the two ounces of pot?"

Better stick to my story, I thought.

"I have a hard time sleeping on the tour bus. I smoke the pot to mellow me out."

He said he would let me know. I took the test, and my urine and blood came back pristine.

He gave me five months in rehab anyway.

When this whole fiasco began back at LAX, I had thought I would get a ticket.

Now I had five months rehab.

Every Monday and Saturday.

Even if I had to fly into town to be there.

Rather than make him stand up and be an adult, I had suffered Sam's consequences for him.

Again.

My first session came up on the Fourth of July. Several weeks earlier, I'd planned a party out by my pool. With a house full of people, I had to leave at 5:30 P.M. My daughter, Ginger, asked me why I had to go. She was only five, but I told her the truth. "I have to go to my first rehab meeting."

Ginger understood what rehab meant. I'd explained it to her when Kevin went through it in Long Beach. But she also knew her dad did not use liquor or drugs. I saw her confusion. I told her we'd talk all about it, but not until she got a little older. Her face clouded up even more, and my anger at Sam spilled out.

"Uncle Sam got in trouble," I said, "and I'm taking the blame."

Then I felt bad about *that*. Ginger adored her Uncle Sam.

"I'm Bill," I said that night in Pomona when it was my turn.

Ted Burnett, the head of the center, waited for me to say: "And I am a drug addict."

When I didn't, Ted said, "And?"

"That's it," I said. "I'm Bill."

Nobody said, "Hi, Bill." They thought I was in denial. So I said it myself: "Hi, Bill."

Then I told them my story. We went to the airport and we got busted. Without mentioning Sam, I said it wasn't my stuff but I'd taken the heat.

"*Bad* start," Ted Burnett interrupted.

I told the story again with a different beginning, but I still ended up at the truth. It wasn't my shit.

This precipitated a lively debate, and *not* the one Burnett was intending to have. Because everyone there had their own story about being set up or framed.

Burnett called me into his office after the session. "You know what this is?" he said, rattling a piece of paper. "This is a memo. I got it before I got you. This memo tells me that that was your brother's shit. I know you're clean. But you're gonna be here awhile. If you don't cause any trouble, then I'm not. You fuck with me, I'll fuck with you."

I saw his point. In time we became good friends. And from that first meeting on, every Monday and Saturday, I sat in a threadbare room in Pomona, hearing confessions from veteran addicts who no longer knew if the stories they told were true. Almost all the people seemed nice—every one was a character. One woman said she drove to visit her boyfriend at L.A. County Jail, decided to smoke some pot in her van before going in, and the smoke poured out her windows. She got arrested on federal property, which is a felony. One guy said he snorted so much cocaine, in his terrible paranoia he drove to the nearest police station. He wanted them to protect him, but forgot to leave home his stash, and they busted him at the desk. One guy stood about six feet six and was certifiably crazy. An American Indian, he called himself Chief. During his lifetime, Chief said, he'd done everything to an extreme: kill the Cong in Vietnam, marry a string of women who later turned out to be whores, father dozens of children he never met. During one of our group discussions on "how to solve the national drug problem," I suggested we get rid of President Bush. It was a joke, a throwaway line.

"I'll do it," Chief volunteered.

"Do what?" I said.

"I'll kill Bush."

"Chief, that's not what I meant."

"I'll kill him. I can do it. I can do it and no one will ever catch me. When's he coming out to L.A.?"

"Chief, hey, take it easy."

Some sessions were interesting. Many were touching. But the circumstances that put me there, the fact that I put Sam's needs in front of my own, and in front of my family's, filled me with resentment toward Sam. We talked about codependence at our rehab sessions. We talked about enabling, any act that helps an addicted person keep shirking responsibility. At some level, I knew they were talking about people like me.

But what do you do with family? I'd ask myself. Do I walk away from a brother who has problems? Who doesn't trust anyone else in the business? Even if Sam doesn't want my help, do

I stop trying to give it? What will happen then, if he thinks nobody cares?

I didn't know the right answers. It was easy to sit in a group and talk about shoulds and should nots. But real life got so messy, and so unclear. Tangling things even more, I was Sam's manager. It was a part of my job to cover for him.

Still, I eventually came to see that I'd let things get out of hand. I'd become so absorbed in cleaning up Sam's problems I hadn't solved my own. In large part from coming to work for Sam, from trying to caretake his life and letting him dictate mine, I lost my marriage, my financial stability, and for a while my good health. I loved Sam completely. We had a lot of laughs. A thousand good times. But my own wife and kid should have come first. I did that, not Sam. And it's something I'll always regret.

When the rehab subject came up, Sam and I had a few fights that summer and fall. Then Sam tried making things right in his usual way, by giving me something material. A few years before, I had bought my mother a 1955 T-Bird. Sam now wanted to buy it from her and give it to me. Our mother quickly agreed. She seldom drove it, and she wanted her sons to make peace. I told Sam I didn't need the car, that he should leave it with mom. If I changed my mind, I could always pick it up then. But Sam's conscience needed cleansing. He wound up wearing me down.

I got the T-Bird. But Sam never got around to paying our mother for it.

Hitting Bottom 16

"It's a strange world out there. Like, mailmen. Mailmen
have been snapping like rubber bands, man. The Son of
Sam was a mailman. People forget that. I didn't know the
connection until several weeks ago. I went: 'Fuck! He was
a postal worker!' The guy with the worst legal defense in
history. A man who stood on nine counts of murder, in front
of a federal court justice, and said, 'Your honor, it was the
dog. The dog literally possessed my mind. He pushed me,
he pressured me—to where I would go out and shoot people at random. He was a *mean* fucking dog, your honor.
He'd bark and he'd bark, in these hideous demonic barks!
Rar-rar-rar-rar!' The judge goes: 'Come here, dog-boy. It
was the fuckin' dog, huh? It never occurred to you to *shoot*
the dog? Get a public defendant next time, fuckhead, all-
right? Jacoby and Myers would have a better defense.' Yeah,
man, justice is fuckin' regional. It really is. Like here in Los
Angeles. Christian Brando said he came home, and he got
in a fight with his sister's girlfriend, and a gun was pulled
out and it went off during the scuffle. Could have happened
to anybody—it went off during the scuffle. So the police

came in and took police photos, and the guy was still sitting in a big chair with the remote control in his hands, in front of the television set, with a hole in his head like he was Gandhi's brother. That pretty much broke up the scuffle theory. So I figure Jim Bakker's gotta be watching this stuff. He's going: 'Let me get this straight now, 'cause I'm a little confused. Let's see, this guy shoots a guy in the head, lies in court, he's out in six years. I fuck a church secretary, I took a little money—FORTY-FIVE YEARS! Now is that because I had my trial in North Carolina, or did I JUST GET FUCKED FOR NO REASON?' I could have overturned that decision. If I was this guy's attorney, if I was representing him in court, I would take Tammy Faye by the hair, or the wig, whatever, take her in front of the jury, and say, '*Look at her! Look at her face!*' They woulda gone, 'Shit, man, I see what you mean. Not only are you free, we owe *you* some fuckin' money.' "

—Sam in concert in Upland, California

"The lawsuit against comedian Sam Kinison over his being fired last year off the movie *Atuk* has been settled. Kinison will pay the studio $200,000, and that will be the end of it. According to sources, Kinison called the settlement a 'small price to pay compared to having to get up early every day for two weeks and go to court.' "

—Mitchell Fink, Los Angeles gossip columnist

Sam elected to settle that summer, just a few weeks after giving his deposition. UA's lawyers got pretty nasty, and Sam really did have a fear of courtrooms and litigation. If he did fight the case and win, Sam also asked his attorneys, would his legal fees exceed $200,000? When his lawyers said yes, he told them to make the deal.

Sam did not tell his lawyers this: He never had any intention of making the payment. He wasn't being a deadbeat; he just didn't believe he was through making movies. If United Artists smelled enough money, Sam felt even they would hire him again. Then they could deduct what he owed them from his salary.

"Look at Dennis Hopper," Sam told *Premiere* magazine. "The guy blew his brains out, and he turns around in the middle of his life, and this town—which probably would have said ten years ago, 'He's out of his mind, he's a loser, he'll never work again'—puts him on the A-list of directors and gives him *Colors.* That's how reliable this town is about who works again and who doesn't."

Shortly thereafter, Sam also ended his spat with Howard Stern. In Atlantic City one morning, Sam and I turned on Howard's radio show. Howard was mocking one of his favorite targets— talk-show host Regis Philbin. Claiming that Regis had turned his back on his web-footed son, Howard always called him a bum. Now, as a gag, Howard was taking "donations" for Regis's kid. So Sam called in and pledged $500.

That broke the ice. Then Sam told Howard he wanted to patch things up. Howard said they could try, but only on his show. The listeners would have to decide.

Sam and I went to New York a week or so later. As each bad boy's fans called in their pointed remarks—"Screw him, he's using ya"—Sam kept his cool most of the morning. Then a phone call came in from Howard's regular chauffeur. "Ronnie the Limo Driver" called Sam a "user." According to Ronnie, Sam used Howard to promote his East Coast concerts. Sam used Jessica Hahn to sell his "Wild Thing" video. Even as Sam was still blowing up at Ronnie, one of Howard's crew said, "Jessica's on the line."

Looking over at Sam, I recognized his expression. He was beginning to feel ganged up on.

"Let's put her on," Howard said.

"Did you feel used by me?" Sam asked Jessica.

"Yeah!" Jessica said.

Regarding their short affair, Sam and Jessica bitched over who leaked what to the tabloids. Then Jessica said, "You open up on the *air* about me."

Except for nervous laughter, Howard Stern and his crew all went silent. I took a deep breath myself. They were about to get into their infamous one-night stand.

Jessica had already talked about it on a recent show of Howard's. Sam had passed out inside her, she told millions of Howard's listeners.

That much Sam had admitted to me himself.

While asleep in their bed, Jessica added, Sam lost control of his bowels.

That one Sam hadn't told me.

"*Wait!*" Sam yelled at Jessica. "*I* opened up about *you?* Aren't you the one that told Howard that I fell asleep inside you? I opened up about you? Don't even start it . . . you *cow-faced loser.* I'll come after you like you can't believe."

"Sam, you wanna come after me?" Jessica said.

"Yeah—no, I don't, man. You got enough preachers on your tail."

After more charges and countercharges, Sam said, "Just because your mom died, you think you're the only one who knows tragedy?"

Jessica's voice quivered, then cracked. "You know, why don't you *fuckin'* go to hell? I hate you."

Howard tried making peace. "Hold it, hold it, hold it, all right, okay, listen."

Sam, knowing that he'd hurt Jessica, let the anger drain from his voice. "Don't expect me to be a friend when you attack me like this, man. I had a small amount of compassion that was absolutely wasted, I guess. Because I know what it's like to lose a loved one, and to have Howard make fun of it the same day."

Howard looked tense. Earlier that summer, while he and Sam were still estranged, he'd supposedly made wisecracks about Kevin's death. Sam heard this secondhand from a few comedian friends. Howard told Sam his friends had the story all wrong, but Sam wasn't sure who to believe, and Kevin was still a tender subject for him.

Although still ostensibly speaking to Jessica, Sam turned toward Howard, sitting just three or four feet away behind his controls. "You didn't know my brother, and neither did *Howard.* You didn't know that I tried to save him for two years, and that I put him in rehab, and that he blew his *brains* out, and that it's not a joke, man. You don't joke about that, man. Joke about Pat Cooper's family . . . joke about Regis Philbin's son, with the flipper feet, man. But not my little brother Kevin, that I tried to save. And I lost."

Gently, Howard recommended they break for commercial.

"*No!*" Sam exploded. "This is the radio you love!"

I could see his rage bubbling up. Sam had come in to make up with Howard. He hadn't planned on Jessica calling in.

"If I set you up," Sam told Howard, "that's a big tragedy. If I set you up with Bon Jovi, that's like, how could you do that? But you could let me walk in here and deal with this, right? That's all right, that's okay, it's okay for you to make fun of my brother's *suicide,* man, and if it wasn't you, Howard, anybody else brother, we'd have a whole different scene happening here."

"All right, okay," Howard said.

Sam said, "Yeah. Trust me, *babe.*"

This was not working out well at all, Howard said. Sam and Jessica argued again, and Howard tried calling a truce. That's when Sam blew.

"You want to play?" he shouted at Howard. "Come on! Come on, be funny, man! *Come on, Howard!*"

A wild, glazed look came into Sam's eyes. For an instant, I thought he might attack Howard. Howard seemed to think so too. Visibly unnerved, he said, "Well, let's not deal with *this*."

Howard's sidekick Robin Quivers said, "I thought we were making up here."

Howard said, "I *thought* we were making up."

After the broadcast, Howard and Sam embraced and reaffirmed their friendship. For its raw, spontaneous emotion, this installment of Howard's show became one of his most famous. Given time to reflect, even Sam called it "great radio."

But after the show that same morning, Sam felt rotten about going off on Howard that way. He also regretted mentioning Jessica's mother. "I didn't mean that to happen in there," Sam told me. "My feelings ran high when I started thinking of Kevin."

Ever since they'd both worked at the Comedy Store, David Letterman and Sam had always been friendly. Once Sam began appearing on his late-night talk show, Letterman always gave him tremendous freedom. Before other stand-ups performed on *Late Night,* they had to submit a tape of the spot they intended to do. Sam did it too on all other TV shows, and yet Letterman never asked him. Letterman wanted Sam to be wild. His wildness was the attraction. But Letterman also trusted Sam not to cross the network line. His first five times on the show, Sam went to that boundary and stopped. On September 8, he trampled it.

Having caroused all night in New York the evening before, Sam was still high for his taping that afternoon. He was very, very high. You couldn't tell by his voice, or the way he moved, but Sam came onstage wearing dark glasses. When he quickly had second thoughts and took them off, his eyes were as red as the light on the NBC camera.

In his unconventional sex life, Sam had recently discovered amyl nitrate. Even more recently, however, the FDA had declared the drug illegal. With his usual candor, Sam tried telling Letterman's audience all about it. "Some guys like to play golf," he said. "I love women. I do. And I'm very disturbed because I heard that a certain, uh, a certain sexual—I gotta word this really cool . . . uh, how do you say Hamburger Helper in the sexual sense? Have you ever heard of amyl nitrate? You know what this is? This little bottle called rush?"

As Sam was still talking, one of Letterman's people signaled a sudden commercial.

"Uh, how much time is there left?" Sam asked. "That's it? Wait a second, I just wanna say one more thing."

The crowd started cheering and clapping at something happening behind him. When Sam turned around, he saw David Letterman marching off his own set. He didn't know if David was angry or fooling around.

"Hey, hey, *David!*" Sam yelled.

Someone gestured to Sam again that his spot was over.

"That *can't* be it," he said. "Is that it? Okay."

Sam looked forlorn, like a little boy whose bicycle just got stolen. He was onstage less than three minutes.

Sam was sitting near Letterman's desk after the break. Probably because he was buzzed, he still didn't seem to know how badly he'd just screwed up. After politely responding to several innocuous questions, Sam rushed right back to the sex and drugs. "David? Have *you* ever had sex on amyl nitrate? Ever? Have you heard about this? I'm just curious."

Letterman, lightning-quick, took refuge in a bit he'd done at the top of the show, on the weekly parking rates in the NBC parking lot. "If you have a *camper,* you can park a camper over there for a hundred and fifty-seven dollars a month."

"I'm sorry," Sam could be heard saying offscreen, while the camera showed the garage. "I was out of line."

When David and Sam returned to the screen, David said, "Sam? Do you *understand* the principle of the parking garage? You know how that works?"

"Uh . . . you know, I've always been fascinated with that."

"Uhhh . . . and now you're living in Malibu."

"Malibu. Don't you have a place out there?"

"Well, I used to," David said.

"I'm out there past Broadbeach," Sam said. "I live out there by Sylvester Stallone."

"Yeah, that's great. Do you fit in out there? Do people *like* seeing you on the beach?"

Everyone laughed and the tension diffused, but when NBC broadcast the show later that evening, it edited out nearly all of Sam's stand-up routine. Sam was irate at himself, not NBC. It was his first terrible spot on the Letterman show, and the first time he'd betrayed Letterman's trust.

"I figured out why no country wants to fuck with us. We feed the world—we might put stuff in their food. Russia got the picture, they're kissing our ass now. They called us up and said, 'Listen, we have problem. We have no jobs and no food.' So we told them, 'Here's a McDonald's. Now hire yourself and make yourself something to eat.' I'm glad we gave them McDonald's, because now McDonald's has another place to try out those funky new fuckin' sandwiches they keep whipping out on *us* all the time. Yeah, man, try it out on the fuckin' Russians—leave us *alone.* But McDonald's doesn't care, they're too ambitious. They do *not* give a fuck, man. They got two guys in a room somewhere, wearing lab coats, going: 'Hey, you think people will eat tree bark if we deep-fry it?' 'I don't know. They ate the McRib.' Yeah, the American Heart Association wants to thank McDonald's for the McRib. That was a great fuckin' idea. Why don't they just call it the McStroke? 'New from McDonald's, it's the Valve Blocker! No one can eat just one.' That's right, I took two bites—'*Oh, oh, I'm having a stroke!*' Ohhhh, man . . . now they got a breakfast fuckin' burrito. They're getting *too* ambitious. This is Southern California. I want Mexican food, I don't think McDonald's is

Living large: Sam surrounded by Malika and Sabrina.

Sam's first HBO special in 1987—a wildman at the absolute peak of his powers.

At one of their friendlier moments, Sam and Comedy Store owner Mitzi Shore.

The concert for Lenny Bruce's mother. Sam, Malika, Doug Bady, and Sabrina.

Sam and I, Christmas 1989. Sam is just sleepy, not buzzed.

My daughter, Ginger, Sly Stallone, and Sam, hanging out at a friend's house.

They used to be teenage preachers: Marjoe Gortner and Sam.

Sam debuts on *The Tonight Show*.
Johnny Carson was clearly tickled
by him.

Sam and his greatest mentor, Rodney
Dangerfield.

Sam's tenderness always came out
around my daughter, Ginger.

Sam, Ginger, and I at the T. J. Martell
Foundation's celebrity softball game for AIDS.

The rock-and-roll comic jams with Billy Idol.

On Grammy night of 1988, Sam and fellow
freethinker George Carlin.

Sam and Julian Lennon.
They would talk about how
it felt to follow in the foot-
steps of a father.

My wife, Sherry, performs with Sam at Spice on Sunset Strip.

Sam with two early fans of his humor: Eric Clapton and Phil Collins.

DAVE PLASTIK

The eye-catching billboard on Sunset for Sam's third album.

Sam's musical finale at the Universal Amphitheater, New Year's Eve, 1989.

Eclectic bunch: Sabrina,
Malika, Sam, Tommy
Smothers, and Pauly
Shore in Atlantic City.

Lita Ford with Sam and
me onstage at the Aladdin
Hotel. This was Sam's last
performance in Las Vegas.

GARY PARSONS

Sam and Ozzy Osbourne—friends from AA.

Sam and his pal Jon Bon Jovi while taping the video for "Wild Thing."

Still tight after all these years: Sam and I at his last show in Las Vegas.

GARY PARSONS

Good times on the set of *Charlie Hoover*. Sam, Ginger, and Tim Matheson.

Sam and Malika get married just five days before Sam's death.

FRANK BAKER

After Sam died, my mother and I at the Fox-TV tribute to him.

Sam's intellectual look.

what I had in mind. Plus, I don't even know what's in it—I don't *wanna* know. These guys might have had another meeting, the guy in the lab coat goes: 'Hey, you think people will eat shit?' 'What do you mean, like by-products or something?' 'No, I mean shit. Real shit. *Our* shit.' 'I don't know, they're eating that breakfast burrito. Maybe they will. Mix it with some other stuff, maybe they won't know what it is.' See, I don't think it's a bad idea. I think we should make shit burgers and sell them to Russia. They've never had meat—they won't know the difference. Sell them our shit, let them eat our shit. 'New from American McDonald's—its the half-pounder. More beef than ever before, you Russkies.' "

—Sam in concert in Houston

Sam had his own reasons for fearing a stroke. Though he didn't care for McDonald's, he ate way too much red meat and greasy fast food. Only five feet eight, he sometimes weighed up to as much as 275. Sam also had too much rage, and while some of that rage was expelled during his shows, a tremendous amount still festered inside him. By 1989, Sam had also been using cocaine for eleven years. At those times when he used most heavily, I would half expect a call from the manager of a hotel: "Your brother has had a heart attack. He's on the floor of his room and we can't get him up."

When the first big cocaine scare did arrive, I wasn't there. It happened on the night of October 17, just five weeks after his first lousy spot on the Letterman show. After Sam snorted some questionable cocaine, his heart started to hammer. His skin felt wet. He feared he might die. The Comedy Outlaws, his partying partners that night, rushed him to the emergency ward of Cedar Sinai Hospital in Beverly Hills. For fear of what I might do, nobody called me or told me. I found out one week later, when Sam couldn't keep it a secret from me anymore. According to

Sam, his friend Mitchell Walters had given him "speedy co-caine." Although Mitchell was one of the long-standing Comedy Outlaws, Sam cut him out of his inner circle. With Sam, it was all a loyalty thing. The bad cocaine had come from Mitchell. Therefore, Mitchell had betrayed him.

Sam was frightened upon his release from Cedar Sinai. And beginning that October—after his grimmest experience ever with cocaine—he drastically cut his consumption. It was a start, an important first step. His loved ones were pleased. But the alcohol was still flowing.

After concerts in Vermont, West Virginia, Indiana, and Michigan, Sam sold out the Civic Center Theater in Peoria on November 17. Afterward, Sam went out for pizza with Malika and Jimmy Shubert. In the course of their meal, they picked up their pretty waitress. They would all meet at Sam's hotel suite after her shift.

Malika called my own hotel room the following morning. She said their suite had two adjoining rooms. In one of them, she had just woken up alone. She was pretty sure Sam and Jimmy were still in the next room, but the door was locked and she had no key. When she pounded and pounded the door, no one responded.

I grabbed a key from the desk, rushed back upstairs, and opened Sam's door. The waitress was gone. Stark naked, Sam was passed out on the floor. Jimmy, up on the bed, was also nude and unconscious. I couldn't rouse either one of them. Apparently, they'd been drinking and doing downers. I tried waking them again. When they didn't stir, I felt a surge of anger and fear. Downers and booze? What were they thinking about?

Downstairs, our tour bus was waiting to drive us into Kentucky. I thought: Get them on the bus, then figure out what to do. Since Sam was a hometown boy, reporters had been hanging out at our hotel. I could already picture the headlines if they saw him like this.

Working with Malika and Sabrina, I somehow managed to dress Jimmy and Sam. Then we wrapped them in hotel blankets, stuck them on baggage carts, and wheeled them onto our tour bus. When I didn't see any press, I hustled back inside to pay our hotel bill. I walked back on the tour bus five minutes later, and Sam was dripping blood from a gash between his eyes. Malika and Gene Hall, our security man, told me what had happened. They tried tilting Sam onto a couch, but he suddenly fell from their grasp and his face struck the wall.

I called a registered nurse, a friend I'd known for years, at St. Francis Hospital in Peoria. "We'd like to keep this private," I said. "We don't want the press coming in. Will one of your doctors come out to the tour bus and stitch him up? It's only a cut, but it looks deep."

She sent over George Bush's plastic surgeon, who worked on staff at St. Francis. He looked at Sam, still out cold. "I could stitch him up here," the surgeon said, "but you really should have him X-rayed. As big as he is, and hitting that wall, he may have a concussion."

At St. Francis Hospital, as Sam and Jimmy still slept, I gathered around me Malika, Sabrina, and Gene. "If Sam ever finds out he got dropped on his face, I'll be the only one left around here," I told them. "The rest of you will be history. I'll tell him he tried taking a pee in his hotel room, and he fell and cut his head."

When Sam woke up, he was still in the emergency ward. I could hear him bellowing all the way in the lobby. "BILL! WHERE'S BILL? SOMEBODY GET MY BROTHER! BILLLL!"

I hurried inside his room. Because of the scare he'd recently had with his heart, Sam was hooked up to a heart monitor. He seemed to be terrified. "BILL! WHAT ARE THEY DOING TO ME?"

"Lower your voice, Sam. You fell down in the hotel, taking a pee. You cut your head. We gotta get it stitched up."

"I wouldn't do this to you, man!"

"Yeah, you would. You got a big cut here. We gotta get it fixed. It won't even show. You got George Bush's plastic surgeon."

"BILL! Don't let 'em do me the way they did Rollie!"

Rollie Keith, the Peoria weatherman who Sam and I had watched as children, had come by to say hello the day before. "I just had open-heart surgery," Rollie had told us. "It was really strange. I went to my doctor one day for a routine physical. Next thing I knew, I was checking into St. Francis and getting a bypass. The sad thing is, I don't even think I needed it."

Waking up in the ER ward, seeing his heart hooked up, Rollie's story was all Sam could think of now.

"BILL! Don't let 'em do me the way they did Rollie! Don't let 'em operate on my heart!"

I promised him nothing would happen without him knowing about it. Sam fell back asleep, then woke up five hours later in a private room. He asked me, again, what had happened to him that morning. To keep him from going ballistic on Gene and Malika, I told him the same lie. Sam wanted out and asked to see a doctor. If Sam took it "easy," the doctor said, he could go.

Easy? I thought. Sam doesn't know the word.

While I gathered Sam's belongings, the plastic surgeon came in and pulled up a chair next to him. "I'm a big fan of yours," he told Sam.

"Thank you," Sam said.

"But I don't want to see you end up like John Belushi. If you continue to go the way you've been going, you won't live another two years."

Nobody spoke after that.

For the whole next week, Sam was scared enough to stay straight. After his show in Kentucky, where he performed with makeup over his stitches, we had a break in our tour, and he mostly relaxed at his house out in Malibu. Having grown up in Illinois, Sam loved peering through his window at the ocean, but he also stayed out there for his own protection. Malibu kept him away from the Hollywood night scene.

"Fox Broadcasting earned its highest ratings ever on Sunday night with a special hourlong of *Married with Children* that featured comedian Sam Kinison."
—Los Angeles Times, December 20, 1989

When Sam taped *Married with Children* the first week of December, it typified his relationship with Hollywood. The cast and crew loved him. The executives held their breath until his performance was in the can.

Sam nearly lost the gig right out of the gate. After drinking all Monday night, he missed a read-through on Tuesday. The producers gave him one more chance, and the rest of the week he behaved. But Sam was still Sam. He had lunch catered every day for the cast and crew. While everyone ate, he hired belly dancers to come in and entertain. After taping the show on Friday night, Sam threw a wrap party in a private room at the China Club. Ed O'Neill had other plans, but Christina Applegate, David Faustino, and Katie Segal all attended.

Sam made it fun. Fun for himself and fun for the people around him. But he was also living up to his reputation. Big spender. Grand gestures. Larger than life.

For their Christmastime spoof of *It's a Wonderful Life,* the producers wrote in a part for Sam as Al Bundy's guardian angel. They'd come to us with the idea, which Sam took as proof that Hollywood wanted him back. He felt certain of this when his guest shot drew record ratings. As Sam resumed dreaming out loud about starring in feature films, I reminded him of something he already knew: Compared to movies, Hollywood views TV as a distant, inferior cousin. That he'd kicked ass on TV wouldn't mean much to the big shots in feature films.

If Sam was open to it, I suggested we go after a sitcom. Maybe something on Fox, since it wasn't afraid of doing TV with an edge, and it already knew what Sam could mean to its ratings. The youngest network, it also seemed most apt to take in a maverick.

Sam gave me his blessing, and I started making phone calls, but I held off on setting up too many meetings. Sam was still going too hard to be completely relied on.

On December 28, despite his strong-arm tactics the previous May, *The Tonight Show* brought back Sam for a second appearance. Two days later we flew to Las Vegas, where Sam had a five-show engagement at Bally's Grand Ballroom. For his five shows in two hectic nights, he figured to earn about $250,000.

To Sam, playing at Bally's meant more than big money. Even once he got his career break on HBO, it had taken him three years to start playing the large casinos. Until then, no one in Vegas believed Sam could sell them out. Even I doubted him, but Sam kept pushing anyway. "My fans are getting older," he told me again and again. "They're getting married and having children. They're becoming Vegas people." In 1988, when Bally's finally agreed, Sam signed a multishow contract for that year, with an option held by Bally's for two more.

It took Sam three years to chase down his dream. Then he nearly blew it all in one night.

Sam in Vegas was like Sam in New York: A little of anything always turned into a lot. This time, Sam went on a bender the instant he stepped off the airplane. He did two shows on December 30, and managed to be outstanding, but he was still binging by early New Year's Eve. He also hadn't slept in forty-eight hours.

Sam had three more shows coming up—at 11:00 P.M to usher

in 1990, and then at 2:00 and 4:30 A.M. on January 1. I went up to his suite at Bally's at 7:00 P.M. Looking upset, Carl answered Sam's door. "Sam's in the bedroom," he said. "You better go in there."

I went inside by myself. Sitting on top of his bed with all his dissheveled clothes on, Sam was drunk and morose. He saw me and started weeping.

"What's the matter?" I asked.

"It shoulda been me, man," Sam said. "I'm the reason he's dead. I killed him, man. I killed Kevin."

"Kevin is gone," I said gently. "All of us feel responsible, Sam. There's nothing we can do, though. No matter how much we want him back, Kevin is *gone*."

"I want him back, man. I miss him."

"So do I, Sam. Every day I think about him."

"Do you?"

"Yeah. You know I do."

Sam stopped crying and wiped his cheeks. For a long time nobody spoke.

"Come on, Sam," I said. "Get up. I don't want you going to bed. You got three shows tonight. You sleep through them, we're fucked."

"What? You think I can't do the show, man?"

"No, I've seen you do shows a lot worse than this. I just don't want you going to bed."

Suddenly, Sam seemed amused. "You worry too much! You worry all the time! Gotta walk on the edge, brother!"

"Just don't go to bed. You won't have to worry about walking on the edge."

An hour before the 11:00 P.M. show, Sam fell asleep. This was no light sleep, either. Not after forty-eight hours without any rest. I finally woke him by shouting into his face.

With two other comics performing before him, Sam took the stage at five minutes to New Year's—a nightmare assignment for any comedian. Sam, of course, had made things even harder for himself. Still drowsy, disoriented, and drunk, he couldn't even count down from ten as midnight approached. After several minutes of bedlam as 1990 came in, he tried doing his stand-up. But he could barely speak, let alone be funny.

Down near the front, a table of twelve rowdy guys began heckling him. Loudly, one guy called Sam a drunk. Sam found the table and stepped to the edge of the stage. "I may be drunk," he angrily slurred, "but you know what the real joke is? I've already got your money. So *fuck you!*"

All twelve guys stood up at once and marched out on Sam. In the Bally's lobby, they all demanded their money back. Sam had sold every seat in the house at $50 a head.

Trying to keep things orderly, I told our copromoter Michael Skivo to collect all their names and hotel room numbers. Tomorrow, we'd issue them total refunds. Inexplicably, Skivo told the twelve guys they were just out of luck.

"*Refund, refund, refund!*" they started chanting.

Hearing all the commotion, more of Sam's crowd came pouring into the lobby. Sam's show was nearly over by then; they figured they could get back their $50 too. I never saw anything like it at a concert. At the same desk where the 11:00 P.M. people were demanding their refunds, the 2:00 A.M. crowd was lining up to buy tickets. Fans coming out told fans coming in: Don't even bother. He gave a horrible show.

I ran backstage and found Sam. Amazingly, he was already sobering up. "Go back to your room," I said. "Take a cold shower and order some food. You go up again at two. What the hell was that up there?"

Richard Sturm, Bally's head of entertainment, called me at 1:00 A.M. in my hotel room. Though it would be a public relations disaster, Sturm wanted to cancel the next two shows. "Sam's just too out of it," he told me.

"Don't do anything rash," I said. "I'll be right down."

Sturm was huddling in the lobby with Barry Fey, our main Las Vegas promoter. It was still a madhouse down there, so we all stepped inside an elevator. "If I can show you he's not out of it," I said to Sturm, "will we still do the shows?"

When Sturm was noncommittal, I said I'd call Sam right now, and Sturm could hear for himself. I told Sturm, truthfully, that Sam didn't know I was calling. This meant Sturm would get the straight story, whatever it was. Sturm shrugged and said, "Let's see what happens." I called Gene Hall on my walkie-talkie. Gene put on Sam, who'd already showered and put some food in his stomach.

"Sam, I just talked to Bally's," I said. "They said you're out of it. They say you can't perform, and they're calling off the two shows."

"*Fuck them!*" Sam shouted. "They're still gonna fuckin' pay me! That was an *act* I pulled out there! Like fuckin' Dean Martin and Foster Brooks! My crowd *expects* me to act like that! If Bally's don't understand that, they can bring in their fuckin' Gallagher and their George Carlin! I'll go somewhere else, man! I can play anywhere on the Strip! You tell 'em that! And you tell 'em they're still fuckin' paying me!"

"Okay, Sam, I'll tell them."

I clicked off with Sam and turned to Sturm. "Well, sounds to me like he's sobered up."

Sam didn't *sound* drunk, Sturm admitted, but he wanted to see him in person. This time I warned Sam we were coming up to his room, where Sam got right up in Sturm's face.

"Look at me," Sam demanded. "Do I look fuckin' drunk to you? Huh?"

Convinced, Sturm moved the 2:00 A.M. show to 3:00, and the 4:30 show to 5:30. When Sam finally came off the stage—after two funny performances—it was daylight in Las Vegas.

The last two good shows could not erase the first one, and the stories spread through the Strip even before we left town: Sam got bombed and cursed his own fans. He's fallen from Bally's good graces, and they're likely to drop his lucrative option. He'll be shunned now by every major casino.

Barry Fey called me the next week with his final accounting. So many people demanded refunds that night, Barry said, he and Bally's were kicking back some of their money. Barry said Sam had to pitch in as well, with $42,000.

"No fuckin' way," Sam said when I told him. "I'm not paying anything back."

"But they're right. It was a horrible show."

"Come on, man. It wasn't that bad."

"I have a tape. I'll give it to you, then you tell me."

Sam watched the tape alone, felt like an ass, and told me to write the check for the $42,000. Then we waited to see if the rumors were true. After it took him three years to conquer the town, would Sam be banned from Las Vegas?

Back in L.A., Sam spent the first week of 1990 completing his third album for Warner Bros. Sam wanted *Leader of the Banned,* due out in the spring, to solidify his reputation as "the rock-and-roll comedian." When I first heard his plan—one side of stand-up comedy, one side of heavy metal—I questioned whether his fans wanted that much music. I said to him, "You're a comic, Sam. Remember?" Engulfed in his rock-and-roll phase, he plowed ahead anyway. As he told the *Los Angeles Times* in a preview of the album, "I've been playing guitar since I was fifteen. I'm not intimidated by these guys. I may not be as good as C. C. DeVille, but it's not like I'm William Shatner doing 'Lucy in the Sky with Diamonds.' "

In terms of craft, the music *was* good. Backed up by several respected musicians–including Slash of Guns N' Roses, Bon Jovi keyboardist David Bryam, Whitesnake bassist Rudy Sarzo, and Poison guitarist C. C. DeVille—Sam recorded straight renditions of Cheap Trick's "Gonna Raise Hell" and the Rolling Stones'

"Under My Thumb." In a comic version of Mountain's "Mississippi Queen," he satirized Jessica Hahn and Jim Bakker. For his final selection, Sam recorded "Are You Lonesome Tonight?" After it played so well on *The Tonight Show,* Sam thought his twisted homage to Elvis would be his next "Wild Thing." He planned to make it his album's first single, which he felt would get heavy airplay on both country and pop.

Then Sam hit a legal snag. Once she heard his new lyrics—"Are you a reptile with a nice hairdo? You lied to me, you sneaky tramp!"—the old woman owning the song rights refused to license them. On the night of January 9, Sam hustled back into the studio for a replacement. He chose a metal classic: AC/DC's "Highway to Hell."

Drinking and recording, Sam and C. C. DeVille stayed up all Tuesday night and into Wednesday morning. In Sam's Corvette, they left about 9:00 A.M. for the house Sam was renting in Nichols Canyon. As he later told it to me, Sam's 'vette hit a patch of slick, wet pavement. Its big custom racing tires skidded. Sam lost control of his car in the winding canyon. It flew up the side of the hill, wedging between a power pole and the hillside. With all four of its wheels off the ground, the two doors wouldn't open because of the 'vette's suspension. Gene Hall and Jimmy Shubert were driving right behind them. They busted open a window, which Sam and C.C. somehow squeezed through. Jimmy drove them all to Sam's house and they called a tow truck.

The police got there first. Sam didn't know it, but a resident down the canyon had called the LAPD. Declaring the 'vette abandoned, the police had it impounded.

Overnight, Sam's car wreck triggered a media feeding frenzy. The following day, on a local TV news show, I heard that the LAPD had an APB out on Sam. I called the police. They said there was no APB, but they did want to talk to Sam when he came to pick up his car. The next day the story went national. On a tabloid TV show, I heard a report that Sam was hiding in

Mexico. "You mean his house?" I said to my TV. Sam hadn't left there once since the accident Wednesday morning.

Sam wound up lying to both the police and reporters. Sparing C. C. DeVille the same public embarrassment, Sam never revealed that C.C. was there that morning. Sam also claimed that he wasn't driving his car; his security man Gene Hall was. Gene had *told* Sam to say that. Gene figured that was part of protecting his boss.

Sam would tell his fans the same thing during his concerts— "Really, I wasn't driving"—but then he'd pretend that his nose was growing like Pinocchio's. Reporters and cops were one thing. As long as they kept laughing, and buying tickets, Sam didn't mind if his fans thought he was a fuckup.

The car crash came only ten days after the drunken debacle at Bally's. In the onslaught of bad publicity, the media portrayed Sam as a man with a death wish. And they didn't know the half of it: In only the past six weeks, Sam had gotten in three other car wrecks. I never found out for sure, but each time he was probably drinking and driving. Miraculously, no one was ever injured.

Were the media right this time? Was Sam trying to kill himself?

In the past, I'd always told myself no. I knew Sam was in terrible pain over Kevin. Even before Kevin died, I knew Sam was prone to self-hatred. And I knew what Sam had told me himself: "I'll never live to see forty."

But I never felt this added up to a death wish. I felt there was still a distinction.

Now, I wasn't quite so sure. And even if Sam wasn't trying, how long could he keep dodging fate? And how long would it be before he hurt someone else?

Rising Back Up

"Jesus had a tough life, man. Jesus is the only guy that came out of the dead that didn't scare the fuck out of everybody. He's the only guy that ever crawled out of a cave and people didn't go: 'OH! AAAAUGH! I JUST SAW SOME FUCKER CRAWL OUT OF HIS GRAVE! I DON'T BELIEVE I'M SEEING THIS SHIT! THIS GUY JUST CRAWLED OUT OF HIS BOX—OH! AAAUGH! THE DEAD LIVE, THE DEAD LIVE! GET A STAKE! PUT A STAKE THROUGH HIS ASS! CUT OFF HIS HEAD! KILL HIM AGAIN!' Jesus comes back, he doesn't get any pressure. No static, nobody's upset. He climbs out, he's walking around, nobody's upset. They can eat with him and everything." Pretending to be Jesus, Sam rolled his eyes back in his head, so the crowd could see only its whites. 'Hey, psst. Isn't that guy dead?' 'Yeah, but he's real stubborn, man. He won't accept it.' Yeah, I read that book, folks. He's on the cross, there's thirty or forty Christians standing around, weeping, going: 'It's a shame that he has to die.' And Jesus is going: 'MAYBE I WOULDN'T HAVE TO IF SOMEBODY WOULD GET A LADDER AND PAIR OF PLIERS!' A ladder, a pair of pliers—

it could have been a different book, folks. Just a little con-
centration, that's all it would've taken."

—Sam at the Roxy Theater in West Hollywood.

"There's no happy ending to cocaine. You either die, you
go to jail, or else you run out."

—Sam on *The Arsenio Hall Show.*

The last week of February, I called Sam's accountant Lester
Knispel. Sam had recently gotten slapped with a pair of judg-
ments, one from United Artists and one from Terry Marrs. In both
cases, he'd failed to make his first scheduled payment. Now Sam
had almost no savings, and almost no cash coming in; he was
drinking so hard that I was reluctant to book him. In the midst of
his ugly binge, Sam didn't even complain that he wasn't working.

I wasn't calling this meeting just for him, though. His money
problems were *my* money problems. It was one thing to work
for free when you could afford it. I couldn't anymore, and the
pressure was taking its toll.

I asked Lester to meet us later that week at a restaurant in
Encino. I asked him to bring Mahalia, another of Sam's accountants. Sam loved and trusted them both. If they explained
his financial meltdown to him, he would believe them. If I tried
by myself, Sam might think his older brother was just trying to
scare him.

Lester must have picked something up in my voice. He asked
me if the meeting was just about money.

I admitted to him it wasn't. With the car wrecks, the embarrassing night in Las Vegas, the split-open head in Peoria, I felt
Sam was hitting rock bottom. And I'd already lost one brother.

"Yeah, Lester," I said. "I'm gonna talk to Sam about joining
AA. I found a meeting in Malibu near his house. It's mostly other
celebrities. If Sam doesn't go, I'm quitting."

"You can't quit," Lester said, stunned. "If you quit, it's all over for him."

"I'm sorry. I made up my mind. Something has to give."

Sam arrived at the restaurant after we did. He looked tired, vacant, defeated. He hadn't shaved in days. Under his stubble, his face looked blotchy and bloated. When Sam sat down, I said the first thing that came to my mind.

"You look like shit."

"Thanks, Bill," he said. "Hi, Mahalia. Hi, Lester."

They explained, for ten minutes, why Sam's financial outlook had never been gloomier. After they finished, Sam turned to me. This time, he looked like he wanted my help.

"Here's the bottom line," I said. "Every problem you have right now—personal, financial, every single one—is related to alcohol and drug abuse. And it's also related to Kevin. I know that. But Kevin is gone, Sam. I miss him just like you miss him."

"Yeah, man, but you're able to handle it," Sam said. "I'm not like you."

That pissed me off. I said, "What, you think I don't hurt? I fuckin' hurt. I cry just like you cry. It's just that I deal with my feelings, I don't drown 'em and drug 'em out."

I thought Sam might start ranting and raving, Hey motherfucker, you used to snort and drink too. He didn't say anything, so I continued.

"I can't work for you anymore, Sam."

"What's that supposed to mean?"

"I'm off this wagon, man. If you're gonna kill yourself, you do it without me. I'm not gonna sit around and *watch* you kill yourself."

Sam looked straight into my eyes. "I know I have a problem," he said.

I felt a rush of hope. Sam had never conceded this before.

I said, "Okay, Sam, listen. I checked around. You don't want to hear this, but I don't give a shit—I'm walking out if you don't, so it's not even an option. They have an AA meeting out in Malibu. It's not far from your house. It's mostly for celebrities. Either you start going there or I'm out. I'm out, Sam."

"When is it?"

"It's eight every morning. Your ass better be there tomorrow."

"I'll be there."

Sam meant it. I could just tell. I said to myself, Okay, let's get to work.

Sam called me the next afternoon to say he'd enjoyed his first meeting. "It was like going to church," he said. "Except Ozzy Osbourne was there."

A lifelong rock-and-roll fan, Sam considered Ozzy a bigger star than he was. Ozzy's presence made Sam feel less self-conscious.

He started attending regularly, but it took him two weeks to get serious. Until then, Sam came to some meetings still drunk from the evening before. Before a few of the meetings, he picked up his friend Corey Feldman, also still drunk. Shitfaced, they sat through the sessions together.

About two weeks into AA, Sam started concentrating on what he was hearing. He started getting healthy. He still had a long way to go. He still had explosions of temper. He still got down on himself. But he didn't reach for a bottle. He rode it out, and eventually his insides would stop churning. By mid-April, Sam had been sober for almost thirty days.

I loved being with him during this time. I could count on him to make plane flights. We could eat dinner together without him ordering liquor, and without ten other guys. Rather than staying home, getting drunk, and watching movies, Sam would call me to go to the theater and see new releases. It didn't happen over-night, but we became close all over again. With the alcohol and cocaine out of the way, we weren't stiff-arming each other emotionally.

During interviews, and in concert, Sam started saying that he was *totally* clean. But it wasn't true. From age twenty-five, Sam had smoked pot almost every day of his life, and he didn't stop now. "Pot doesn't count," he joked in private. "These are natural herbs from the ground." On those nights when he couldn't sleep, when coming off booze and cocaine made him feel jittery, sometimes he took a Valium. But Sam never came close to getting hooked. He didn't take them often enough.

Not all of his fans wanted him straight. After telling his crowds that he'd stopped doping and drinking, he'd always receive a mixed reaction. "Folks," Sam would say, "I've been sober for seventeen days." When half the crowd booed, he'd say, "Not all in a row!"

In a more serious vein, Bob Costas asked Sam on *Later* about his reputed cocaine use.

"Drugs are not a fashionable topic now," Costas said. "Even though a lot of comics have used drugs in the past, and common sense tells us a lot *still* use it without acknowledging it, you're the only guy who pretty much openly says, 'Hey, still do it.' "

"Well, that was up until recently," Sam said. "Until I decided to basically step away from them."

"What made you reach that decision?"

"I thought I was about to have a heart attack one night. I was doing . . . what they call cocaine, and I was like . . . I don't want to die. I knew I went too far. I said, 'If I survive this, I'm never doing this stuff again.' Because I *don't* want to die, and I don't want to go to jail."

"Did you know Belushi at all?" Costas asked.

"I met him twice, yeah, before he passed away."

"Wasn't his experience enough of a cautionary tale to push you and others away from it before you came that close yourself?"

Sam couldn't hide a grin. Though he knew how carried away with cocaine he could get, he always felt he and Belushi were in different leagues. "I'm not trying to smile," Sam told Costas, "but the difference between me and him was that this guy could do a line from here to that wall."

Throughout that spring, as Sam attended AA, he was told again and again to avoid troublesome places. So unless the gig was simply too good to pass up—a *Letterman* spot, a Stern show, a high-paying stand-up date—we both agreed not to book him in New York. When Sam did perform there, he stayed fifty miles from the city, down on the shoreline. Even when he had the Stern show in the morning, he just woke up extra early and made the drive in.

Unfortunately, Sam couldn't count on Malika for any support. A heavy drinker herself, she refused all suggestions that she get some help. Sam asked her several times to come with him to AA, and so did her sister, Sabrina. "You have a bigger problem than Sam does," Sabrina said. "You need to get cleaned out just like Sam."

"I don't have any problem," Malika insisted. "I'm not like *him*."

One night, on an airplane flight to Canada, I was sitting with Sam while Malika sat with Sabrina. Drinking alone, Malika finished a bottle of champagne. When she ordered a second, I pointed it out to Sam.

"I know," Sam said. "She's having a hard time handling this."

"Handling what?"

"Everything, I guess. Me not drinking."

"Brother, the whole thing is, I'm worried about you. I don't know how you're gonna stay straight when you're living with a woman who always stays drunk."

"She'll get it, Bill. It's a little harder for her."

But Malika's problem went untreated. Sometimes, in public, she drank from Evian bottles filled with vodka.

                              *   *   *

Sam wasn't drinking or snorting that spring, but he still needed his kicks. Or as he put it, "I'm still not exactly Tim Conway."

Sam got a *huge* kick out of driving down Sunset Strip, past the eye-catching billboard for his new album. Replicating the cover art for *Leader of the Banned,* it featured Sam in a takeoff on *The Last Supper.* Standing at the head of a long banquet table, he was surrounded by twelve sexy women in lingerie. Before the billboard went up, Sam was given several choices for its location. To thumb his nose at Mitzi Shore, he had it placed directly across from the Comedy Store.

Banned came out that spring to lackluster reviews. Although most critics liked the one side of comedy, they were unimpressed by the back side of heavy metal. Personally, I felt *Banned* would have sold better with stronger promotion by Warner Bros. But I also considered Sam's first two albums funnier. That wasn't so odd: Whether it be a comedian or a rock band, it's frequently hard to top those earliest albums. Once an artist becomes successful, he doesn't get or take as much time to create new product. Sam's first album, for example, was really "the best of Sam" in his first five years in L.A.

Despite a few obstacles, *Banned* ending up selling about 100,000 records, still a success compared to most comedy albums. By Sam's own high standard, however, his third album was a failure.

Still, it did have great liner notes. Including Irving Azoff, Sly Stallone, Julian Lennon, Johnny Carson, David Letterman, Rodney Dangerfield, Sean Penn, Rob Lowe, Gary Busey, Moon and Dweezil Zappa, several musician pals, and Howard Stern and his crew, Sam thanked numerous friends and mentors over the years. Then, off to the side in capital letters, Sam wrote: "AND VERY SPECIAL THANKS TO JOE ESZTERHAS FOR WRITING HIS LETTER TO MIKE OVITZ."

*   *   *

Clearly, Sam still had his irreverence. He still had the balls to poke fun at powerful people. What Hollywood wanted to know: Could he be relied on? Could he make a clean break from his past?

In trying to keep Sam's career from jumping the tracks, I had always downplayed his problems with liquor and drugs. That spring, I could finally stop conning and bluffing. But rather than try to convince people myself, I invited several important executives to attend Sam's concerts in Southern California. This time the rumor mill worked in his favor: "Kinison looks good. He's getting clean." After a long drought, we started receiving feature-film scripts again. There was also loose talk of Sam starring in his own sitcom.

It was nice, for a change, to have a little peace in our turbulent lives. But then, on the night of June 6, Elton John put an end to our three months free of uproar.

It happened in New York, while Sam was hosting the 2nd Annual International Rock Awards on ABC. By then, though Sam was still doing jokes about gays, he was doing it much less than ever before, and he'd completely stopped making light of the AIDS epidemic. Sam did this partly out of self-interest and partly out of a heightened sensitivity. Sam had fought so many battles with the gay community, his reputation for controversy was obscuring his reputation as a comedian. A little older and wiser, he wanted to put the focus back on his humor. At the same time, two events helped sensitize Sam to the issue of AIDS: Ryan White passed away, and Sam's best friend, Carl's, father contracted AIDS. Sam had known for years that Carl's father was gay, but he'd never really known anyone with the disease.

The morning of the International Rock Awards, Sam told the *New York Post:* "I came to terms with the fact that death isn't funny. It's something I shouldn't have made fun of in the first place. It should be dealt with compassionately. I hadn't been around anybody who had AIDS. And that's my fault. It's my fault for being drunk and high the last five years and being ignorant to people's pain."

During that evening's live broadcast on ABC, Elton John appeared onscreen via satellite from L.A. About to present Eric Clapton with a lifetime achievement award, first he called Sam a pig on national television. "I'm doing this show under protest," Elton John said. "I'd like to congratulate Sam Kinison on being the first pig ever to introduce a rock-and-roll show." In a passage bleeped out by ABC, he also chided the show's producers to get "decent fucking people" to host the show in the future.

Since Elton John made his remarks on a satellite feed, Sam and everyone else at the show saw only a blank blue screen. Sam found out the next morning, when the national media called him in his hotel room. When they read him Elton John's comments, Sam kept his cool. He remained diplomatic the following week, issuing this statement through his publicist: "It was unprofessional and irresponsible for Elton John to take the spotlight away from Eric Clapton with his remarks about me."

Sam fumed in private for several more days, until finally erupting one night in concert. After calling Elton John a "disco dinosaur," Sam moved on to his odd collection of hats. "What's that all about with those fuckin' hats? He looks like a gay Shriner. Yeah, I was doing the International Rock Awards, he came on live television and said I was a pig. I did nothing to this guy. Never met him. I even used to buy his albums. Yeah, I bought his albums—FIFTEEN YEARS AGO! I was naive, I didn't know what they meant. I bought albums like *Brown Dirt Cowboy*. I liked the songs, this was good music, but why would you call an album *Brown Dirt Cowboy?* I get it NOW. 'Don't Let the Sun Go Down on Me'? NOW, I understand!"

Sam couldn't help himself. He might not be snorting and drinking, he might actually be doing some growing up, but he was still ferocious when someone embarrassed him. He also thought the Elton John stuff was *funny,* and sometimes that was as far as Sam's criteria went. ''I'm not a politician,'' he used to say. ''My job is to make people laugh.''

Scandal, in Context

"Comedian Sam Kinison's bodyguard was arrested and booked yesterday for investigation of rape after the entertainer's girlfriend was assaulted and shot at her attacker at Kinison's home, police said. Kinison was in the Hollywood Hills house at the time but did not know about the incident until after the shooting and was not harmed, said police and the entertainer's spokesman Jeff Albright. Booked at the Hollywood police station was Unway Carter, 22, described by Detective Gil Jones as Kinison's 6-foot-4-inch, 300-pound bodyguard. 'The victim was attacked in her bedroom in the residence,' said Jones, who said Kinison was asleep in another room. 'After the rape was completed, the victim, in her 20s, excused herself to go to the bathroom,' Jones said. 'She walked through the bathroom and entered another adjoining bedroom, where she knew there was a gun. She returned and fired four shots at Carter, but missed him,' said Jones."

—A wire-service story in the *Hollywood Reporter,*
June 22, 1990

That's the story that ran in most of the papers, but there was a lot more to it. In some ways, I felt there was also much less.

Even before this, June turned into an awful month for the Kinisons. First, our stepfather, A.D., died. Just one day after his burial, our mother's father passed away. At the end of the second funeral, Sam and I talked in Tulsa before he flew back to L.A.

"We both gotta hang around, Sam," I said. "We can't go anywhere. It's just you, me, Richard, and mom now."

Tears flooded Sam's eyes. He tried to speak, but he couldn't.

I spent the next two weeks in Tulsa, consoling my mother and helping her tend to her church. Back at my home in Upland on June 21, my phone rang at 10:00 A.M. Sam's close friend Dan Barton said Sam hadn't shown up for their meeting that morning.

"I just tried calling his house," Dan told me, meaning the house Sam was renting in Nichols Canyon. "The police answered the phone."

My first thought: Sam's dead. He's had a terrible relapse.

An LAPD detective answered Sam's phone. I identified myself and asked him to put Sam on. Sobbing and drunk, he muttered something incomprehensible.

"I can't understand you, Sam. What are you saying?"

"Raped, man. Malika was raped."

"What? By who?"

"Fuckin' guy, man."

"Sam, put the detective back on."

I asked the detective, "What's going on out there?"

"We have an alleged rape," he said. "We're taking the woman to the hospital."

"Is she hurt?"

"No. But we're taking her in to be examined. We're taking Sam too. He's in no condition to stay here. We couldn't even wake him up. We had to throw water into his face."

When I got to Cedar Sinai, Malika was being examined. Sam was out cold again but otherwise intact. I figured he could sleep it off at home, so I drove him back toward his house in Nichols Canyon. Winding my way up the mountain, I saw cameramen and reporters hanging out at the bottom of Sam's driveway. So he wouldn't be spotted, I pulled over before I got there, lowered his seat all the way back, and hid him under my coat. Then I drove right past the media up the driveway. I realized at the top that Sam couldn't stay there; his place was surrounded by squad cars. I left him in my car, hoping he wouldn't be seen by any reporters. I went inside to grab his clothes and sundries, and to see if I could get some more information. After that, we'd drive back to my house in Upland.

About fifteen policemen from the Hollywood Division were investigating his home. After I identified myself, a pair of detectives showed me the four bullet holes. As we walked and talked, they told me something surprising. After the alleged rape that morning, after the shooting, both Malika and Carter called the police. Each called from the homes of Sam's neighbors. When the first unit arrived, the police found Carter standing outside in Sam's driveway.

"Why would a guy that just raped somebody call the police?" I asked the detectives.

Neither one answered, but one detective gestured as if to say, "I don't know."

Back outside at my car a few minutes later, several uniformed cops were talking to Sam. Angry, confused, uncooperative, and still drunk, Sam called them liars for not letting him see Malika at Cedar Sinai. "We weren't even there," one angry officer told him. Before we drove off, Sam was also told not to leave town.

Sam fell back asleep on the ride out to my house. After her release from Cedar Sinai, Malika called there around 2:00 P.M. I asked her what happened, and this is what she told me:

The night had begun at the Rainbow, then moved to the rock club Gazzari's, where Sam met this guy Unway Carter. She and Sam were fighting, and she and Sabrina left Gazzari's without him. Malika went back alone to the house on Nichols Canyon. Sam came home with Carter the following morning. Sam and Malika argued again, then Sam passed out in the guest room. Malika started crying. Carter went to her as if to console her, but then carried her into Sam and Malika's bedroom. Terrified, she did whatever Carter wanted. After he raped her two or three times, she asked Carter if she could go to the bathroom. She wanted to clean herself up. Carter said yes, and Malika went to the bathroom. When she returned to the bedroom, Carter continued to rape her. She asked him again later, and again Carter allowed her to use the bathroom. This time Malika went through the bathroom and into Sabrina's bedroom. She grabbed Sam's loaded .44, rushed back toward the bedroom, and started shooting. She wanted to kill the guy, but by then he was gone. She ran outside to a neighbor and called the police.

Malika never cried as she told me this. She never became emotional at all. She sounded composed, matter-of-fact, and I found this startling. As a preacher for seventeen years, I had spent time with several rape victims. I saw them experience rage, fear, hysteria, shame, and shock. I never recognized calmness.

After she told me the story, Malika said she was leaving Sam.

"That's probably a good idea," I said.

Later that afternoon, with Sam still sleeping, I watched the local TV news shows mangle the story. One anchor referred to Unway Carter as a man "Sam Kinison knew quite well." Another called Carter Sam's "longtime bodyguard." It wasn't all the media's fault, though. At first, a police captain came on the screen and gave an accurate statement: Sam had only met Unway Carter the night before. Then Jeff Albright, described as Sam's publicist, contradicted the policeman. Ordinarily, Mitchell Schneider was Sam's personal publicist. But Mitchell didn't drive out to Sam's house that crucial morning. Mitchell's assistant Jeff Albright did.

"The connection is that Mr. Carter is Sam's bodyguard," Albright told the knot of reporters.

Prodded by one skeptical writer, Albright admitted that he'd never actually seen Sam with Carter.

"Have you ever met Carter yourself?" the same writer asked.

"No, I haven't," Albright said. "That's the only comments I can make at this time."

Too late. The public perception was forming. Sam had the alleged rapist on his payroll. Sam knew Unway Carter "quite well."

At about 6:00 P.M., Sam woke up insisting I take him home. He wanted to see Malika, but he was afraid to call her, so I called her for him, telling her what time we planned to be at Sam's house. On the ride back into Hollywood, he told me what he recalled from the night before:

After three months of not drinking, he'd had a relapse. He didn't really know why. He and Malika were fighting, but that wasn't unusual. At Gazzari's, several people were bothering Sam for his autograph. He wasn't in the mood to be social. Sam met Unway Carter. Two people Sam knew said they'd met Carter before—the club owner, Bill Gazzari, and porn star Ron Jeremy. After Malika left, Sam kept drinking heavily. He paid Carter $100 to keep the crowd from his table, and to make sure that Sam got home in one piece. Carter and Sam came home together that morning. Sam and Malika fought again, then Sam passed out in the guest room. He never heard any gunshots. He never heard anything. When Sam woke up, he was staring at several cops.

At the bottom of Sam's driveway, Malika and Sabrina sat parked in Sabrina's convertible Mustang. Malika sat shotgun and Sam tried talking to her. Malika went wild, screaming at him and cursing. She ordered Sabrina to leave, but Sam draped his body across the hood of the Mustang. Sabrina drove about forty feet, then slammed on her brakes. Sam nearly flew off the hood, and

I started hollering bloody murder. Sabrina pressed on the gas, then screeched to another stop. I threatened to kick all three of their stupid asses. Sabrina sat idling as Sam climbed off the hood. All four of us were shouting as they sped away.

I stayed with Sam for the next hour or so. I showed him the four bullet holes, and I told him what *I* thought had happened that morning:

Malika took her first shot while still inside Sabrina's bedroom. But she shot through the closed bedroom door that led to the *hallway,* and not the door to the bathroom. Malika opened that door and went into the hallway. She shot downstairs, piercing a first-floor window. She walked down the hallway until she stood outside the master bedroom. The door was closed and she shot through it twice. But she shot through the *top* of the door; that's why both bullets lodged in the bedroom ceiling. When Malika stepped into the bedroom, Carter had already gone out through the balcony. Her last shot went through the balcony's sliding glass door.

Sam didn't want to hear it, but I told him anyway. "This morning, Malika told me she wanted to kill this guy. But she had no intention of even shooting him. She shot up the entire house, man. She knows your bed is right on the other side of your door. If she wanted to shoot him, she'd have gone right there, then shot straight through the door. Big as he is, she couldn't have missed. But she shot through the top of the door, into the ceiling. And that was after two shots that weren't even near your bedroom."

Sam always had an answer for everything. But this time he played dumb. "I don't understand what you mean," he said.

After I left, Sam called a cab and went to a strip joint. Binging now for the second straight night, he picked up two strippers, then brought them back to his house when they were done working.

By morning, Sam was humiliated in headlines from coast to

coast. Using Jeff Albright's term, the Associated Press sent out a story referring to Unway Carter as "Sam Kinison's bodyguard." In *Daily Variety,* an important trade publication read throughout Hollywood, the headline called Unway Carter a "Kinison Aide."

When I called Sam that afternoon, he sounded smashed. He said the two strippers were there, and I could hear them carrying on in the background. I told him I'd call him later, but when I did his machine was on. It was probably better that way. I had something important to say. With Sam boozing, this wasn't the time to say it.

The next time we spoke was Saturday night, at his concert at the Celebrity Theater in Anaheim. Sam arrived, sloshed, just minutes before his show. He brought the two strippers, who were now staying with him at his house in the hills. They escorted Sam onstage at the start of his show, a role usually played by Malika and Sabrina.

When the concert ended I told him we needed to talk. We went to a distant corner away from the backstage crowd.

"This thing with Malika," I said. "Do you think you can get her to drop the charges?"

Just like that, he was angry. "No fuckin' way! Why the fuck should she?"

"Because she can't win, Sam. I don't know what happened that night. I wasn't there. But *whatever* happened there, I don't think Malika is telling the truth."

Sam shot me a killing glare, but I kept talking. "If she goes to court on this, Sam, she is *not* going to win. If the defense does their job at all, they're gonna destroy her story."

"Listen, man . . . "

"No, Sam, you gotta fuckin' listen. Malika seems perfectly healthy to me. I talked to her that *day.* She wasn't even upset. This thing is embarrassing our whole family, and I don't believe it even happened!"

"Forget it," Sam fumed. "She was raped, and I was drunk, and

I should have been there for her that fuckin' night. I'm not gonna ask her to drop the charges."

Sam called me a few nights later and asked me to join him at Spice, another of his favorite Hollywood haunts. After one solid week of partying, he'd straightened back out. Malika had moved back in and the two strippers were history. As to when he and Sabrina resumed sleeping together, I don't know if it happened quickly or not for a while.

On the restaurant side of Spice, Sam's intentions were obvious. He wanted to stack the case against Unway Carter.

Sam told Ron Jeremy, who was also a buddy of mine, to deny ever meeting Carter before that night at Gazzari's. Sam also told a young woman he knew, a regular on the club scene, to testify that Carter had once slapped her around.

After watching Sam coach a few more witnesses, I pulled him off to the side and asked him who he was kidding. "That stuff won't stand for a second," I said. "You don't think the defense attorneys know what they're doing? You really want to go through with this thing? The best thing to do is just be honest."

Sam blew me off.

He and Malika kept saying, "We're getting this guy."

From where I stood, they were working themselves into a state of hysteria.

Then Sam called me at home the first week of July. He wasn't mad at me anymore. Now he was enraged at Malika.

"You pick up *People* magazine lately?" Sam said.

"No."

"Well, pick it up. You're not gonna believe what this fuckin' bitch did this time."

"What's going on now, Sam?"

"She sold her story to *People* for five thousand dollars. She never fuckin' told me. I just fuckin' found out when I went to the store."

I bought the new *People* after Sam's phone call. Under the section entitled "Crime," the headline read: "Sam Kinison's girlfriend claims that while the comic slept off a hard night, she was being raped by his bodyguard." The full-page story made titillating reading. Unless your last name was Kinison, that is. And unless you were Unway Carter, possibly looking at doing hard time.

The district attorney was livid. He told Sam at their next meeting, "Malika just tried my case in *People* magazine!"

As the rape case moved toward a trial date, Sam and I had several bitter arguments. I was also pissed off at his friends. Almost without exception, they fully agreed that Carter was getting set up, and that Sam and Malika should quietly let this thing drop. But nobody told this to Sam, because everyone was scared to. Sam might see this as betrayal, and then they'd be banished.

"Marriage is tough, it's so fuckin' tough. It's tough to stick together, folks. I respect people that can make it work. I've been through it a few times and . . . I set myself up for it, I know that. I go for the fuckin' women that are just gonna rip my heart out. I'm attracted to heartbreakers—I am. I imagine it's tough to be married in this town especially. Hollywood. Jesus. Because I'll tell you, if you want to meet interesting women, if you want to meet that neurotic ball of psychosis you've been waiting for your whole life, this is the town. Psycho-bitch headquarters of the entire world— Hollywood, California. There's women going around, they're two days away from having a nervous breakdown, and they're just waiting for a new guy to come into their life who they can BLAME IT ON! AH, HA, HA, HA! And there's no better place to do it than right next door, at the Rainbow Bar and Grill. Where the possessed go to mingle! Yeah, where demons go to hang! I know, I should get the good kind of woman. I know that. A woman that will *be* there, be my friend, love me, be partners—but women like that scare me. They're too good. They're scary. Really, seriously. I've seen women who don't cheat, they don't flirt on you, they're lovely, they're wonderful, they're faithful, they're committed, they're right there for you, but they do one sneaky fuckin' little thing. What they do is, they put on like five to seven pounds every year—nothing you notice immediately. Nothing you notice right off, boy. And then about nine or ten years, you realize you're LIVING WITH THEIR MOM! OH, AAAUGHH! OH, YOU TRICKED ME! YOU DIDN'T TELL ME YOU WERE GONNA LOOK LIKE THIS—DEMON! DEMON!"

—Sam in concert at the Roxy

I'd first felt the tenderness in my face the night after Malika's alleged rape. The soreness had set in by morning, but I'd put off calling the doctor. Though the discomfort kept building, I kept avoiding doctors for several more weeks. I figured I'd wake up one morning and it would be gone.

In early August, one side of my face erupted in shingles. It was probably caused by stress, my doctor said.

I told Sam a few days later. By then, about six weeks after Malika's alleged rape, Sam was back in AA. He was keeping himself clean, behaving fairly responsibly. But this wasn't about a few weeks or even months. I was feeling all the years of sibling rage and frustration.

"I'll be your manager," I told him. "But I ain't fuckin' dying for you."

Sam didn't quite understand what shingles was. He seemed to think I was being melodramatic.

"Hey, man," he said, "I'm not asking you to die. You gotta take care of yourself."

"From now on," I kept going, "I'll make you aware of every

situation. I'll tell you what time your shows are, what time we should meet at the airport. If you show up, fine. If you wanna stay straight and take care of business, fantastic. If not, it's *your* problem now."

"Okay," Sam said. "I hear you, man."

And from that period on, Sam fulfilled about 95 percent of his obligations. I thought: Shit. I should have said this before. Why did I wait until I got sick?

Unway Carter's alleged rape case moved through the system quickly. On October 25, just four months after his arrest, his trial resulted in a hung jury. According to what the DA told Sam, it was not a narrow decision by the jury. The case was dismissed, and the district attorney chose not to try it a second time.

Malika seemed relieved to put it behind her, but Sam had a harder time letting it go. To assuage his guilt over not "being there for Malika," he'd become obsessed with Carter's conviction. During his stand-up act, and on shows like Arsenio Hall's, Sam began telling women in his audience: "If you're ever raped or assaulted, pull out a gun and blow them away. Just blow 'em away, man. Because the court system is for criminals."

Privately, Sam and I talked about why that incident happened in the first place: He'd fallen off the wagon and lost control of events.

"I gotta stay straight," Sam would say. "I can't live with this shit anymore."

A New Direction

"The last time I went on this show, the censor went away with a nub for a finger. 'Oh! OH! AAAAUGH! THAT KIN-ISON!' Yeah, folks, the censors get a little nervous when I'm on . . . but that's changed now. Because my goal now is to be part of family entertainment. Oh, go ahead, laugh. Scoff if you will. Wait till you see this next bit. What about those Teenage Mutant Ninja Turtles, huh?"
—Sam's first time back on *Late Night with David Letterman* after NBC censored him for extolling the virtues of sex while on amyl nitrate.

Sam was obviously playing with Letterman's crowd, but he did have a real desire to alter his image. Sam's rebellion had started when he was a child. Like anything else done too long, it was getting old.

He was also feeling anxious about his career. By the fall of 1990, it was declining for several reasons:

The cumulative effect of bad publicity, beginning with *Atuk* and culminating in Malika's alleged rape.

His own addictive nature. Had Sam not partied so hard, had

all these incidents not kept piling up, the media might still be talking about his comedy.

The natural order of show business. Artists get hot, artists cool off, the media moves onto the next "sensation." Nobody dominates show business forever. There's too much talent out there.

Underexposure in sitcoms and movies after *Atuk;* overexposure on the stand-up comedy circuit. In order to rebuild the demand for their concerts, most comics will take time off from the road. Sam couldn't do that because of his heavy debts. Since becoming a star in 1985, he'd been touring for four straight years. We hit every major market once a year, and some markets twice. There was bound to be some drop-off by 1990.

From my standpoint as his manager, there was one other factor in Sam's popularity dip. We talked about it the first time that November, after Sam returned home from a concert swing through the Northeast. He'd just grossed about $10,000 a night, compared to the $50,000 he averaged during his peak. This meant he was playing to crowds of about a thousand, rather than five times that size.

Sam felt humbled when he came back to L.A. "I want to get back in the mainstream," he told me.

"Then you have to make some changes," I said.

"What kind of changes?"

"Well, you're thirty-seven years old, and you're jamming onstage with Slash. You used to be a comedian. Now you dress like a pirate—people think you're a rocker."

Along with a dangling earring, and flashy fuck-you rings on every finger, Sam had taken to wearing bandannas around his head.

"You gotta lose that look, Sam," I said. "You have to get rid of the band, and the Comedy Outlaws. I know they're your friends, but your fans don't pay to see four other comics before you. They don't pay to see you play music. People come to hear you do stand-up. Stand-up is what made you. I think you should go back to it. Or else you'll have tours like you just did. You'll be playing rock-and-roll clubs the rest of your life."

"I can't get rid of everyone," Sam said.

"I know. I don't mean Carl. But just keep it you and him. It'll be like the old days."

While Sam was considering this, I got a phone call one month later from Bernie Brillstein. Back when *Saturday Night Live* was in its prime, Brillstein had managed John Belushi and Lorne Michaels. Still a major industry player in 1990, Brillstein was now a top producer as well as manager. This way, he could use his own clients to package TV shows, while inserting him and his partners as producers. At one time or another, his clients included Dana Carvey, Dennis Miller, and Garry Shandling.

"You look great," Brillstein told Sam when we stepped into his office. Brillstein wasn't feeding him Hollywood bullshit. Sam really did look terrific. At my suggestion, he'd just dismissed the band and all the comics but Carl. Without his big entourage, it was easier for Sam to avoid liquor and blow. That's why Brillstein had called us in the first place. He already knew all this from the Hollywood gossip machine.

Brillstein wanted to discuss a weekly series.

"I'm ready for a series," Sam replied. "I want a normal life. I'm looking at forty years old in a couple years. I don't want to be onstage jamming with Slash."

Brillstein and his associates pitched a sitcom idea. Sam would play the mischievous inner voice, the pleasure-seeking id, of a middle-aged executive. The rest of the cast could not see Sam, only this executive and all the viewers. Through special effects, Sam would appear on TV looking twelve inches tall.

It was hard to have any strong feelings at this early stage, but for two reasons we were enthusiastic. On a weekly series, Sam could entertain millions of people without leaving Los Angeles, at a time in his life when the road was becoming a drag. He could prove he could behave professionally, so Hollywood would let him back into the movies.

Using Sam's name as the lure, we gave Brillstein permission to shop around for a deal.

After his performance in Reno on New Year's Eve, Sam and our mom flew back to L.A. in the morning. They called me that afternoon from his new West Hollywood apartment, just a block or so north of Sunset. Although he still owned the house in Malibu, Sam no longer rented the house in Nichols Canyon. Wanting to put its bad memories behind him, he'd left it shortly after Malika's alleged rape.

Even on the telephone, Sam was normally loud. Now his voice sounded small and thin. I asked him if anything was wrong.

"I don't know," Sam said. "I feel real bad in my chest."

"Don't take any chances, Sam. Have Mom drive you straight to Cedar Sinai. I'll meet you there."

One hour later, I found Sam hooked up to a heart monitor in the ER ward.

"How you doing?" I asked.

"Well, I was just trying to decide whether or not I should get back in the ministry."

"You feel that bad huh?"

Sam let out a deep breath. "I been laying here praying, telling God I'll do whatever he wants me to do. If he wants me back in the ministry . . . "

Sam wasn't dying. The ER doctors, in fact, found nothing wrong with his heart, so they sent him to see a cardiologist. Arrhythmia was detected. Sam was put under a doctor's care and prescribed medication.

Although worried enough to stay on his medication, Sam ignored his doctor's warning to change his eating habits. He kept eating burgers and steaks, heavy sauces and greasy fast foods. After concerts, in hotel rooms on the road, Sam kept smoking joints and watching movies, and then ordering room service up at three in the morning. Sam often talked about changing his diet, but he never really got on it.

In the first few months of 1991, in his hope to become a part of "family entertainment," Sam devoted less time onstage to sex, gays, and drugs. In search of new subjects, he turned his dark wit on the Gulf War.

"I tried to feel bad for the Kurds. But I couldn't. The Kurds are the dumbest people on earth. They are, they're fuckin' idiots. I've never seen two million idiots together, in one place. Usually they're spread out, one to a village. I *wanted* to have some compassion for the Kurds. And then I read that eight of them died by being hit in the head . . . by relief boxes dropped from our planes. I'm not making this up. How dumb are you to stand there under the box and say, 'I don't know. Could be sammiches, could be medical supplies—*bam!*' Eight of them dead. From getting hit in the head by a fuckin' sandwich. And is it me, or do these people look a little familiar? Because I coulda sworn WE JUST HAD A WAR WITH THESE ASSHOLES! Goddam, I cannot believe the gall of these countries we have war with. A week later they come back: 'Hey, can you help us out? Our cities are all fucked up. Our economy's shit, the people are out of work.' Yeah, yeah, that was basically our *plan.* That was our military *objective.* THAT'S WHY THEY CALL IT A WAR! See, we wouldn't have had to do that. If you pulled your troops out of Kuwait, instead of setting those seven hundred oil wells on fire, and dumping oil in the ocean and killing all those fish! SO BREATHE YOUR BLACK AIR, EAT YOUR POISON FISH, FUCK YOU, AND KISS MY AMERICAN ASS!

"Yeah, let's help the Kurds. You see those commercials? Kiss my ass. Help the American farmer. Help Willie Nelson. Seventeen million dollars in back taxes? Oh, man—poor Willie. See, he thought he owed *Texas.* That's why he threw that party every

year, that July Fourth party for free. He's like, 'COME ON
DOWN! WOO! IT'S WILLIE'S FREE PARTY! EVERYTHING'S
FREE! COME ON DOWN TO WILLIE'S FREE TEXAS FOURTH
OF JULY PARTY! COME ON DOWN! WOO-HOO!' Then the
government said, 'No, you don't owe Texas. You owe taxes.'
'What? What are you talking about? I thought I owed Texas.'
'No, you owe taxes, Willie. Seventeen million.' 'Oh *fuck,* man.
I threw that party every year for free!' Yeah, man, he doesn't
even sing the same way anymore. He's a bitter fuckin' guy now.
Yeah, help Willie before you help the Kurds. They're from Iraq,
let's not forget that.

"It wasn't even a war! It was like an *impression* of a war for
us. You don't fuck with us. We have the SMART bomb. You do
not fuck with the SMART bomb. It's the most highly technically
advanced radar missile in history—and we have it. Then again,
the American sense of humor . . . because we're a riot in a war,
folks. We're very funny. We're a real crackup. Those guys in the
Defense Department are going: 'You know what might be funny?
If we put a video camera right on the top of it.' Come on, you
know those American generals were getting drunk at night, going: 'REWIND IT! REWIND IT! Stop, this is my favorite part!
FREEZE FRAME, FREEZE FRAME!'

"Of course, we had to face *their* doomsday machine. We had
to face their weapon of death . . . the SCUD missile. If K-Mart
was a weapons dealer, the SCUD missile would be their blue-
light special. It's *kind* of like the smart bomb. You fire it out of
the trunk of your car, then you go home and watch CNN to see
where it landed. I love that threat, too: 'The fourth-largest army
in the world.' Oh, OH, AAAAUGGH—NOT NUMBER FOUR!
How scary are you if you're fuckin' number four? Not to mention
that, if two of these guys had outfits that matched, *maybe* I
woulda been a little more afraid. This was the shittiest-dressed
army I've ever seen. Terrible outfits. I saw one guy supposed to
be an Iraqi soldier . . . he had Bermuda shorts on, one shoe, and

a T-shirt that said 'I just wanna eat.' These guys were *waiting* to surrender. I swear to God, they kissed the feet of our soldiers. One guy brought in two thousand soldiers, all he had was a video camera. The military said, 'What'd you use, some kind of bazooka, some kind of missile launcher?' The guy said, 'Nah. All I had was this Quasar camcorder. I ran into two thousand Iraqi soldiers. I said, Come on, guys, LET'S GO! DON'T MAKE ME RECORD! DON'T MAKE ME DO IT! You in the back, knock it off—I'VE GOT ZOOM, I'VE GOT ZOOM!

"Come on, the ground war was over in one hundred hours. I've had parties that went on longer that that. It's kind of embarrassing, actually. I've had parties that went on longer than World War III. Guys will be meeting each other five years from now, going: 'Hey, were you in World War III?' 'NO, BUT I WAS AT ONE OF KINISON'S PARTIES ONCE! WENT ON FOR SIX FUCKIN' DAYS! I'M LUCKY TO BE ALIVE! DO I STILL HAVE MY NOSE?' I have my own theory why the war only lasted a hundred hours. I think our guys got over there and said: 'Hey, what do you say we end this war and go home before Bob Hope comes back with another shitty fuckin' show of loser, has-been celebrities—let's go! Hey, I love Bob Hope. He's a great man, a wonderful American—but he's ninety. How funny can the fuckin' guy be? He's ninety years old. He's got a thing on his wrist that goes, 'HELP! I'VE FALLEN AND I CAN'T GET UP! JESUS CHRIST, I BROKE MY SPINE! MY LEGS ARE LIKE PRETZELS—I'M NINETY!' The guy's up there wearing Depends! This is who we send! To entertain our guys who are fighting for freedom! What ever happened to Playgirl of the Month? What happened to Marilyn Monroe? The guys are going: 'We got fucked in this war! There's Bob Hope—he's farting onstage! We got *fucked*!' They did, man. Bob Hope's gotta go out with a fuckin' walker, he can't read the cue cards, they gotta skywrite his jokes with an F-14, and he's wearing *Depends!* The fuckin' headliner's wearing *Depends!* He's got a load of shit in his pants, singing

'Thanks for the Memories,' and we want to know why the war lasted one hundred hours!"

There was more to Sam's bit about Hope than Sam's fans were aware of. Feeling patriotic that winter, and truly believing Saddam needed his ass kicked, *Sam* wanted to entertain our troops. But without any explanation, the State Department said no.

Early that spring, Sam felt another tremor inside his heart. This time, it was emotional.

The trouble began in New Jersey, on a rare day off between concerts on the East Coast. Malika and Sabrina were traveling with us. Malika asked Sam if Sabrina could borrow some money. He wanted to know what it was for. Sabrina had gotten pregnant, Malika said. She'd already had the abortion, paying for it herself, but she was expecting "her boyfriend" to pay her back. Now the guy wouldn't give her a cent and Sabrina was broke.

Sam went nuts, stomping and screaming, and beating the hell out of furniture in his hotel room. I said to Sam when he settled down: "Malika tells you Sabrina has a boyfriend. You throw a fit. How could Malika *not* know by now?"

But according to Sam, Malika still had no clue he was having sex with Sabrina.

"Sabrina's only nineteen," Sam explained. "Malika just thinks I'm being overprotective."

The rest of that trip was hell, especially in our pressure-chamber-like tour bus. Feeling betrayed, Sam shot an arrow at Sabrina with every comment he made. He owned a tape by the Traveling Wilburys, and he kept replaying one song over and over: "Congratulations for breaking my heart, congratulations, you tore it all apart." Each time he played it, Sam dedicated the song to Sabrina. He did this *in front of Malika*. And yet, astonishingly, we all kept playing the game.

About a week or so later, Sabrina told Sam she loved him. She said she was sorry she'd hurt him. She promised that as soon as we got to L.A., she'd break it off with her other boyfriend. Sam was still crazy about her. He forgave her on the spot, and they resumed sleeping together.

On May 3, after his show in Lake Tahoe, Sam and I went to his hotel room, where he put in a call to Malika back in West Hollywood. Malika said she thought Sabrina was dating that guy again. She hasn't been staying here much, Malika explained.

Sam got that burn in his eyes. "Throw her ass out the next time she comes over!" he ordered Malika.

Oddly enough, Sabrina walked in while Malika was still on the phone.

"Then throw her out now!" Sam demanded.

Malika kicked out her own sister, and Sam lost the third love of his life. He and Sabrina never got back together.

We spent the next few weeks in Tulsa, visiting our mom at her annual preachers' convention. On May 21 we flew to Las Vegas, where Sam had been reembraced since making a serious effort to clean up his life. One night at the Dunes casino, however, I found Sam playing keno and power-drinking free cocktails. Feeling heartsick and sentimental, he couldn't stop talking about Sabrina. Sam said, "She's the one I love. Loved her, man . . . she betrayed me. I taught her everything. I taught her how to cheat!"

"You think Malika knows?" he asked me a few minutes later.

"Yeah, Sam. I've thought that for a long time."

"I don't think so. I think we fooled her."

"Sam, you'd go out for a video and come back three hours later."

"I'm telling you, man, she doesn't know. . . . I can't believe I lost fuckin' Sabrina."

"Sam, listen to me. If you really think Malika doesn't know? Then tell her yourself. Tell her right away."

"How come?"

"Because somewhere along the road, now that you and Sabrina are broken up, Sabrina *will* tell Malika. Or else someone else will. You told just about everybody you know! You told Robin Quivers, for godsake." Robin was Howard Stern's sidekick.

"If it comes down to you or Sabrina," I said, "whoever tells Malika first will look like the good guy. Whoever holds out will be the shit."

"Man, you know how violent she is."

Who could forget? In a nasty recent fight in Pennsylvania, Sam and Malika had blackened each other's eyes. Until I calmed everyone down, Malika had threatened to have Sam arrested.

"You still gotta tell her," I persisted. "You think she's violent now? If she finds out you slept with her sister for almost two years? And she hears it first from Sabrina?"

Already loaded, Sam said, "Okay, I'll tell her. But I'm getting drunk first."

Before he told Malika, I advised Sam to remove all the knives from their fancy suite at the Dunes. "Get rid of *every* sharp object," I said. "Everything she can hurt you with. Then sit down and tell her and let her do what she wants."

Sam kept drinking and playing keno and drinking. It was almost 5:00 A.M by the time he called Malika. Rather than tell her upstairs, screw around with all the sharp objects, he had Malika meet him in the hotel bar. Sam gave her the news down there.

Later, that afternoon, I saw Malika. She said, "Bill, do you know how much courage that took for Sam to tell me?"

As I had predicted, Malika was less tolerant toward Sabrina. She called Sabrina that night at their mother's L.A. apartment. First, Malika called her a younger sister a whore. Then she threatened to "beat your ass whenever I see you!" After Malika slammed down the phone, her mother called her right back. Berating Malika for turning on her own sister, her mother blamed Sam for the whole sordid affair. When that conversation ended,

Sam called his accountants. He told them to cut off Malika's mother and brother. Up until then, Sam had been supporting them too.

In the weeks after that crazy day:

Sam stopped drinking again.

Sabrina stopped coming by the apartment.

Malika and Sabrina stopped talking completely.

Sam's accounting firm stopped sending checks to Malika's mother and brother.

Sam remained obsessed by Sabrina. One moment he couldn't live without her. The next moment he hated her. Then he loved her *and* he hated her.

Beginning that summer, Sam started telling me and a few close friends, "I might marry Malika after all. Wouldn't *that* piss Sabrina off?"

On August 2, Sam had his most exciting day of the summer: *The Howard Stern Show* in the morning, *The Joan Rivers Show* early that afternoon, *Late Night with David Letterman* at 5:00 P.M.

And the evening before, he went out and got blasted. It was the old Sam all over again, the Sam who always failed as flamboyantly as he triumphed.

After carousing around New York with Carl LaBove and Majid Khoury, an on-again, off-again friend, Sam showed up still drunk at *The Howard Stern Show*. When one of Howard's staff popped some champagne, Sam started hitting that too.

"How are you gonna get sober in time for Joan Rivers?" Howard asked Sam on the air. "Tell everyone the plan."

"How do you know I'm drunk?" Sam said, blowing smoke. "People expect a certain behavioral pattern out of me, and I'm only trying to supply them with what they think the image of me is."

Robin Quivers said she had just received a fax from one of

their listeners. This guy said *he* felt drunk from hearing Sam.

Sam said, "Who said that, who said that? Bob Goldthwait?"

At 11:00 A.M., I got a call in my room at the Plaza Hotel. Joan Rivers had dispatched a limo to pick up Sam, her only scheduled guest on her hour-long program. Joan taped her shows every Friday for broadcast the following Wednesday.

"I'm here to get Sam," one of Joan's employees told me. She said she was standing downstairs in the Plaza lobby. I said, "Sam isn't ready, and anyway you're early. We don't tape until two."

"No, we tape at noon. We need him at noon."

"What are you talking about? We were told two o'clock."

"I don't know how that happened, because it's at noon. Is he there?"

I told her no, but to call me back every ten minutes or so. "Sam should be here soon. He's probably still schmoozing with Howard after their show."

Sam, although I didn't know it yet, was actually having more drinks at a restaurant on Fifth Avenue. He banged on my door about thirty minutes later. We argued about the mixup over the times, then I asked him how long he'd need to get ready for Joan.

"Gimme thirty minutes," he said. "That's all I need."

The woman called me again. To give Sam a cushion, I told her we'd be downstairs in forty-five minutes. When I went to his suite ten minutes later, I found Sam lying half-asleep on his bed. Malika and two of her girlfriends were doing their best, but he kept saying he wanted another five minutes. Carl and Majid came in next, but they were as drunk as Sam. The woman downstairs kept calling my mobile phone. I kept stalling and making excuses. Sam kept ignoring me when I told him to jump in the shower.

"Come on, man," I said, getting more and more irritated with him. "Get in there. Clean up. Let's go."

"I'll go when I'm ready," Sam slurred.

"Bullshit. Get your fat ass off the bed."

"That's it!" Sam exploded. *"Get outta my fuckin' room!"*

"No! I'm not!"

"I said, get out!"

"I'll tell you what, Mr. Big Fuckin' Ass Star, why don't you throw me out?"

Actually, I wasn't feeling all that violent. I just wanted to goad him out of the bed.

"I will throw you out," Sam said, still reclining.

"Come on! I'm half your size! Try throwing me out!"

"All right, motherfucker, I will!"

Now my anger was real. *"What* did you call me?"

Sam scrambled off the bed, ready to fight. I took three quick steps toward him and drew back my right fist. Majid tackled Sam and Carl grabbed me. Sam escaped Majid's grasp and ran into the bathroom. I heard the shower running, but Sam had been pulling that trick since he was a kid.

"I know where you are, Sam!" I yelled. "You're lying down on the floor blocking the door."

I kept hollering into the door, but Sam wouldn't answer. From her head of public relations to her producer, Joan Rivers's staff kept calling me every ten minutes. Then Joan started calling herself around 1:00 P.M.

"Hey," she said stiffly. "I've done stand-up for an hour here in the studio. We have three-hundred people waiting, and I still have a show to tape. Where the hell is he at?"

Another hour came and went. Joan called me a fifth time at 2:00 P.M. Sam had fallen asleep by then on the bathroom floor. We could all hear him snoring.

"He's not coming in, Joan," I said. "It's not going to happen."

After she finished cursing, Joan said, "He *better* not do *Letterman*! If he doesn't do my show, he doesn't do *Letterman*."

"I don't think you have to worry," I said. "I don't think Sam'll be doing anyone's shows today."

I went downstairs into Trump Plaza. My head was spinning; I

needed some food. Eating lunch mellowed me out, and I started feeling bad about what had happened. For a moment there, I'd really wanted to kick the shit out of Sam. He must have been serious too. It was the closest we'd ever come to actually throwing punches.

While paying my bill, I spotted Joan Rivers marching into the lobby! An entire camera crew was trailing behind her. With or without Sam, she still had a show to tape for the following Wednesday. So she was devoting it now to why Sam had stiffed her.

I hustled up to my room without Joan seeing me. Carl was sleeping in there, so I spoke to Majid. "Don't answer my door," I told him. "Don't pick up the phone. Joan Rivers is here looking for Sam. I think she's trying to nail him."

I ran over to Sam's room. He was awake but still drowsy and tipsy. It was like a Three Stooges routine: While I was smuggling Sam to a room on another floor, Joan was knocking on the door of the room we'd just fled. Joan tried my room next, and Majid answered the door despite what I'd told him. Majid, still drunk, came out of my room wearing no shoes. He sat on the corridor floor with his back against the wall.

Joan Rivers *loved* it. She even knelt down beside him.

"So what was the problem with Sam?" Joan asked Majid.

"I think it was bad Chinese food," he said.

"Do you need a doctor?" Joan asked, meaning a doctor for Sam.

"No, I feel all right," Majid said.

This became part of the story too: Kinison cancels on Rivers because of bad Chinese food.

Later that afternoon, Sam also missed the Letterman show. When he woke up the next day and realized what he'd done, he needed a scapegoat. So Sam called Howard Stern at his house on Long Island.

"You better get me outta this fuckin' mess," he screamed at

Howard. "If it wasn't for that champagne, man . . . if it wasn't for *you!*"

Howard told Sam to calm down. He'd call up Joan himself, during his show, and she and Sam could make up then.

On the Stern show Tuesday morning, Sam and Joan argued for several minutes. But then they professed their mutual love. The next afternoon, her embarrassing show on Sam was broadcast nationally. In addition to running her tape from the Plaza Hotel, Joan interviewed several staff members about what it was like to wait around for Sam Kinison all day. Joan also brought on a psychologist, who gravely dissected "Sam Kinison's drinking problem." But Sam wasn't the only embarrassed Kinison. When Majid came out of my hotel room—drunk, wearing no shoes, and blaming Sam's absence on bad Chinese food—the graphic on the screen read: "Bill Kinison, Sam Kinison's older brother and manager."

"Jesus Christ!" I said. "Everyone thinks that's me!"

It was not a production mistake. It was Joan's way of getting some payback on me too. Because Joan knew exactly who I was and what I looked like. We'd met just a few months before, in Las Vegas.

Joan wasn't content to bury Sam once. Her office also issued a press release on his no-show. Then Joan started swiping at Sam during interviews with the press. Soon the tabloid TV shows were gleefully taking their shots. It wasn't enough for them to report that Sam missed Joan's show. They actually ran old clips from Malika's alleged rape trial.

I was irked at Sam too for blowing off Joan. The day it happened, we nearly got in a fistfight. But I never dreamt Joan would do such a number on him. She and Sam had always been very friendly. Now she seemed intent on driving him out of the business.

Although he did it in private, Arsenio Hall backed up Sam. An old buddy of ours from the Comedy Store, Arsenio called me himself during Joan's vendetta.

"Hey, man, don't take no shit off this bitch," Arsenio said. "She did the same thing to me. Canceled out on my show because she had 'Vegas throat.' What the fuck is that? How come she can do it to other people, but when it happens to her she goes crazy?"

Later that week the network ratings came out. Joan's hatchet job on Sam was the highest-rating show she'd ever had. Shrewdly, Joan invited Sam back. Graciously, he accepted. But that didn't mean he forgot.

"Hello, Houston. My God, he showed up! Not like *The Joan Rivers Show*. He actually showed up. Okay, I did fuck up recently in show business—let's get this out of the way, because I know you might be a little curious. I mean, I didn't think it was that big of a fucking deal. There's bigger news stories happening, you know. There's a guy in Milwaukee with heads in his icebox, but our top story is 'Sam Kinison Missed *The Joan Rivers Show*.' It's not like I'm the only guy who's fucked up in show business lately. There's a couple guys out there that I think have outdone me a little *bit*. Like Rick fuckin' James, for starters. I missed a show! I didn't torture a woman with a fuckin' base pipe. I'm not out on five hundred thousand dollars bail, all right? I'm not Axl Rose, who has a warrant out for his arrest in the state of Missouri for inciting a riot, three hundred thousand dollars' worth of damage, sixty people injured—I missed a show! These guys make me look like fuckin' Pat Sajak. I missed a show! I missed a show that has six fuckin' viewers, okay? Come on, who watches the fuckin' *Joan Rivers Show?* Bedridden people and housewives. Yeah, that's my audience. That's my demographics. And I was at a show the other night, and somebody yelled out, 'Fuck Joan Rivers!' And I was going, 'Well . . . I would.' I know me, I know me! I would, I'd do her. Come on, guys, some of us have done worse. If I was at her house, we were alone, we were drunk, we had some Stolly, the pictures of Edgar were turned face-down—yeah, I'd do her right *there*!

"Come on, I'm not the only guy who's messed up in show business lately. It's not like I'm Pee-wee Herman, who has to live with his mistake the rest of his life. Here's a man who had it made. Here's a man with a children's show—*Pee-wee's Playhouse.* Here's a man that parents all over America thought they could trust. 'We can trust him with our children, dear. That's Pee-wee.' Yeah, it was the Pee-wee they *thought* they knew. In real life, he was in an adult theater, going: 'Nurse Nancy, ohhhh. Nurse Nancy, oh yeah. Make my Pee-wee hard, willya, baby?' Nasty fuckin' little guy in a plaid suit and a red bow tie. I think he should get the sternest punishment they can dish out. Execution. Execute Pee-wee. Make an example out of him for other people that are involved with children's programming. EXECUTION! HANG HIM! HANG HIM! Make an example out of his ass.

"Hey, there's been other people in children's programming. Look at Captain Kangaroo. This man had to be Captain Kangaroo for thirty fucking *years*! No scandal, no controversy—drank a lot. You would, too. Fuck, man, I don't think the guy knew the show was gonna go on for *thirty* fuckin' years. He looked like a *heavy* fuckin' drinker. He's at home, going, 'I thought the gig would last two or three years. I was an actor. Jesus Christ, I was in the Actor's Studio. I wanted to do *Death of a Salesman.* I wanted to play Willie. My God, I'm CAPTAIN KANGAROO!' But he kept it together! Sure, he was fuckin' discouraged all the time. Never saw him excited. He was like, 'Good morning, boys and girls. Hey, let's take the Walk of Death and go over here and talk to Mister Grandfather Clock. Hold up, hold up, here's Mister Bunny. How does it feel to have a hand up your ass, you little fuck?' He was *very* depressed, but he never fuckin' snapped—he held it together! Mister Greenjeans took his own fuckin' life. Couldn't handle it. Woke up one day and said, 'My God, I'm sixty-three . . . AND I'M MISTER GREENJEANS!' He's dead. Greenjeans is dead. He snapped. He snapped like a rubber band. Kangaroo kept it together. He's retired now . . . he can have a *normal* haircut. Remember that fuckin' haircut they made him wear? The guy was fifty-nine, and he looked like a mongoloid. That bowl on his head? That fuckin' cut, man? Lamb chops? He looked like an *ass*. He did! His wife probably gave him shit: 'I married a loser! Look at you. God, you told me you were an actor. You're Captain Kangaroo! People *laugh* at us when we go out.' 'I can't help it, you fuckin bitch. I'm under a contract. I DIDN'T KNOW THIS SHOW WOULD LAST THIRTY YEARS! CBS STANDS FOR COCK-SUCKING BASTARD SONSABITCHES! I'M IN HELL! OH! AAAAUGH!'

"He handled it, though. He didn't snap. No controversy. He wasn't in a fuckin' adult theater, going, 'Nurse Nancy.' HE DIDN'T DO THAT! He loved the kids so much! Kangaroo kept it together, he didn't fuck up. *I* can fuck up. People *expect* that from me—I'm not on a lunch box. There *are* no Sammy dolls. I'm family entertainment on another level. My fans would have been disappointed if I *woulda* showed up at *The Joan Rivers Show*."

—Sam in concert in Houston, a few weeks after missing
The Joan Rivers Show

In private, Sam wasn't so cavalier about his highly publicized relapse. As usual, there were industry repercussions.

Along with Tim Matheson, Sam was planning to star in *Charlie*

Hoover, the sitcom we'd been pitched by Bernie Brillstein. All the contracts were signed and the players were set. Brillstein-Grey would coproduce with New World Productions, which was putting up the front money. Taping would start in September. The series would air on Fox TV, probably later that fall as a midseason replacement.

Except Fox also carried *The Joan Rivers Show.* And now everyone wanted to know, from Brillstein to New World to Fox: Is our star a loose cannon, or was this an aberration?

A meeting was set in L.A. for Sam to prove he was healthy. It was planned for a Monday, the day after his concert in Cincinnati. But before Sam's show that Sunday night, his ex-wife Gail showed up with her husband. Gail and Sam had once sung in a church choir together. Now she wanted his help on a song she was recording. After his concert, Sam spent all Sunday night in a recording studio with Gail and her husband. On Monday morning, with our meeting that afternoon, I couldn't locate him.

I called Brillstein's people. I gave them some bullshit story about rotten Midwestern weather and half-canceled plane flights with only so many seats. Since I didn't think Sam was partying— Gail and her husband were straight—I suggested we move back the meeting only one day. Brillstein's people agreed, but I still couldn't find Sam by Tuesday morning.

I called Brillstein's office again and fed them another line. I said, Everyone's pissed at Sam, and now he's got a newtork TV show at risk. This is too important a meeting. We can't attend it without Elliot Roberts. (Elliot worked at a management firm we were thinking of teaming up with.) Unfortunately, I said, Elliot unexpectedly had left town.

Brillstein's people passed the word back to him. In a conference call that afternoon, Bernie Brillstein lost his famous temper.

He told me, "Look, everyone in the world has been fighting for Sam Kinison. Now, when we're treated like stupid *fuckheads,* which is the way we're being treated, we really . . . stop . . .

fighting. Because it ain't worth it after a while. And I have to know if you guys want *in,* or if you want fuckin' out. If you want out, it's easy. It's one phone call. But this bullshit—I'm not gonna live with it for six months. Life is too fuckin' hard. And New World has too much *goddam* money invested in this. We'll get someone else. Show business *will* go on, believe it or not. So I gotta know where you guys stand. This is *bullshit!*"

I blew off some steam of my own, telling Bernie he *had* no show without Sam. Sam's character, "Hugh," was supposed to be the bad boy inside Tim Matheson. "Sam *is* Hugh," I told Bernie. "Fox won't settle for anything less."

When he asked me again if we were still in, I told him yes. "Today's meeting wasn't Sam's fault," I added. "I screwed up this one."

Brillstein had heard that one. He might have used it himself when he managed Belushi.

His associate Mark Gurvitz jumped in. He had a large stake in this too, since he and his brother were slotted to be the producers. Gurvitz mentioned to Brillstein what I'd told Gurvitz that morning: I felt Elliot Roberts needed to be there, but Elliot had just left town.

Brillstein's reply was vintage Hollywood. He said, "Who gives a shit about Elliot Roberts? I *love* Elliot Roberts, but who the fuck needs him? He invented show business now, too?"

We bickered again and hung up. Gurvitz called back within the hour, playing good cop to Brillstein's hard guy. While I was still talking with Gurvitz, Sam finally called in on my other line. Stone sober, and still back in Ohio, he'd just gotten a phone call from a friend. According to this friend, who was watching CNN's entertainment report, Sam was about to be fired from *Charlie Hoover.* Sam felt certain that "our team" planted the item, meaning Brillstein's office or New World's.

I told Sam to simmer off. If what he'd heard was even accurate, it only meant CNN had the story wrong. "I've got Gurvitz on the line now," I said. "The deal isn't dead. Where the hell have you been?"

"I was still helping Gail. I'm sorry I didn't call you. You know I hate fuckin' meetings. And now I'm glad I didn't go! Obviously, they've released *some* kind of statement to try and make me look bad. Our own guys! If that's the way they want to play, there will *be* no fucking meeting. The next meeting will be with my attorney. Call me right back, I'm getting ready to leave."

I came back to Gurvitz, but never told him I'd just spoken to Sam. Thanks largely to Eric Tannenbaum at New World, everybody chilled out and another meeting was set for the week coming up. Sam showed up sober, rested and friendly, if not quite contrite. Walking into the conference room at New World, his opening line was: "You guys got Chinese food here?"

That dissolved the tension. Sam was very much "on" the rest of the meeting. *Charlie Hoover* was salvaged.

> "I want to show people that there's a side of myself other than just the outrageous comedian. I hope this shows that I can do family entertainment, that my comedy doesn't just depend on vulgarity. I'm just glad I made the transition from when I could have overdosed or when I could have fallen asleep at the wheel and run off a cliff or something. It's good to have survived those years. I'm just happy to be here. I'm just happy to have the chance."
> —Sam in the *Los Angeles Times* in a preview of
> *Charlie Hoover*

One morning that September, I picked up the phone at my house around eight-fifteen.

"It's me," Sam said, sounding sloshed. "I'm too out of it, dude. I'm not going in to work."

I nearly spilled my coffee. It was only his first week of taping *Charlie Hoover.*

Sam said, "Bill, I'm bullshitting you! I'm in my car, on my way there now. I'm straight as an arrow. I'm excited about this thing."

It became a running gag, Sam calling me from his car phone as if he was drunk, but actually his attitude was great. Sam showed up every morning. He showed up straight. He put in the long hours of weekly television. He really enjoyed his costar Tim Matheson. Even as the producers refused his funny suggestions, even as writers kept leaving the show and scripts got progressively worse, Sam was still a team player. His reputation was finally starting to turn. Sam knew this wasn't the time for the angry-young-man thing.

When the show aired in November, he felt embarrassed by it. Still doing concerts on weekends, he was concerned his fans might think he'd sold out. So Sam started joking onstage about his own sitcom.

"You gotta believe me, folks. They lied to me to get me to do this show. They said, 'Sam, how would you like to play the twelve-inch guy?' I'm going, 'Yeah! Yeah! Sam Kinsion, the twelve-inch guy! What a crazy fuckin' network you Fox guys are. First it was *Married—with Children,* then *In Living Color,* now it's Sam Kinison, the twelve-inch guy!' I could see the merchandise. The twelve-inch guy! I had visions, man. Women at the airport, going, 'That's him, that's him! He's got the twelve inches!' I got down to Fox and they went: 'No, we want you twelve inches *high.* You'll be about the size of a Ken doll. Your dick will be like the eraser on a Number 2 pencil.' I said, 'Great. That's just the fuckin' image I had for myself. Thanks, guys!'"

Sam had another reason for keeping his sense of humor about the show. With it fated for cancellation, we were already talking to Fox about Sam's own variety show. If it all came together, *The Sam Kinison Family Entertainment Hour* would be patterned after the old *Jackie Gleason Show.* In a nod to *The Honeymooners,* there'd also be one skit a week in which Sam spoofed Ralph

Kramden, with Richard Belzer and Sandra Bernhard playing Ed Norton and Alice. Sandra still looked iffy, but Belzer wanted in. The executives at Fox were serious about it. Sam and I were too. Only *Charlie Hoover* stood in the way, since Sam was exclusive to it.

That Christmas Eve should have been upbeat. It was Sam's favorite holiday. Our mother was flying in from Tulsa. With his career back on track, his haywire life-style mostly behind him, Sam wasn't so mad at himself anymore.

Unfortunately, he still lived with a heavy drinker.

When our mother entered their Sunset Plaza apartment that afternoon, she found Malika already tanked, an embarrassed Sam scrubbing a filthy kitchen, and a Christmas tree without any decoration. Sam promised they'd buy all the trimmings and dress up the tree later on. When they returned from the store early that evening, his telephone rang.

It was Marvin Mitchelson calling.

On Christmas Eve.

He told Sam he was "returning Malika's call."

With Sam and our mom standing right there, Malika told Mitchelson: Everything is worked out now. I don't need to talk to you anymore. Thank you very much.

"What the fuck's going on?" Sam said when Malika hung up.

Malika said she'd called Mitchelson "for a friend." Sam didn't buy it, and he and Malika shouted at one another. Our mom came to Sam's defense, and Sam started crying. He told our mom, "You're the first one who's ever stood up for me with her."

That was probably true. Most people, including me, let Sam and Malika fight their own battles. Those times when I did intervene, I always tried making the peace without taking sides. If I said anything bad about Malika, I knew Sam would come back to me once they'd made up. He'd probably say, "Hey, *pal,* let's talk about what you said."

Later that night, Sam and our mom wanted to stay home and dress up the tree, but Malika kept whining, "I wanna party. It's Christmas Eve." So they all went to Dan Tana's, a restaurant/bar on Sunset. Sam sipped Diet Cokes. Malika had to be carried out to the car. Back at the apartment, Sam and our mom stayed up laughing and crying, reminiscing about Kevin and decking the tree. It was 5:00 A.M. before they slept.

After a three-month run, *Charlie Hoover* was canceled in February. Although pleased—he could now star on Fox in his own variety show—Sam didn't regret his involvement with *Charlie Hoover*. Critics had singled him out as the show's only spark, and the weekly exposure helped kickstart his stand-up career. As he had when he was on top, that winter Sam sold out a few five-thousand-seat venues.

With Hollywood back in his corner, we also had a two-movie deal in the works with New Line Cinema. It called for a concert film first, something along the lines of Eddie Murphy's *Raw*. Then Sam would do a comedy. But rather than seek a starring role, we planned on teaming him up with a proven actor. We figured it this way: Let the other guy bear the brunt of Hollywood's expectations and investment. Then Sam can steal the movie from him.

There was talk about Rick Moranis or Arnold Schwarzenegger. Sam said he'd be happy to work with either.

It was all part of our plan to get Sam off the road, and away from temptation. In the future, we hoped, Sam would only do comedy tours during the summer. Even then, we'd only book ten or twelve dates. The rest of the year, he would just play the major casino resorts: Vegas, Atlantic City, Reno, Lake Tahoe, and Laughlin, Nevada.

Sounds of Silence

I N THE FIRST SEVERAL WEEKS OF 1992, AN ELECTION YEAR, SAM'S act began changing again. It wasn't a radical shift; he just wanted to be more political in the future. It was another way of moving back toward "the mainstream."

During the presidential primaries, Sam began tapping into the doubting mood of the country. "I'm just curious. Is anybody following the Democratic campaign? Bill Clinton. Yeah, now there's a cool fuckin' guy. Why doesn't he just campaign like this?" Sam put his microphone down by his crotch, then pointed it straight out like a hard-on. Grinning and speaking like Clinton, Sam said, " 'You know, in my home state . . . oops, sorry about that, folks. I didn't know that was hanging out there! I want to apologize—I know it's got that *big* old Razorback Arkansas head on it. I hope I didn't scare any of those *young* female voters sitting up in the front there.' Get your *mind* off fucking pussy, Clinton. This guy looks like he's thinking about pussy *all the time.* 'Well, folks, I'd like to be more concerned about America's problems . . . but I'm just thinking about pussy.'

"And Jerry Brown. Yeah, yeah. I love that fuckin' turtleneck, man. What is that turtleneck about? Am I watching a presidential candidate, or an old episode of *I Spy?* What the fuck is that? He's either wearing the turtleneck, or the turtleneck with the plaid shirt. It's like—hey, either you want be a logger, or a president. Pick one, okay? 'I want to be a logger *and* a president.' Well, that's too fuckin' bad. You're taking the Abraham Lincoln thing a little too far here, okay?"

One morning in late February, Sam called me from his hotel suite in La Jolla. In a voice devoid of emotion, he said Malika was pregnant. They were going to have the baby and get married.

I was surprised on two counts. First, that Malika was pregnant. I was pretty sure neither one of them used protection, and in five years of living together they hadn't conceived. Second, that Sam seemed to mean what he said about getting married. He'd been promising it to Malika for almost a year, ever since that morning in Las Vegas when he told her he'd been sleeping with Sabrina. But I never took Sam seriously. I thought it was just a revenge fantasy: Marry one sister to punish the other.

On the other hand, I also knew Malika was constantly hounding him.

She'd always tell him, "I know you won't marry me, I know you aren't gonna marry me."

Sam would reply, "I told you I'd do it, we'll do it. We'll do it in Vegas."

When Malika wasn't around, Sam would tell me and a few close friends, "Even if we split up, she's not gonna just walk away. She's already talked to Marvin Mitchelson. I'm basically stuck with her. If marrying her will make her easier to live with, then that's what I'll do."

In early March, just a few weeks after Sam's phone call from La Jolla, Malika had a miscarriage. The day she found out from her doctor, I happened to be at their apartment.

"Now you're not gonna marry me!" she told Sam.

Sam said, "Everything's staying the same. We're still getting married. In a few months, we can start trying to have a baby again."

I tried comforting Sam as he walked me out to my car. I also said I'd tell Sherry to call up Malika. Before we had our daughter, Ginger, Sherry had once miscarried too.

"I'm okay," Sam said, sounding almost relieved. "I've felt every feeling in life, and this is one more. I don't really want a kid anyway."

This surprised me too. I'd always thought Sam wanted to be a father. It was nothing he ever said to me. It was just something I always felt when I watched Sam with Ginger.

I was struck by a thought that night when I was alone: Maybe Sam *expects* his life to be full of loss. Maybe he's numb to the pain.

In the past four years, Kevin, A.D., and our grandfather all had died. Sam had also lost his love affair with Sabrina. In an unguarded moment with a reporter, he had recently talked about all the hurt in his life. "It seems to be one tragedy followed by another," he said. "Just about the time you think life's perfect, something else comes up that breaks your heart, devastates you. And then you gotta get over that and try to trust again, believe again, and set up for the next tragedy."

Sam started to worry me early that spring. Even without all the booze and drugs, he seemed to believe that *he* wouldn't be around long. Since he was always concerned about his arrhythmia, I suspected that he was afraid of a heart attack. Although Sam never told me this, keeping his fears to himself would be just like him. Sam believed bad thoughts would come true if you said them out loud. It was one of his superstitions since he was a boy.

I thought I saw the first bad sign the last week of March, when we met with a pair of independent producers, who told us Sam's film deal with New Line had just gone through. I was elated for him, and proud of the part I had played. In both the media and in Hollywood, Sam always had people waiting for him to fail. After *Atuk,* his detractors said he could forget about making movies. Working together, Sam and I were starting to silence all the doubters. He not only had a two-movie deal, he had it with New Line, a company known in the business for being first-class. Among its recent hits were *The Player* and *Damage.*

Now New Line wanted Sam, and he didn't seem capable of enjoying it.

"It sounds good," he told the two producers. "If you can work things out with my brother, then we'll do it."

Then Sam walked out of the meeting before it was over. That night, there was no celebration at Spagos. There was no calling all his friends to tell them the news. It was weird, and extremely disturbing.

By the end of March, Sam and Malika had vague plans for a wedding the first week of April. One day that week, Sam asked me to make a doctor's appointment for him after his honeymoon.

Sam said, "I just want to get checked out."

I said, "*You* want to get a physical?"

I'd been fighting with him for years to start having them.

The strangest thing of all happened Friday, April 3. Our mother flew into New Orleans, where Sam gave a concert at Tulane University, and afterward we all went back to the Hyatt. On the elevator ride up to our hotel rooms, our mom looked like she had something to say. There was a long, uncomfortable silence. And then she said it. In a dream she'd just had the other night, her late husband A.D. had told our mom that Sam would not be around long. Better tell Sam, A.D. said, to get his affairs in order.

I waited for Sam to say, "Yeah, yeah, yeah. You had too much to eat that night."

But Sam never flinched. He just looked at her.

When our mom went back to her room, I stopped by Sam's for a while. Our mom had already told him she didn't approve of the wedding. I asked Sam now if he really wanted to do this.

"She's been through a lot, man," he said. "The rape, the thing with Sabrina, now she's lost the kid. She's been through it all with me, man."

"Those are good reasons, Sam—if you love someone. You've never once said that you loved her."

"Why can't you just be happy for me?" Sam said.

"I *will* be happy for you if you tell me you love her. Otherwise, I'm not gonna bullshit you. Why marry someone you don't even love?"

"She's been through a lot," Sam said.

I let it drop. Sam knew how I felt. And it was his life, not mine.

The following evening I flew into Las Vegas. Sam had planned the wedding for after midnight, when April 4 would become April 5. If he had to get married, he wanted it to be on his father's birthday.

Sam was funny that night in his suite at the Vegas Hilton. Smoking pot and drinking champagne, he said he wanted to do this night like a bad tattoo. "I wanna get blitzed, get married, wake up the next morning, and go, 'I did *what*?' "

As the night went on, as more friends filtered in, Sam kept vanishing into the bedroom, where we could all hear him bickering with Malika. People kept asking him, "When are we doing this thing?" At about 1:15 A.M., about fifteen of us started out for the Candlelight Chapel. I rode in the limo with Sam and Malika and her bridesmaid. It wasn't a pleasant ride. Sam and Malika argued all the way to the courthouse, all through the marriage application, then all the way back to the chapel.

"This doesn't feel like a wedding," Malika said, stepping out of our limo, onto the Strip. "It feels more like a funeral," she said.

Up at the altar, Sam seemed sullen and distant. He barely smiled. He rarely looked at Malika. Then, after Sam recited his vows, tears streamed down his face. It was very odd. Sam never blinked as he cried. The water just dripped from his eyes.

Sam dabbed his cheeks and kissed Malika. He turned back to the minister who'd just married them.

Sam said, "God bless you, Brother James."

Their honeymoon was brief. On Monday, they flew from Las Vegas to Honolulu. They got a hotel there that night, then flew to Kona on Tuesday. After staying two full days at the Mauna Kea Beach Hotel, they got back home on a red-eye Friday morning.

When Malika called my house around 8:30 A.M., I was a little surprised to hear they were back. Beginning that Friday night, Sam had three sold-out shows that weekend in Laughlin, Nevada. But I figured that once he got to Kona, Sam might decide to stretch his vacation. At minimum, I wasn't expecting to do the Friday-night show.

Malika's first words floored me.

"We've been married five days," she said. "Is it too soon to get an annulment?"

"What?"

"If it's too soon for that, can we get a divorce?"

I said, "What are you guys doing now?"

She said, "Sam thought I was asleep at our hotel room. He told all his friends that I made him marry me. He told them he didn't want to marry me. I want a divorce."

"Put Sam on."

When he came to the phone, I said, "Sam, what's going on over there?'

"Ah, she's fucked."

"Yeah, well, she says she wants a divorce."

"She's full of shit. She thinks you live together for five years, everything's different once you get married. Well, it's not. It stays the same. Don't worry about her. I'll take care of her."

We talked about our travel plans to Laughlin, a riverfront gambling town just a few miles east of the California border. There were five of us going that weekend: Sam, Malika, myself, Carl, and Majid. I'd booked flights for Sam and Malika into Las Vegas, where a limo would take them the rest of the way into Laughlin.

Sam said, "Nah, man, I want to drive."

Laughlin was almost three hundred miles from L.A., but this wasn't peculiar for Sam. Airplanes still made him nervous. He always preferred to drive when he had the choice.

Sam said he and Malika would meet us in Barstow, about halfway to our gig. They left around noon in his white '89 Trans Am. This was earlier than they had to, but Sam liked taking the long way, through the cool green Angeles Forest. At about 2:00 P.M., I left with Majid and Carl in a rented van. Sam kept in contact by phone, calling three or four times as we all cruised north on Interstate 15. The latest plan was to eat together at Barstow.

"Where you guys at?" Sam asked me the last time he called.

"Five miles from Barstow," I said. "Where you at?"

"About fifteen miles behind you."

"How did you get behind us?"

Sam didn't answer.

I said, "You *ass*. You already ate."

Busted, Sam started laughing. "We stopped in Victorville," he admitted. "You guys go on and eat. We'll probably be there by the time you get through."

We were sitting outside in a strip mall when they pulled up. Watching me polish off my banana split, Sam wanted to know if he had time for one. He did, and while he ate his ice cream I updated him on business. On Tuesday, we had a meeting with New Line to sign the movie contracts. The variety show on Fox was a done deal too. Fox wanted the show to be part of their next fall lineup. To promote it, they were talking about a special airing that May. I'd also closed a nice deal with the Las Vegas Hilton. For the next three years, Sam would be headlining there four weeks a year.

Sam seemed all fired up as he listened to me. I thought: Maybe I've been misreading him. Maybe the flame will come back into his eyes.

After sitting outside for almost one hour, Sam handed me *Double Trouble,* his favorite tape by Steve Ray Vaughan. He said, "Listen to this. It'll take you back to church."

As our caravan started due east on Interstate 40, I popped in Stevie Ray about 4:30 P.M. That four-lane stretch of 40 was nearly deserted. Sam kept speeding past us, then slowing back down, then whizzing by us again. He loved driving fast in the desert, and his special-edition Trans Am was his hottest car. I called him on his phone to see how fast he was going.

"About one-forty," Sam said.

He slowed down a few minutes later and pulled up next to our van. We talked through our open windows. Malika was sleeping and he looked tired too. They'd flown all night on a red-eye.

"You want me to drive?" I asked.

Sam said, "Nah, I'm fine. We're almost there anyway."

"You have a show tonight, though. I don't want you to be tired."

"Yeah, but I only got one show. That ain't nothing for me, bro."

One exit before State Highway 95, where we would turn north toward Laughlin, we pulled off for gas. As we talked about business again, Sam asked me to take Russo with us in our van. A waitress on Sunset had given Russo, a white Lhasa apso, to Sam and Malika when he was a puppy. They took him wherever they went, they seemed to love him, but they never housetrained the little wacko. Out on the road, this dog cost us thousands of dollars in damages. At the Dunes Hotel, Russo once went hog wild on the Cary Grant Suite.

I asked Sam why he wanted us to take the dog. Russo never traveled with *anybody* but them, and we were nearly to Laughlin. Sam said he wanted the dog to have more room. Carl was sleeping in back, and Russo lay down beside him.

Just before getting back into his car, Sam admired my sunglasses. They were Oliver Peoples, tinted blue, about $300.

"These are all I have left," Sam said, pointing to his own rose-tinted pair. "Everyone comes in the house and steals my fuckin' glasses."

"Well, do you want these glasses?" I said.

"Are you going to give them to me?" he said.

"Sure. If you want them, I will."

After we made the switch, he turned to Majid.

"Majid," Sam said, referring to me, "this is the most honest guy I've ever met in my life."

As we turned north on 95, a narrow, twisting highway with one lane in each direction, Sam took the lead with Malika sleeping next to him. Majid sat shotgun near me in the van. Carl and Russo dozed in our backseat. The sun had already set. The afterglow was beautiful. It was about 7:20 P.M.

Only four miles past the gas station, Sam slowed to forty-five miles per hour. An hour or so ago, he'd been going 140.

"We're thirty miles away," I said to Majid. "Why is he going so slow? I wanna get there already."

That's when I first noticed the truck up ahead of us. It pulled into Sam's lane, speeding in his direction, about half a mile away. I figured the truck was passing somebody else. Why else would it be in our lane?

This highway had almost no shoulder. To the side of the shoulder, a steep embankment dropped down into scorched earth and cactus. Sam had no room to pull off.

He slowed to twenty-five, then fifteen miles per hour. I did the same. I was following about fifty feet behind Sam.

I kept expecting the truck to pull back into its lane.

Sam wiggled his car's front end to get the driver's attention. But the truck kept barreling down. Sam braked. He braked again, when suddenly the truck was nearly in front of him.

I yelled, "Watch out for this guy! Sam! Watch out for him, Sam!"

Sam hit his brakes hard and veered right, deciding to take his chances down in the desert. The truck driver swerved left. The car and truck smashed violently, head-on.

I shouted, "Oh my God!"

Majid reached Sam's car first, but he couldn't open the mangled door.

"Move the fuck out of the way!" I yelled at him.

I jerked open Sam's door. Still conscious, he was lying between the two bucket seats, with his head almost in the back. Sam hadn't been wearing his seat belt.

The only blood I could see, at the corner of his lips, made it appear as if Sam had bitten his tongue. On his forehead, he also had three fingernail-like scratches.

My first thought: He's hurt but he'll be okay.

Then I heard Sam speak, and I was frozen with dread.

"Why?" Sam asked. "Why now?"

The exact same words he'd said when I told him that Kevin was dying.

But you're *not* dying, Sam, I silently said.

And I didn't believe he was. Sam's eyes weren't glazed. There was almost no blood.

Sam suddenly tried sitting up. He wanted out of his car.

I told him, "Don't move. Please, Sam, stay where you are. We're gonna get you some help."

He never acknowledged me. He never acknowledged Carl or Majid. He didn't seem to know that any of us were there.

I looked at Malika, who'd been sleeping before the car wreck and still wasn't moving. I ran around to her side and screamed at her to wake up. She didn't, but I felt her pulse at her wrist and it seemed strong. Unconscious but still alive. Both of them were alive.

"There's gas all around the truck," I heard Majid shout.

I saw the teenaged driver fumbling with his front door. I ran to the truck and forced it open. The kid stumbled out wearing no shirt. It was established later that he'd been drinking beer at the river, but he wasn't legally intoxicated.

The kid said to me, "Look at my fucking truck. Look what he did to my fucking truck."

Incredulous, I didn't react for a moment. Then my fists balled up in rage. I screamed at the kid to shut up and sit on the curb.

About two minutes had passed. Sam was still fighting to leave his car.

"You gotta lay still, Sam," I said. "Don't move. We got help on the way."

Sam didn't seem to hear me. He kept moving around, so I told Majid and Carl to help him out of the car. As carefully as they could, they laid him on the ground next to his door. I rushed to my van, but my mobile phone wouldn't get service out in the desert. I began stopping cars and trucks on the highway, telling drivers we needed someone to phone for help.

I ran back to the guys. Carl was holding Sam's head. Majid gripped one of his hands.

Sam said again, "Why now?"

Then he said, "I don't want to die."

But Sam was not fearful. He sounded like he was arguing with someone.

I said, "Sam, you'll be okay."

Sam said more softly, "Why?"

I ran back to my van and tried my mobile again. And then I knew. Sam had stopped breathing.

I yelled, "Carl, has he quit breathing?"

Carl, in shock, put his ear over Sam's chest. Carl said, "Yeah, man, yeah! He's quit breathing!"

Sam's eyes were closed when I returned. I put my mouth over his and performed CPR. I reached inside his mouth and drew out some mucus, but it was still bubbling up from deep inside him.

I screamed, "Does anybody else here know CPR?"

The kid driving the truck told me he did. He gave Sam mouth-to-mouth, but it was no use. As I started pounding Sam's chest, I looked up and saw Malika. She was standing on the other side of Sam's car. She saw me pounding on Sam and became hysterical. A passing motorist sat her down in a lawn chair.

I heard the sirens first. Then I saw the first police car snake through the winding road. The officer knew CPR, but by then Sam's face was covered by phlegm. I turned away, working for breath. I felt my heartbeat increasing. I stomped around in a circle and turned back to Sam. Almost four minutes had passed.

Another police car arrived, and then paramedics. I knelt next to the technician working on Sam.

I asked him, "Are we doing any good?"

He just looked at me. He just looked at me without speaking.

I said, "Okay."

They wouldn't let anyone ride along with Sam, so I rode in the same ambulance with Malika. At Needles Desert Communities Hospital, a woman asked me to fill out some papers.

"Before I fill out anything," I said, "I want to know how my brother is."

My mind knew. But my heart . . .

The woman said someone would talk to me in a moment.

I called Sherry on a pay phone. For the first time in my life I could recall, I began stuttering. Sherry asked me to calm down.

I said, "Well, I am calm, except I can't hardly form words."

Sherry said, "How bad is it?"

I couldn't say it.

I told Sherry, "I think he's in critical condition. I don't know if he'll make it. I'm going to call you right back."

A coroner came out with an executive from the hospital.

One of them said, "Your brother has passed away."

I asked if they knew what had killed him.

Not yet, they said.

They were cleaning him up, they told me. I could see him then if I wanted.

I told them I needed an office with a phone. I called Sherry back and told her. She'd known Sam since we were all kids. She met him before she met me, when she and Sam were both about thirteen. Sherry was inconsolable.

At about 8:30 P.M., I was told I could see Sam. They took me into the room and then left us alone. Sam was lying on a table beneath a white sheet. He had his hair slicked back, the same way he looked when he came out of the shower. I thought, He looks so big under there. I didn't realize he was that big.

I wanted to say things to him. But my words kept going away.

I tried again. I still couldn't speak through the lump in my throat.

Whenever we hugged, Sam loved to kiss me on the cheek.

"Man, don't do that," I used to tell him. Sam was the brother who always showed his emotions.

I leaned over him and kissed his cheek. *I love you,* I silently said.

"We want you to tell her," the coroner said, coming into the office where I was making phone calls. In the X-ray room, Malika was screaming. She wanted to know if Sam was dead.

"You want me to tell her?" I said.

They both nodded their heads.

I said, "Oh, man!"

Malika saw me and knew. She was lying on a table under a sheet. She jumped up and attacked me. I tried wrapping her up, but it took three men and a nurse to finally restrain her. When Malika calmed down, she said she wanted to see him. Since she had a concussion, they didn't want her walking. So they brought Malika into Sam's room on a gurney. I went in with them, and Sam looked even bigger than he had before. I realized then: Sam was bleeding inside and the blood had no place to escape.

As Malika bent down to kiss Sam goodbye, she turned his cheek so it faced her. A blue-black fluid gushed out of his mouth. It threw Malika back into hysterics.

Before they took Sam to the mortuary, Carl and Majid wanted to see him too. It was almost 9:20 P.M. by the time they left him. To avoid the fans and reporters in all the waiting rooms, Sam was taken out a side entrance. I went back to the office, dreading my next phone call. How do you tell a mother she's lost another son?

Terry Presley walked in crying. Elvis Presley's cousin, Terry was an old friend of our family's. He had just driven from Las Vegas to see Sam's concert in Laughlin. Our promoter had told him that Sam had been hospitalized. I gave Terry a savage hug, and then the telephone rang. It was Todd Smith, Sam's former agent from Creative Artists Agency.

Hollywood already knew.

But why would Todd Smith call me? Four years earlier, when *Atuk* fell apart, Todd Smith had dropped Sam like a stone. He never even told Sam he was dumping him as a client. He never returned our phone calls. A few years later, when we tried getting Sam back into CAA, several industry people told us that Todd Smith kept nixing him. One time, I called him myself and he hung up on me.

Todd Smith told me now: I just heard Sam passed away. I'm sorry. If you need an agent to handle the rights to the book on Sam's life or the movie . . .

Sam had been dead two hours.

"You fucks!" I screamed. "Four years, you try putting him out of the business! Now before the body is even cold? You fucks! You vultures!"

When I put down the phone, Terry Presley said, "Who was that?"

"That was Hollywood," I said.

Five minutes later I called Terry Jones, my mother's neighbor in Tulsa. My mom never had any girls of her own. She always called Terry "my daughter." Without telling Terry why, I asked her to go to my mom's house. I didn't want Mom alone when I gave her the news.

Terry said she could be there in five minutes. I waited fifteen, then called my mother. It was almost midnight in Oklahoma. But Sam wasn't the only night owl in our family. To a lesser extent than Sam, we were all that way.

My mom sounded happy and wide awake. She sounded full of life. She told me her daughter Terry had just stopped by.

I said, "Mom, this is the hardest phone call I'll ever have to make to you."

"What happened? What happened?" And she was crying.

"Sam was in a head-on collision tonight. We were going to a show. It was on the highway from Needles to Laughlin."

"How bad is it?" my mother asked.

"He's dead."

She started sobbing.

We talked for fifteen more minutes. But I couldn't soothe her.

Bill Kinison

Afterword

THAT SAM DIED YOUNG DIDN'T SURPRISE ME. HOW HE DIED WAS a terrible shock. When I entered my house the next morning, I still hadn't cried.

Nobody was home, since Ginger was staying with Sherry. In my kitchen, I had thirty-three messages on my machine. Many had come from stand-up comedian friends. They were people I'd known for years, people I'd seen toughened up by the business. When I heard them going to pieces on my machine, something hard broke inside me. I walked into the bedroom, lay on top of my bed and started to weep.

Four days later, a memorial service was held at Forest Lawn Memorial Park in the Hollywood Hills. This service was nonreligious, by invitation only, a chance for Sam's show business friends to bid him farewell. About four hundred people attended, including Jim Carrey, Tommy Chong, Dabney Coleman, Rodney Dangerfield, C. C. DeVille, Vince Neil, Ozzy Osbourne, Luke Perry, Joan Rivers, Axl Rose, Bob Saget, Rudy Sarzo, Garry Shandling, Pauly Shore, Slash, Chris Squire, Alan Thicke, Steven Tyler and Aerosmith, Joe Walsh, Richard Belzer, Billy Idol, Robin Wil-

liams, Charlie Sheen, Tommy Lee and Heather Locklear, Julian
Lennon, Tim Matheson, Pat McCormack, Chuck McCann,
Richard Lewis, Corey Feldman, Dan Aykroyd, Lita Ford, Billy
Gibbons, and Arsenio Hall.

When Malika arrived, I spoke to her in private.

I said, "We're going to view the body after everyone else clears
out. It'll just be close friends and family."

Malika said, "I'm going to the Rainbow." She meant the bar
and restaurant on Sunset.

I said, "All right, that's up to you. The rest of us are staying,
then we're all flying to Tulsa tonight on a red-eye. I've arranged
for Sam to fly on the plane with us. We're all gonna fly together.
I've got a first-class ticket for you."

"I'm not going," Malika said.

"You're not going to your own husband's burial?"

"No."

"Well . . . that's up to you too."

The service began. In her strong, reassuring voice, Sherry sang
"Walk Around Heaven" and "The Battle Hymn of the Repub-
lic." Six people eulogized Sam in addition to me: His best friend
Carl LaBove, Billy Gibbons of ZZ Top, Robin Williams, Richard
Belzer, and Pauly Shore. Robin Williams went first, setting the
tone for the day by keeping his comments light. After Robin,
every speaker got laughs with recollections of Sam.

I thought it was great. The humor, the laughter. People talked
so much about Sam's life-style, the interest groups he offended,
his famous scream, sometimes they lost sight of what was most
important: Sam made people laugh. He made them laugh *hard*.
And few things in this life are more healing than laughter.

Later that evening, I flew with Sam's body to Tulsa. On Monday, April 20, we gave him his religious service, with all the
singing and preaching. The Hollywood Sam had been said goodbye to last week. As I told the overflow crowd at my mother's
church, this day was meant for the Tulsa Sam.

I preached that morning running on pure emotion. My message, however, was carefully chosen. I wanted to preach for Sam as I thought he would preach for me had I died before him. So I tried being honest. I did not prettify Sam's life. But I also spoke of love and salvation, redemption and forgiveness. Like Sam, I didn't believe in a hell. God loves all his children, I told the crowd. God loves Sam. Why would he choose to punish Sam? Sam's spirit has ascended. Sam is in Heaven.

I saw some shaking heads in the congregation. I knew what those people were thinking: Sam Kinison was a backslider. Certainly he went to hell.

But my conviction was strong. I kept thundering forward, preaching hard, preaching with everything I had. When I felt emptied out, when most of the shaking heads were beginning to nod, I turned to the gospel chorus. They sang the roof off my mother's church. Later that day, at the cemetery, we said more prayers and sang more hymns. We buried Sam near his brother, Kevin, his father, Sam Sr., and his stepfather, A.D.

The week after Sam died, Howard Stern and his crew aired a touching four-hour tribute. In a full-page tribute to Sam in *Rolling Stone,* Howard said, "He was a major talent with a brilliant comic mind. Sam's bad night was a lot more interesting than just about anyone else's best night. I don't usually like having comedians on my show, because they're for the most part just personas, one shtick line after another. Sam was totally different— he was utterly real." Robin Williams said Sam was "absolutely fearless. He was like a comedy combination of Chuck Yeager and Evel Knievel. Most people go to the edge and then stop. Not Sam. He'd see the edge and then just keep going. And I think that scream he was famous for was just the sound he made on his way down." "He'll definitely be remembered," Rodney Dangerfield said, "because someone that funny and wild you don't forget." The members of Mötley Crüe were quoted too. "If

God didn't have a sense of humor before, he does now."

Richard Belzer said in *Entertainment Weekly,* "His perform-ance style was overpowering, with his screaming and wildman appearance, and it disturbed a lot of people. But to me the screaming was eloquent. It was a vent of rage. It added power and depth to his material."

The producers of *Prime Time Live,* while putting together their own segment on Sam, told me his death had received more me-dia coverage than the death of any other performer since Elvis Presley. I had known Sam was popular, but this came as a sur-prise.

Since I was his manager, the financial mess he left did not surprise me at all. Two weeks before his death, Sam made his final payment to Terry Marrs. But he still died about $1 million in debt. Using round numbers, Sam owed $500,000 to the IRS, $200,000 to United Artists over *Atuk,* and $160,000 to American Express. The rest was assorted debt.

When the stories came out, I joked a few times in the press: "If a guy died $1 million in debt, then you know he had a good time." That was the Kinison way, using gallows humor when life turned darkest. But Sam also left his family with serious head-aches. Despite all his debt, he had made almost no preparations for dying. He had no mortgage life insurance on his house in Malibu. He had no life insurance at all. Sam, in fact, became enraged if anyone even mentioned it. If he bought life insurance, Sam always said, then he *would* die. Although he did have a will, his estate was insolvent.

Sam died at the age of thirty-eight. Unlike Morrison, Joplin, Belushi, and Hendrix, he did not die of excess. At the end, Sam had a real desire to clean up his act. Sometimes he still couldn't help himself, but he was trying.

That isn't to say he died pristine. His autopsy reports showed traces of marijauna, codeine, Valium, Xanax, and cocaine.

Only the cocaine caught me off-guard.

From the time he discovered drugs, Sam smoked pot almost every day.

For about the last year, he took codeine for a sharp chronic pain he felt below his left shoulder. Sam thought it came from his heart, but a large amount of bile had been found in his gallbladder. Sam's discomfort might have stemmed from there.

He very seldom took Xanax and Valium. He began using them after cutting drastically back on booze and cocaine. At the time, Sam had been finding it hard to sleep.

When I heard about the cocaine, I thought: He must have gone wild on his honeymoon. Because Sam had virtually quit since learning he had arrhythmia. One day I drove out to the coroner's office and he explained the toxicology report. He said Sam's cocaine traces were very small. So small, he said, that they might have been in Sam's system for up to two months. He said the same was true for the codeine, Valium, and Xanax. Only the pot had been found at high toxic levels.

The autopsy report stated that Sam died of "multiple traumatic injuries." I asked the coroner what that specifically meant. He said Sam died with a broken neck, a fractured skull, a lacerated heart, and a lacerated small bowel. He said any one of those injuries could have been fatal.

For many weeks after Sam's death, I couldn't stop replaying his car accident in my mind. At night, it was the last image I saw before I slept. It was the first each day when I woke. I am still haunted by witnessing my brother's death. I always will be.

Some days, I missed Sam so badly I wept. Some days, I found comfort in pictures of him. In one of my favorites, taken in Peoria, our parents are not divorced yet. My father and I haven't moved out of the church. Sam is already troubled, but he still lives with his whole family. He looks about five, maybe six years old. Bending down to pat his skinny dog, Doughnut, Sam is grinning shyly at the camera. It is 1958 or 1959, and nobody dreams that Sam will be famous one day. No one has called him the screamer. A brave man. A misguided missile. A generous soul. A prick. A truthteller. A con man. The most controversial comic of his generation. An American original.

In the photograph of him, Sam is still a little boy, petting his dog. Sam is home.

Index